NUTSHELL

CW00525524

YOU'VE GOT IT
CRACKED

Nutcases – your essential revision and starter guides

- Provides you with in-depth case analysis of the facts, principles and decision of the most important cases in an area of law

- Incorporates colour to help distinguish cases and legislation and aid ease of use

- Presents the text in bite-size chunks and includes bullets where appropriate to aid navigation, assimilation and retention of information

- Breaks the subject down into key topics to enable you to easily identify and concentrate on particular topics

- Opens each chapter with a short introduction to outline the key concepts covered and condense complex and important information

- Highlights Court of Appeal and House of Lords cases to enable you to easily identify the relative significance of the cases examined

- Includes boxed "think points" at the end of each chapter providing further case analysis

- Fully indexed by individual cases and topics

Available from all good booksellers

NUT**SHELLS**

Evidence

SIXTH EDITION

by
DR MICHAEL STOCKDALE
Principal Lecturer
School of Law
Northumbria University

and

ADAM JACKSON
Senior Lecturer
School of Law
Northumbria University

SWEET & MAXWELL

THOMSON REUTERS

Published in 2011 by Sweet & Maxwell, 100 Avenue Road, London NW3 3PF
part of Thomson Reuters (Professional) UK Limited
(Registered in England & Wales, Company No 1679046.
Registered Office and address for service:
Aldgate House, 33 Aldgate High Street, London EC3N 1DL)

Typeset by YHT Ltd, London
Printed in Great Britain by Ashford Colour Press, Gosport, Hants

*For further information on our products and services, visit www.sweetandmaxwell.co.uk

No natural forests were destroyed to make this product;
only farmed timber was used and re-planted.

A CIP catalogue record for this book is available from the British Library.

ISBN 978-0-414-04593-4

Contents

Using this Book

Welcome to our new look NUTSHELLS revision series. We have revamped and improved the existing design and layout and added new features, according to student feedback.

NEW DETAILED TABLE OF CONTENTS for easy navigation.

REDESIGNED TABLES OF CASES AND LEGISLATION for easy reference.

NEW CHAPTER INTRODUCTIONS to outline
the key concepts covered and condense
complex and important information.

Other Statutory R.

......

NATIONAL MINIMUM WAGE AC

The National Minimum Wage Act 19
minimum hourly rate of pay for all v
'tate to determine and ame'
 are set: one

**DEFINITION CHECKPOINTS, LEGISLATION
HIGHLIGHTERS AND EXPLANATION
OF KEY CASES** to highlight important
information.

Witness anonymity order

LEGISLATION HIGHLIGHTER

Section 88 of the **Coroners and J**

A criminal court may make a witnes
C&JA 2009 if three conditions are
order must either be necessary to
another person or to prevent seri
necessary to prevent real harm to
the identity of an undercover
the measure

the HL reversed tin.
ot customary and did need t

DEFINITION CHECKPOINT
Procession
The **Public Order Act 1986**, s.16
sion in a public place. This is not o
nition can be found in the case of *Fl*
at 502, where Lord Goddard C.J.
body of persons: it is a body,

DEFINITION CHECKPOINT
Assembly
The **Public Order Act 1986**
mbly of two or

KEY CASE

CARMICHAEL V NATIONAL POW
Mrs Carmichael worked as a gu
required" basis, showing group
tion. She worked some hours m
wore a company uniform, was s
vehicle, and enjoyed many of th
question for the court to determ'
"umbrella" or "global" emplov
which she worked and the ir

Held: (HL) During the
 her duti

DIAGRAMS, FLOWCHARTS AND OTHER DIAGRAMMATIC REPRESENTATION to clarify and condense complex and important information and break up the text.

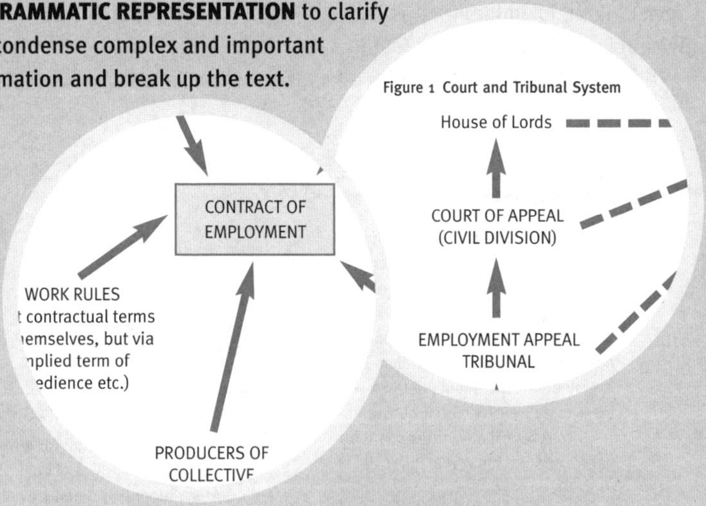

Figure 1 Court and Tribunal System

House of Lords ▬ ▬ ▬ ▬

CONTRACT OF EMPLOYMENT

COURT OF APPEAL (CIVIL DIVISION)

WORK RULES
t contractual terms
hemselves, but via
nplied term of
edience etc.)

EMPLOYMENT APPEAL TRIBUNAL

PRODUCERS OF
COLLECTIVE

END OF CHAPTER REVISION CHECKLISTS outlining what you should now know and understand.

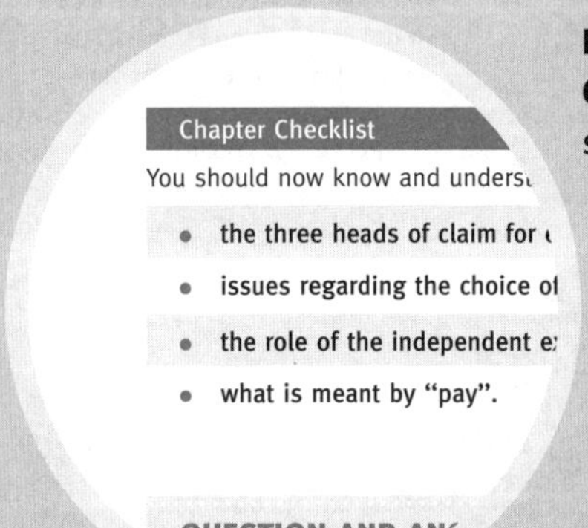

Chapter Checklist

You should now know and unders

- the three heads of claim for
- issues regarding the choice of
- the role of the independent e
- what is meant by "pay".

QUESTION AND AN

END OF CHAPTER QUESTION AND ANSWER SECTION with advice on relating knowledge to examination performance, how to approach the question, how to structure the answer, the pitfalls (and how to avoid them!) and how to get the best marks.

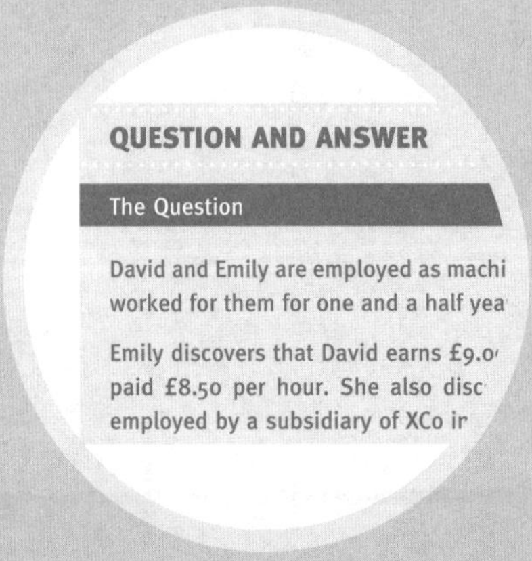

QUESTION AND ANSWER

The Question

David and Emily are employed as machi
worked for them for one and a half yea

Emily discovers that David earns £9.0
paid £8.50 per hour. She also disc
employed by a subsidiary of XCo in

HANDY HINTS AND USEFUL WEBSITES
– revision and examination tips and
advice relating to the subject features
at the end of the book, along with a list of useful websites.

HANDY HINTS

Examination questions in employmei
either essay questions or problem ques
format and in what is required of the ex
of question in turn.

Students usually prefer one type
normally opting for the problem ques
examinations are usually set in a wa'
least one of each style of questior
Very few, if any, questions
ows about a topic, and it '
make a n

USEFUL WEBSITES

Official Information
www.parliament.uk—very user-friendly.
www.direct.gov.uk—portal for governme
www.opsi.gov.uk—Office of Public Secto
and statutory instruments available
www.dca.gov.uk—Department for Con
www.dca.gov.uk/peoples-rights/hum
Unit at the Department for Con
www.homeoffice.gov.uk/police/
the Police and Criminal

NEW COLOUR CODING throughout to
help distinguish cases and legislation
from the narrative. At the first mention,
cases are highlighted in colour and
italicised and legislation is highlighted
in colour and emboldened.

are an ethnic group (*Seiu*
ypsies are an ethnic group (*CRE*
Rastafarians are not an ethnic group
ment [1993] I.R.L.R. 284)
(d) Jehovah's Witnesses are not an ethnic o
Norwich City College case 1502237/97)
(e) RRA covers the Welsh (*Gwynedd CC v Jone*
(f) Both the Scots and the English are covere
"national origins" but not by "ethnic or
Board v Power [1997], *Boyce v British Ai*

It should be noted that Sikhs, Jews, Je
ians are also protected on '
Equality (Religion or P

Table of Cases

Table of Statutes

Burden and Standard of Proof

Introduction

In legal proceedings, whether civil or criminal, it is necessary to determine which party has the burden of proving the facts in issue and what standard of proof is required. The rules concerning burden and standard of proof differ greatly depending on whether the proceedings are civil or criminal in nature. This chapter will consider the position in relation to both types of proceedings. This chapter will also deal with the various types of "presumptions" and the consequences of their operation in legal proceedings as well as considering the nature and significance of the taking of "judicial notice".

CIVIL PROCEEDINGS

Burden of proof

> **DEFINITION CHECKPOINT**
>
> In civil proceedings, the position is essentially that the party who raises an issue bears the legal burden of proof in relation to that issue (i.e. the burden of proving the issue raised) (*Wakelin v London and South Western Railway* (1886)).

Thus, for example, if the claimant asserts that he and the defendant formed a contract and that he suffered loss in consequence of the defendant's breach, it is for the claimant to prove that the contract was formed, that it was breached by the defendant and that he did suffer loss in consequence of that breach.

What is the effect of the defendant denying the claimant's assertions?

If the defendant merely denies the claimant's assertions, this does not impose a burden of proof upon the claimant. Thus, for example, if the defendant claims that no contract was ever formed between himself and the claimant it is still the claimant who is required to prove the existence of the contract and not the defendant who is required to establish its non-existence. The claimant may fail to satisfy the burden of proof imposed upon him even if the defendant adduces no evidence and even though defence counsel does not cross-examine the claimant's witnesses. As a matter of sensible tactics, however, the defendant will normally do all that he can to rebut the claimant's case, where appropriate both cross-examining the claimant's witnesses and calling his own witnesses.

What is the position where the defendant raises an issue?

Where the defendant puts forward a defence which goes beyond a mere denial of the claimant's case and actually raises new issues which the claimant did not raise, then the defendant does bear the burden of proving the relevant facts in issue. This will be the case where, for example, the defendant relies upon the defence of self-defence in civil proceedings (*Ashley v Chief Constable of Sussex Police* (2007)). Equally, where the defendant claims that the contract which he made with the claimant was frustrated, it is for him to prove that a frustrating event made its performance illegal or impossible. In such circumstances the defendant's assertion does not impose a burden of proof on the claimant, though, again, as a matter of sensible tactics, the claimant will normally do all that he can to negate the defendant's defence.

Does the concept of burden of proof become more important where there is little or no evidence in relation to an issue?

Where there is little or no evidence in relation to an issue, the court may be unable to determine which version of the facts is correct. In such circumstances, the party who bears the legal burden of proof in relation to the relevant issue must have failed to satisfy it.

At times it may be unclear where the legal burden of proof lies with regard to an issue in relation to which little or no evidence is available. In such circumstances, when the court determines where the legal burden of proof lies it may also effectively be deciding the case before it. For example, in *Joseph Constantine Steamship Line Ltd v Imperial Smelting Corp Ltd* (1942), the House of Lords was required to consider whether, where a defendant had raised the defence of frustration, he was merely required to prove that a frustrating event had taken place or whether the defence failed unless the defendant also proved that the frustrating event was not his fault. The case concerned the loss of a ship and there was little evidence before the court in relation to the issue of fault. If the burden of proving absence of fault fell on the defendant, then it would be difficult or impossible for defendants to maintain the defence in such circumstances. Conversely, if the burden of proving fault in order to negate the defence of frustration fell on the claimant, then, in such circumstances, the defence of frustration would, potentially, be available to defendants. The House of Lords, for a variety of reasons, held that the burden of proving fault lay on the claimant.

Standard of proof

The standard of proof in civil proceedings is proof on the balance of probabilities. Thus, the evidence adduced by the party who bears the legal burden of proof must persuade the judge (or the jury where, exceptionally, the claim is tried by a jury) that it is more probable than not that the facts were as that party asserts (*Miller v Minister of Pensions* (1947)). Consequently, where the evidence before the court equally supports the version of the facts put forward by the party who bears the legal burden of proof and the version put forward by the other party, the party who bears the legal burden of proof has failed to satisfy it (*Wakelin v London and South Western Railway*). Equally, even though the evidence adduced by the party who bears the legal burden of proof is more persuasive than that adduced in rebuttal by the other party, the party who bears the legal burden of proof still fails to satisfy it if the evidence which he adduces does not persuade the judge that his version of the facts is more probably true than not (*Rhesa Shipping Co SA v Edmunds* (1985)).

Where serious allegations (i.e. allegations of criminal conduct) are made in civil proceedings the requisite standard of proof remains the civil standard, not the criminal standard (*In Re H and Others (Minors) (Sexual Abuse: Standard of Proof)* (1996)). This having been said, if the alleged conduct is of a type which is unlikely to have taken place, the court can take the fact that the conduct is unlikely to have taken place into account when determining whether the allegations are probably true (*In Re D* (2008); *In Re B (Children) (Care Proceedings: Standard of Proof)* (2009)).

Exceptionally, the standard of proof required in civil proceedings may be the criminal standard of proof, namely, proof beyond reasonable doubt. Thus, for example, it appears that the criminal standard of proof is required in order to prove contempt of court in civil proceedings (*Bramblevale Ltd, Re* (1970)). Similarly, the criminal standard of proof is applied by magistrates when they are determining whether to make anti-social behaviour orders (*R. (on the application of McCann) v Crown Court at Manchester* (2002)).

CRIMINAL PROCEEDINGS

Burden of proof

In criminal proceedings, the position is essentially that, subject to limited exceptions which are considered below, the legal burden of proof lies on the prosecution (*Woolmington v DPP* (1935)). This rule is sometimes known as the "presumption of innocence" or the *Woolmington* principle". Thus, for example, if the accused is charged with murder, it is for the prosecution to prove that the accused unlawfully killed the victim with malice aforethought.

KEY CASE

WOOLMINGTON V DPP (1935)

Viscount Sankey, giving the leading judgement in the *Woolmington* case, formulated the classic explanation regarding the burden and standard of proof in criminal proceedings;

> "Throughout the web of the English Criminal Law one golden thread is always to be seen, that it is the duty of the prosecution to prove the prisoner's guilt subject to what I have already said as to the defence of insanity and subject also to any statutory exception. If, at the end of and on the whole of the case, there is a reasonable doubt, created by the evidence given by either the prosecution or the prisoner, as to whether the prisoner killed the deceased with a malicious intention, the prosecution has not made out the case and the prisoner is entitled to an acquittal."

This explanation has become known as the *"Woolmington* principle" or is otherwise referred to as the "presumption of innocence".

What is the effect of the accused denying part or all of the prosecution's case?

If the accused merely denies part or all of the prosecution's case, this does not impose a burden of proof upon the accused. Thus, for example, if the accused claims that he did not kill the victim, it is still the prosecution who is required to prove that the accused did kill the victim and not the accused who is required to prove that he did not. The prosecution may fail to satisfy the burden of proof imposed upon it even if the accused adduces no evidence and even though his counsel does not cross-examine prosecution witnesses. As a matter of sensible tactics, however, the accused will normally do all that he can to rebut the prosecution's case, where appropriate both cross-examining prosecution witnesses and calling his own witnesses.

What is the position where the accused raises an issue?

Where the accused puts forward a defence which goes beyond a mere denial of the prosecution's case and actually raises new issues which the prosecution did not raise, then, even so, the accused will not normally bear the legal burden of proving the relevant facts in issue. Rather, provided that there is some evidence before the court upon which a properly directed jury would be entitled to find that the accused's defence was established, the normal rule is that the legal burden of rebutting the defence lies on the prosecution.

In other words, in such circumstances, the accused may be said to bear the "evidential burden" of adducing sufficient evidence to raise the defence, but if sufficient evidence to raise the defence is before the court then the prosecution bears the legal burden of disproving it. In reality, however, even if the evidence adduced by the accused fails to raise such a defence, the trial judge should still leave the defence to the jury if it is raised by evidence adduced by other parties (e.g. by evidence given by prosecution witnesses) (*R. v Bullard* (1957)). Thus, for example, where the accused relies upon the defence of self defence, if the evidence before the court raises the defence of self defence, the prosecution bears the legal burden of disproving the defence, the accused does not bear the legal burden of proving it (*R. v Lobell* (1957)).

In what circumstances does the accused bear the legal burden of proving facts in issue?

There is only one common law exception to the *Woolmington* principle, which is that the accused bears the legal burden of establishing the common law defence of insanity (*McNaghten's Case* (1843)). This rule is sometimes known as the "presumption of sanity". Otherwise, the accused only bears the legal burden of proving facts in issue if this is imposed upon him by statute. For example, s.2(2) of the Homicide Act 1957 expressly places the legal burden of proving diminished responsibility on the accused.

Where a statute does not expressly place the legal burden of proving facts in issue upon the accused, it may do so by implication, though a judge should not readily infer that a statutory provision is of this effect (*R. v Hunt* (1987)). Essentially, it appears that where statute prohibits conduct of a certain type other than in specified exceptional circumstances, it will be for the accused to prove that he falls within the relevant exception (*R. v Edwards* (1975)). Whether a statutory provision does have this effect, however, fundamentally depends upon the construction of its specific provisions (*R. v Hunt*). The common law principles stated by the House of Lords in *Hunt* and by the Court of Appeal in *Edwards* apply in the context of trial on indictment and effectively equate with the position encountered in relation to summary proceedings, which is governed by s.101 of the Magistrates' Court Act 1980.

For example, where an accused is charged with selling liquor without a licence, the prosecution, in order to succeed, are merely required to prove that the accused sold liquor and are not required to prove that, at the time of the sale, the accused did not possess a licence (*R. v Edwards*). Rather, if the accused wishes to rely upon the possession of a licence in answer to the case against him, it is for him to prove that he did possess one at the relevant time.

Does the concept of burden of proof become more important where there is little or no evidence in relation to an issue?

Where there is little or no evidence in relation to an issue, the court may be unable to determine which version of the facts is correct. In such circumstances, the party who bears the legal burden of proof in relation to the relevant issue must have failed to satisfy it.

In *R. v Edwards* (considered above), neither party had adduced evidence to prove that the accused did or did not possess a licence to sell intoxicating liquor. Thus, if the legal burden of proving that the accused did not possess such a licence had fallen on the prosecution, then the prosecution would have failed to prove an essential ingredient of its case. As was noted above, however, the Court of Appeal held that it was for the accused to prove that he did possess a licence if he wished to rely upon such possession in answer to the case against him.

Where a party to criminal proceedings bears the legal burden of proving facts in issue it is for the jury (or the magistrates in the context of summary trial) to determine whether the party has proved the relevant issue to the standard required by law. Normally, the jury will decide whether the party has satisfied the burden of proof following consideration of all of the relevant evidence (both that adduced by the prosecution and that adduced by the defence). At times, however, following completion of the prosecution's case, the accused may submit that there is no case for him to answer. In such circumstances, if the prosecution has not adduced sufficient evidence to raise a prima facie case then the judge will withdraw the case or, as appropriate, the relevant count, from the jury (*R. v Galbraith* (1981)). The prosecution may be said to have failed to satisfy the "evidential burden" (i.e. the burden of adducing sufficient evidence to entitle a properly directed jury to make a finding on the prosecution's behalf).

Standard of proof

Where the legal burden of proof lies on the prosecution, the standard of proof in criminal proceedings is proof beyond reasonable doubt. In other words, if there is more than a remote possibility of the accused's innocence, then he should be found not guilty (*Miller v Minister of Pensions*). Another way of expressing this standard of proof is to state that the jury must be "satisfied so that they feel sure" of the accused's guilt (*R. v Summers* (1952)).

Where the legal burden of proof lies on the accused, the standard of proof in criminal proceedings is proof on the balance of probabilities (*R. v Carr-Briant* (1943)).

The incidence of the legal burden of proof determines which party to legal proceedings is required to prove which issue or issues. In civil proceedings the party who raises a fact in issue bears the legal burden of proving that issue. In criminal proceedings the legal burden of proof is generally borne by the prosecution meaning the prosecution must prove the accused's guilt and disprove any defences raised. This is subject to limited exceptions, for example where the defences of insanity (the only common law exception) or diminished responsibility (an example of a statutory exception) are raised.

The standard of proof determines the strength of the evidence that is required in order to prove the issue. A party bearing the legal burden of proof must reach the required standard of proof in order to discharge that burden. In civil proceedings, again subject to limited exceptions the standard of proof is proof on the balance of probabilities (i.e. the party bearing the burden of proof must demonstrate that it is 'more probable than not' that the facts were as asserted).

The standard of proof in criminal proceedings is proof beyond all reasonable doubt (the jury are usually told that they must be "satisfied so that they feel sure" (*R. v Summers*) of the defendant's guilt). Where, in criminal proceedings, an exception applies and the burden of proof rests with the defence the standard of proof required of the defence is the same as the civil standard—proof on the balance of probabilities.

Human rights

The presumption of innocence is embodied in art.6(2) of the European Convention on Human Rights. Thus, where statute or the common law imposes a legal burden of proof upon the accused, this is capable of giving rise to a violation of art.6(2).

The only common law defence which imposes a legal burden of proof upon the accused is the defence of insanity, and the Commission of Human Rights held (in *H v UK* (1990)) that requiring the accused to prove this defence did not give rise to a violation of art.6(2).

In relation to the statutory imposition of a legal burden of proof upon the accused, whether or not this results in a violation of art.6(2) will depend upon whether the statutory requirement, requiring the accused to prove the relevant facts in issue, falls within reasonable limits (*Salabiaku v France* (1988)). Thus, it appears that there will be no violation of art.6 in circumstances in which statutory derogation from the presumption of innocence is justified and imposing a legal burden of proof upon the accused is proportionate (*R. v Lambert* (2001)). The Convention requires, however, that there is a reasonable balance between the public interest and the interests of the individual and a reverse burden of proof will only be acceptable if there is a compelling reason why it is fair and reasonable to deny the accused the protection of the presumption of innocence (*R. v Johnstone* (2003)). In circumstances in which imposing a legal burden of proof upon the accused would result in an art.6 violation, it appears that the effect of s.3(1) of the Human Rights Act 1998 in this context is that the court may be required to "read the statutory provision down" such that the accused is only required to satisfy an evidential burden in order to satisfy the statutory requirement, the legal burden of proof being borne by the prosecution (*R. v Lambert*). It is not, however, the court's task to determine whether a reverse burden of proof should be imposed on the defendant but, rather, the role of the court is to determine whether the imposition of a reverse burden on the accused had unjustifiably infringed the art.6(2) presumption of innocence (*Sheldrake v DPP* (2004)).

In considering whether a statutory requirement which imposes a legal burden of proof upon the accused does fall within reasonable limits, it is necessary to consider matters such as:

- whether the statutory requirement requires the accused to disprove an essential element of the offence with which he is charged;
- the purpose of requiring the accused to prove the relevant fact in issue;
- how difficult it will be for the accused to prove the relevant fact in issue;
- the potential consequences for the accused if he is found guilty of the offence with which he is charged;
- the accused's rights;
- whether requiring the accused to prove the relevant fact in issue achieves a fair balance between the public interest and the protection of the human rights of the individual; and
- Parliament's view concerning what is in the public interest (*R. v DPP Ex p. Kebilene* (1994)).

Thus, for example, in *Sheldrake v DPP*, the House of Lords held that the imposition upon the accused, by s.5(2) of the Road Traffic Act 1988, of the burden of proving that there was no likelihood of his driving whilst the proportion of alcohol in his breath remained likely to exceed the limit was directed at the legitimate object of preventing persons from causing death, injury or damage by driving vehicles whilst unfit to do so, and that the imposition of this reverse burden of proof on the accused was not unreasonable or arbitrary and did not go beyond that which was necessary, it being more appropriate for the accused to prove, on the balance of probabilities, that he would not have been likely to drive, a matter within the accused's knowledge, than for the prosecution to prove, to the criminal standard of proof, that the accused would have been likely to drive.

In contrast, in *R. v Lambert*, the House of Lords, applying s.3(1) of the **Human Rights Act 1998,** held that the burden imposed upon the accused by the defence created by s.28(2) of the Misuse of Drugs Act 1971, concerning the accused's knowledge of matters alleged by the prosecution, was only an evidential burden, the prosecution bearing the legal burden of disproving the defence if evidence sufficient to raise it was before the court. The s.28(2) "defence" concerned an essential element of the offence with which the accused was charged (his knowledge of the matters alleged against him), if the accused was found guilty the maximum sentence was life imprisonment and, whilst it might be difficult for the prosecution to disprove the defence, requiring the accused to prove the defence was a disproportionate response to this difficulty.

Similarly in *Att Gen's Reference (No.4 of 2002)* (2004), the House of Lords held that whilst s.11(2) of the Terrorism Act 2000 (which required the accused to prove that the organisation of which he was alleged to have been a member had not been a proscribed organisation when he began to be a member and that he had not taken part in any of its activities whilst it was proscribed) had a legitimate end (i.e. that of deterring people from joining proscribed terrorist organisations), s.11(2) was to be read down as merely imposing an evidential burden upon the accused because a person who was innocent of blameworthy or criminal conduct could fall within s.11(1) of the 2000 Act and imposing the legal burden of exonerating themselves on the balance of probabilities was not a justifiable and proportionate response on the part of the legislature.

PRESUMPTIONS

The term "presumption" is used in a variety of ways:
   (1) The term "presumption" is used to describe certain rules which concern the incidence of the legal burden of proof (e.g. "the presumption of innocence" and "the presumption of sanity", which were considered above).
   (2) The term "presumption" is sometimes used to refer to a "rebuttable presumption of law". This is, essentially, a rule of law (which may be derived from common law or from statute) the effect of which is that if a party to legal proceedings proves a "primary fact", the court will presume that a "presumed fact" has also been proved unless the other party to the proceedings satisfies the burden of rebutting the presumption. Whether a party is required to discharge a legal burden of proof or merely an evidential burden in order to rebut a rebuttable presumption of law depends upon the nature of the specific

presumption. Whether a rebuttable presumption of law requires the accused in criminal proceedings to do more than discharge an evidential burden (i.e. whether it imposes a legal burden of proof on the accused) will depend upon whether the presumption forms a statutory exception to the *Woolmington* principle (see above) and whether requiring the accused to discharge the legal burden of proof that the presumption imposes would result in a violation of art.6 of the **European Convention on Human Rights** (see above). Examples of rebuttable presumptions of law, created by s.11 of the Civil Evidence Act 1968 and s.74 of the Police and Criminal Evidence Act 1984 (PACE), are encountered in Chapter 8, below.

Example

An example of a rebuttable presumption of law can be found in s.11 of the **Civil Evidence Act 1968**. Where a party to civil proceedings proves that a person has a relevant and subsisting previous conviction, the effect of s.11 is that the civil court must presume that the person convicted committed the offence unless the other party to the civil proceedings proves on the balance of probabilities that the person convicted did not commit the offence. See Chapter 8 for more detail on the operation of this presumption.

---

(3) The term "presumption" is sometimes used to describe an "irrebuttable presumption of law" (which may, alternatively, be described as a "conclusive presumption of law"). This is, essentially, a rule of law the effect of which is that if a party to legal proceedings proves a "primary fact", the court will be required to conclusively presume the existence of a "presumed fact", and the other party to the proceedings will not be entitled to adduce evidence in rebuttal.

Example

An example of an irrebuttable presumption of law can be found in s.13 of the **Civil Evidence Act 1968**, (again encountered in Chapter 8, below). The effect of the presumption is that, if a party to defamation proceedings proves under s.13 that the claimant has a relevant and subsisting previous conviction, this amounts to conclusive evidence that the claimant committed the offence of which the claimant was convicted.

---

(4) The term "presumption" may be used to refer to a "presumption of fact". This is merely an inference that the tribunal of fact (i.e. the jury or magistrates or the judge in civil proceedings) is entitled but not obliged to draw upon proof of a primary fact. An example is provided by the "presumption of intention" (see s.8 of the Criminal Justice Act 1967) the effect of which is merely that a jury, when deciding whether the accused intended or foresaw a result of his actions, is entitled to draw such inferences from the evidence as appear proper in the circumstances.

JUDICIAL NOTICE

Courts are entitled to take judicial notice of "notorious facts" (see, for example, *Vehicle Inspectorate v Nuttall* (1999), in which the House of Lords indicated that magistrates are entitled to take judicial notice of the notorious fact that, for various reasons, drivers sometimes feel compelled to exceed reasonable periods of driving). Where a court takes judicial notice of a fact, the court will not require evidence to prove the fact and will not admit evidence to disprove it. Thus, in *R. v Luffe* (1807), the court took judicial notice of the fact that where a husband did not have access to his wife until a fortnight before her child was born, the husband could not have been the child's father. Where a judge sitting with a jury takes judicial notice of a fact, the judge will direct the jury as to the existence of the fact.

A court, in taking judicial notice of a fact, may refer to reference books or documents and may receive "evidence" from witnesses (i.e. from expert witnesses). Thus, in *McQuaker v Goddard* (1940), the court, in considering whether a camel was a domestic animal or a wild animal, was entitled both to hear from expert witnesses and to consult reference books. Equally, in *Duff Development Co Ltd v Kelantan* (1924), the court took judicial notice of the fact that Kelantan was a sovereign independent state. The court had sought this information from the British Government; the reply from the Secretary of State being conclusive in relation to the point.

Revision checklist

You should now know and understand:

- **who bears the burden of proof in civil and criminal proceedings;**

- **the required standard of proof in civil and criminal proceedings;**

- **the exceptions to the general position in criminal proceedings that the prosecution bears the legal burden of proof;**

- the importance of human rights in the context of the presumption of innocence;

- the different meanings of the term 'presumption' in the context of civil and criminal proceedings; and

- the meaning of the term 'judicial notice'.

QUESTION AND ANSWER

The questions

1) Dan is charged with murder. The prosecution allege that Dan killed Martin following a fight outside of a bar. Dan wishes to rely upon the defences of self defence, as he asserts that he was attacked by Martin, and diminished responsibility, due to the fact that he is a diagnosed schizophrenic.

2) Alison is bringing an action in negligence against Malcolm. Alison is seeking damages following an incident in which she was injured after a collision with Malcolm's car at a junction. Alison claims that Malcolm pulled out from the junction without looking to see if the road was clear. Malcolm denies that he was negligent and claims that Alison was driving too fast and was not paying attention. If the court decides that Malcolm was responsible he wishes to rely upon the defence of contributory negligence claiming that the manner of Alison's driving contributed to her injuries. Furthermore the trial judge wishes to take judicial notice of the fact that motorists emerging from a junction must give way to oncoming traffic.

Identify and discuss the position in relation to the burden and standard of proof in relation to the above two scenarios.

Advice and the Answer

General guidance
Almost all evidence problem questions will require you to consider the incidence of the burden of proof and the required standard of proof. Your starting point is to identify whether the question relates to civil or criminal proceedings. Once you have identified the type of

proceedings you are dealing with you can start your answer by outlining the general position in relation to the burden and standard of proof. It is important that you support your explanation with reference to relevant authority, for example if the question relates to criminal proceedings it will be important to refer to the *Woolmington* principle (*Woolmington v DPP* (1935)).

After outlining the relevant general principles, next you need to apply those principles to the facts of the scenario you are dealing with. Be careful to identify any exceptions to the general principles that are raised by the scenario, for example, by identifying the significance of any defences raised.

Model answers

Question 1)

In criminal proceedings the prosecution bear the burden of proving the accused's guilt (*Woolmington v DPP*) to the criminal standard of proof. The prosecution must therefore prove beyond all reasonable doubt (*Miller v Minister of Pensions*) that Dan murdered Martin. The jury will usually be directed that they should be "satisfied so that they feel sure" of the defendant's guilt (*R. v Summers*).

Dan can be said to bear an "evidential burden" in relation to his defence of self defence. This means that he should adduce some evidence to show that he was acting in self defence. In reality if there is evidence of self defence, even if Dan does not raise it, the judge will leave the defence to the jury (*R. v Bullard*). The burden of disproving Dan's defence of self defence will rest with the prosecution (*R. v Lobell*) who must disprove his defence to the criminal standard of proof (beyond all reasonable doubt). Dan does not bear the burden of proving his defence.

Section 2(2) of the **Homicide Act 1957** imposes a burden of proof on the defendant in relation to the defence of diminished responsibility, this is a statutory exception to the *Woolmington* principle. Where the legal burden of proof lies on the accused, the standard of proof in criminal proceedings is proof on the balance of probabilities (*R. v Carr-Briant*). Dan must therefore prove his defence of diminished responsibility but only to the civil standard of proof.

Question 2)

In civil proceedings the burden of proof rests with the party that raises an issue (*Wakelin v London and South Western Railways*), the standard of proof is proof on the balance of probabilities (*Miller v Minister of*

Pensions). By bringing the action in negligence Angela raises the issue of fault in relation to the accident. Angela must therefore prove the elements of her claim on the balance of probabilities. The fact that the issue in the case could potentially lead to criminal liability (e.g. careless driving) does not alter the standard of proof (*Re H*). The first element of Malcolm's defence is simply a denial of the claim. Because the denial does not raise any new facts in issue the burden of proving the claim remains with Alison.

The second element of Malcolm's defence, contributory negligence, does raise new facts in issue (i.e. that Alison contributed to her injuries through her own negligence) and so Malcolm must prove his defence of contributory negligence (*Ashley v Chief Constable of Sussex Police*). The standard of proof remains proof on the balance of probabilities.

The trial judge is entitled to take judicial notice of the fact that motorists emerging from a junction must give way to oncoming traffic because it is a "notorious fact", because of this the court will not require evidence to prove the fact and will not admit evidence to disprove it (*R. v Luffe*).

Competence and Compellability

Introduction

In this chapter we will consider the competence and compellability of witnesses in criminal and civil proceedings. Essentially questions of competence and compellability concern whether a witness is able (competent) to give evidence and, if so, whether the witness can be required (compelled) to do so.

Most persons are both competent to give evidence in civil or criminal proceedings and can be compelled to do so. In this chapter we will consider those exceptional classes of person who either are not competent witnesses (i.e. persons who cannot give evidence) or who, whilst competent witnesses, are not compellable (i.e. persons who may choose to give evidence but cannot be required to do so).

Where a person is competent and compellable, the person may be compelled to attend court via the issuance of a witness summons, the potential sanction where a person fails to attend court to answer a witness summons being punishment for contempt of court.

CRIMINAL PROCEEDINGS

As regards the issue of competence, the general rule in criminal proceedings is that, under s.53(1) of the Youth Justice and Criminal Evidence Act 1999 (YJ&CEA 1999), all persons, whatever age they may be, are competent to give evidence. In relation to compellability, the general rule is that a witness who is competent is also compellable. The remainder of this part of the current chapter is concerned with exceptions to these general rules.

LEGISLATION HIGHLIGHTER

Section 53(1) and (3) of the **Youth Justice and Criminal Evidence Act 1999**

Section 53(1) creates a presumption that in criminal proceedings all persons, whatever their age, are competent to give evidence. This is subject to a test laid down in section 53(3) of the 1999 Act which provides;

A person is not competent to give evidence in criminal proceedings if it appears to the court that he is not a person who is able to—
(a)   understand questions put to him as a witness, and
(b)   give answers to them which can be understood.

Persons who cannot understand questions or give answers which can be understood

In criminal proceedings, under s.53(3) of the **YJ&CEA 1999**, a person will not be competent if it appears to the court that the person cannot both understand questions put to him as a witness and give answers to those questions which can be understood. There is, however, no minimum age below which a witness cannot be competent, provided that the witness can understand questions put to him as a witness and give answers to those questions which can be understood, the test being that laid down by s.53(3) of the 1999 Act (*R. v Powell* (2006)). Thus, if a four year old child can speak to strangers in basic English and can understand questions put to him thereby, it seems that the child will be competent (*R. v MacPherson* (2006)). Moreover, in order to satisfy the test imposed by s.53(3), it is not necessary for a witness to have 100 per cent understanding of the questions put to him and it is not necessary that the witness's answers be 100 per cent understandable, it being for the judge to consider the witness's performance as a whole (*R. v Sed* (2004)).

Whether the issue of the competence of a witness is raised by the court or by one of the parties, s.54 of the 1999 Act provides that the party who called the witness bears the burden of proving on the balance of probabilities that the witness is competent. Section 54 also provides that proceedings to determine the competence of a witness will take place in the absence of the jury, that expert evidence may be received for the purpose of determining the witness's competence and that any questioning of the witness for this purpose will be conducted by the judge.

In practice, the competence of a witness will normally be determined before the witness is sworn and, where a video recorded interview is tendered as a witness' evidence in chief, the judge should watch the recording and/or ask the witness questions (*R. v MacPherson*). Moreover, s.54 provides that where the court gives or intends to give a special measures direction (see Chapter 5, below) in relation to a witness, the court must take this into account when determining the witness's competence. Where a witness is permitted to give evidence in chief (e.g. in the form of a video recorded interview admitted under a special measures direction) and it then transpires that meaningful cross-examination of the witness is not possible, the court may find it necessary to review the issue of the witness' competence (*R. v B* (2010)).

Sworn and unsworn evidence

Section 55(2)(a) of the **YJ&CEA 1999** provides that a witness under the age of 14 may not give sworn evidence in criminal proceedings. Moreover, under s.55(2)(b), a witness aged 14 or more may not give sworn evidence in criminal proceedings if the witness does not sufficiently appreciate the solemnity of the occasion and the particular responsibility of telling the truth which taking an oath involves. Section 55(3) provides that if a witness is able to give intelligible testimony (i.e. is able to understand questions and to give answers which can be understood (s.55(8)), the witness is presumed to sufficiently appreciate the above-mentioned matters unless evidence to the contrary is tendered by a party.

Whether the issue of whether a witness may give sworn evidence is raised by the court or by one of the parties, s.55 provides that the party who desires the witness to be sworn bears the burden of proving on the balance of probabilities that the witness is aged 14 or more and that he sufficiently appreciates the above-mentioned matters. Section 55 also provides that proceedings to determine the competence of a witness will take place in the absence of the jury, that expert evidence may be received for the purpose of determining whether a witness may be sworn and that any questioning of the witness for this purpose will be conducted by the judge.

The accused

Can the accused testify for the prosecution?

LEGISLATION HIGHLIGHTER

Section 53(4) of the **YJ&CEA 1999** provides as follows.

"A person charged in criminal proceedings is not competent to give evidence in the proceedings for the prosecution (whether he is the only person, or is one of two or more persons, charged in the proceedings)."

The effect of s.53(4) of the **YJ&CEA 1999** provides that the accused is not a competent prosecution witness. Indeed, where several persons are charged in the proceedings, none of them are competent to give evidence for the prosecution. Thus, if A and B are charged in the same proceedings, neither A nor B are competent to give evidence for the prosecution. The effect of s.53(5) is, however, that B is competent (and may be compelled) to give evidence for the prosecution against A if B is no longer liable to be convicted. This will be the case if B pleads guilty, if B has already been acquitted of the relevant charge or charges or if the proceedings against B have been discontinued. Moreover, B may be compelled to give evidence for the prosecution against A if A and B are being tried separately.

Can the accused be a defence witness?

LEGISLATION HIGHLIGHTER

Section 1(1) of the **Criminal Evidence Act 1898 (CEA 1898)** provides as follows.

"A person charged in criminal proceedings shall not be called as a witness in the proceedings except on his own application."

The effect of s.1 of the **CEA 1898** is that the accused is a competent defence witness but cannot be compelled to give evidence. Thus, if A and B are tried in the same proceedings, B may choose to give evidence for the defence but cannot be compelled to do so by A. If an accused does not testify in his own defence, however, the court may be entitled to draw an inference from his silence (see Chapter 4, below).

The spouse or civil partner of the accused

The competence of the accused's spouse (husband or wife, not unmarried partner (*R. v Pearce* (2002)) or civil partner in criminal proceedings is governed by s.53 of the **YJ&CEA 1999**. The compellability of the accused's spouse or civil partner is governed by s.80 of **PACE**.

Can the accused's spouse or civil partner testify for the prosecution?

Under s.53(4) of the 1999 Act (considered above), the accused's spouse or civil partner is not competent to give evidence for the prosecution if the spouse or civil partner is charged with an offence in the proceedings. Since the spouse or civil partner is not competent in such circumstances the spouse or civil partner, of course, cannot be compelled to testify (that this is so is made clear by PACE s.80(4)).

Even if the accused's spouse or civil partner is competent to give evidence for the prosecution (i.e. where the spouse or civil partner is not charged with an offence in the proceedings), the effect of s.80(2A)(b) of the 1984 Act is that the spouse or civil partner can only be compelled to give evidence for the prosecution if the offence charged is of a type specified by s.80(3) of the 1984 Act (for example, if it involved an assault on the spouse or civil partner or on a person under the age of 16 or if it is a sexual offence alleged to have been committed in respect of a person under the age of 16). In such circumstances, the spouse or civil partner can only be compelled to give evidence in respect of the specified offence.

Can the accused's spouse or civil partner be a defence witness?

The accused's spouse or civil partner is competent to give evidence for the defence (both for the accused and for any other persons charged in the same proceedings). Under s.80(2) of the 1984 Act, the accused's spouse or civil partner may be compelled to give evidence for the accused unless the spouse or civil partner is charged with an offence in the proceedings (in which case the effect of s.1(1) of the **Criminal Evidence Act 1898** and of s.80(4) of the 1984 Act, both considered above, is that the spouse or civil partner will not be compellable). The extent to which a defendant other than the accused (i.e. a co-accused) may compel the accused's spouse or civil partner to testify is governed by **PACE** s.80(2A)(a). The effect of s. 80(2A)(a) is that the accused's spouse or civil partner may be compelled to give evidence for a person charged in the same proceedings as the accused only if the offence charged is of a type specified by s.80(3) of the 1984 Act (see above). In such circumstances, the spouse or civil partner can only be compelled to give evidence in respect of the specified offence. Moreover, under s.80(4) of the 1984 Act and s.1(1) of the 1898 Act (both considered above), the accused's spouse or civil partner is not compellable to give evidence for a person charged in the same proceedings as the accused if the spouse or civil partner is charged with an offence in the proceedings.

Former spouses/civil partners and spouses/civil partners who refuse to testify

Section 80(5) of the 1984 Act provides that a former spouse/civil partner of the accused is competent and compellable as if the accused and the former spouse/civil partner had never been married. Finally, s.80A of the 1984 Act provides that the prosecution cannot comment upon the failure of the accused's spouse or civil partner to testify.

Admissibility of hearsay evidence of a spouse/civil partner who refuses to testify

Where the accused's spouse or civil partner is not compellable and refuses to testify, the court may be prepared to admit hearsay evidence of statements made to the police by the spouse or civil partner under a hearsay exception such as section 114(1)(d) of the Criminal Justice Act 2003 (*R. v L* (2008)). See Ch.12, below.

DEFINITION CHECKPOINT

Witnesses cannot give sworn testimony in criminal proceedings if;
- they are under the age of 14; or
- they do not have a sufficient appreciation of the solemnity of the occasion and the particular responsibility to tell the truth which is involved in taking an oath.

Where a person is competent to give evidence in criminal proceedings but may not give sworn evidence due to the operation of s.55 of the 1999 Act, s.56 of the 1999 Act provides that the witness will give unsworn evidence.

CIVIL PROCEEDINGS

Limited mental ability and communication difficulties

A person called to give evidence in civil proceedings who, in the opinion of the judge, does not sufficiently appreciate the seriousness of the occasion or does not realise that giving evidence under oath involves more than the everyday duty of telling the truth is not competent (*R. v Bellamy* (1986)). In determining the competence of a witness, the judge may examine the witness and hear expert psychological evidence (*R. v Deakin* (1994); *R. v Hampshire* (1995)). Indeed, if the witness is mentally ill, it may be that the judge, having heard the evidence of the expert, can deal with the issue of competence without the necessity of examining the witness (*R. v Barratt*

(1996)). If the witness's incapacity is only short term (e.g. when it is caused by drink or drugs) the judge may be prepared to adjourn (*R. v Baines* (1987)).

<blockquote>

■ DEFINITION CHECKPOINT

In civil proceedings the test for whether a witness is competent is same test for whether the witness can give sworn evidence. The civil courts will not receive unsworn evidence from a witness (except in the case of children—see below) and so a witness who is incapable of swearing an oath will not be competent to give evidence in civil proceedings.

</blockquote>

A person incapable of communicating his evidence to the court (e.g. because the person is deaf and dumb and is incapable of communicating by sign language through an interpreter) is also incompetent (*R. v Whitehead* (1866)).

Children

In civil proceedings a child (a person under the age of 18 Children Act 1989, s.105) may be competent to give sworn testimony. This will be the case if, in the opinion of the judge, the child sufficiently appreciates the seriousness of the occasion and realises that giving evidence under oath involves more than the everyday duty of telling the truth (*R. v Hayes* (1977) and *R. v Campbell* (1983)). Secondly, if a child is not competent to give sworn testimony in civil proceedings, the child may give unsworn testimony if, in the opinion of the judge, the child both understands that he is under a duty to speak the truth and has sufficient understanding to justify the reception of his evidence (**Children Act 1989** s.96). Finally, if a child is neither competent to give sworn testimony nor competent to give unsworn testimony in civil proceedings then the child is incompetent and its evidence may not be received.

Revision checklist

You should now know and understand:

- **that in criminal and civil proceedings there is a presumption that witnesses are both competent and compellable;**

- **the test for competence in criminal proceedings;**

- **the main exceptions that apply to general presumption of competence in criminal proceedings;**

- **the main exceptions that apply to compellability in criminal proceedings;**

- **when a witness may give sworn evidence in criminal proceedings;**

- when a witness may give unsworn evidence in criminal proceedings;
- the test for competence in civil proceedings;
- the rules governing the reception of unsworn evidence from children in civil proceedings.

QUESTION AND ANSWER

The Question

Andy is charged with causing grievous bodily harm to Tony, the prosecution allege that Andy "glassed" Tony outside of the local pub, the Oxgate Arms. Whilst walking home from school past the Oxgate Arms, Rebecca and her sister Claire witnessed the incident take place. The prosecution wish to call both girls to give evidence about what they saw. Rebecca is 13 years old and of above average intelligence, Claire is 16 years old but has cognitive difficulties which impair her understanding although she is able to communicate.

The prosecution also wish to call Pam, Andy's wife, who was present when the incident occurred to testify that Andy "glassed" Tony. Andy is concerned that the prosecution may attempt to call him as a witness.

Consider whether Rebecca, Claire, Pam and Andy are competent and compellable witnesses for the prosecution.

Advice and the Answer

General guidance

It is important that you first identify what type of proceedings you are dealing with as the tests for competence and the question of whether the witness may give sworn or unsworn evidence differ between criminal and civil proceedings. Once you have identified the type of proceedings remember that in both criminal and civil proceedings there is a presumption that the witness will be both competent and compellable. You should therefore address the issue with competence and compellability if you are dealing with a situation that appears to fall outside of the general rules, for example, if you are asked about the competence and compellability of the accused in criminal proceedings or you are dealing with a witness who may have difficulty communicating.

Answer plan

1 Andy is charged with a criminal offence so the competence of witnesses will be governed by s.53 of the **Youth Justice and Criminal Evidence Act (YJ&CEA)** 1999. Section 53(1) creates a presumption that all witnesses, regardless of age, are competent witnesses. A competent witness is also presumed to be compellable.

2 Rebecca appears to be a competent and compellable witness i.e. she is able to testify and can be required to testify. Rebecca is under 14 years of age and, consequently, under s.55 of the **YJ&CEA 1999**, she may not give sworn evidence. Even though Rebecca cannot give sworn evidence, she may give unsworn evidence under s.56 of the 1999 Act as she appears to be a competent witness. [Note: you will see in Chapter 5, below, that the court will probably make a special measures direction in relation to Rebecca—so her evidence in chief will probably take the form of a video recorded interview and she will probably be cross-examined and re-examined via a live link.]

3 Under s.53(3) of the 1999 Act, Claire will not be a competent witness if it appears to the court that she cannot understand questions put to her and give answers to those questions that can be understood. This does not require the witness to have 100 per cent understanding of the questions put to her and it is not necessary that the witness' answers be 100 per cent understandable, it being for the judge to consider the witness' performance as a whole (*R. v Sed*)

4 If the issue of Claire's competence is raised, either by the court or by one of the parties, s.54 of the 1999 Act provides that the party who called her (i.e. the prosecution) bears the burden of proving on the balance of probabilities that she is competent.

5 Claire is old enough to give sworn testimony (as she is over 14) but may be prevented from doing so by virtue of s.55(2)(b) of the 1999 Act if she does not have "a sufficient appreciation of the solemnity of the occasion and of the particular responsibility to tell the truth which is involved in taking an oath".

6 If Claire is unable to give sworn testimony the court will be able to receive her unsworn testimony under s.56 of the 1999 Act provided she is competent to testify.

7 In general, the spouse of the accused is a competent prosecution witness but cannot be compelled to testify (**YJ&CEA** 1999 s.53; **PACE** s.80). Pam is not charged with an offence in the proceedings and so is competent to testify (s.53(1) of the 1999 Act).

8 The spouse is a compellable prosecution witness if the offence with which the accused is charged falls within s.80(3) of the 1984 Act (i.e. if it is a "specified offence"). Andy is not charged with a "specified

offence" and therefore it would appear that Pam is a competent but not compellable prosecution witness.

9 Andy is charged with an offence in the proceedings and so, by virtue of s.54 of the 1999 Act, is neither a competent nor compellable prosecution witness. Andy is competent to testify in his defence but cannot be compelled to do so. [Note: you will see in Chapter 4 below that if Andy does not testify the jury may be entitled to draw an inference in respect of his failure to testify.]

Corroboration, Unreliable Witnesses, Identification Evidence and Lies Told by the Accused

Introduction
In this chapter we will consider a number of things. We will start with corroboration, essentially the use of one piece of evidence to confirm the reliability of another. This will be followed by an examination of the separate but related issues caused by unreliable witnesses, identification evidence and lies told by the accused. We will consider the need for the judge to give a clear direction to the jury as to how they should approach each of these different types of evidence.

CORROBORATION

> **DEFINITION CHECKPOINT**
>
> **What is corroboration?**
> Essentially, one item of evidence is corroborated by another when the reliability of the former is confirmed by the latter. In English law, however, in order for one piece of admissible evidence to be capable of corroborating another, the former piece of evidence must, as was recognised by the Court of Criminal Appeal in *R. v Baskerville* (1916), satisfy two fundamental requirements:
> (1) The corroborative evidence must be independent of the witness whose evidence requires corroboration.
> (2) The corroborative evidence must connect the accused with the commission of the crime by confirming in a material particular both that the crime was committed and that it was committed by the accused.

Corroboration is now rarely required by English law
In English law, corroboration is only required in those exceptional situations in which statute still imposes corroboration requirements. For example, a person cannot be convicted of speeding if the only evidence that he was

speeding is the uncorroborated evidence of a single witness (Road Traffic Regulation Act 1984 s.89). Thus, D cannot be convicted of speeding solely upon the evidence of W, who is prepared to testify that he saw D exceeding the speed limit, but D may be convicted if W's evidence is confirmed by X, who was with W when D's car passed them, or if W's evidence is confirmed by some mechanical means (e.g. by the speedometer of W's car or by a speed gun) (*Nicholas v Penny* (1950)). A corroboration requirement is also imposed in the context of perjury by s.13 of the Perjury Act 1911.

. . . .

UNRELIABLE WITNESSES

In circumstances in which there is an evidential basis for suggesting that the evidence of a witness is unreliable, the judge possesses discretion to give the jury a warning (*R. v Makanjuola* (1995)). This might be the case where, for example, there is evidence that a witness who is a sexual offence complainant has made false sexual offence complaints in the past or where there is evidence that a witness has a grudge against the accused or has a purpose of his own to serve. Thus, for example, such a warning is likely to be required where a co-accused gives evidence against the accused.

So far as the nature of the warning is concerned, their Lordships in *Makanjuola* indicated that when a trial judge in the exercise of his discretion decides that a warning is required, the warning should form part of his review of and comments upon the evidence, and the nature of the warning is for the judge to determine. Thus, their Lordships in *Makanjuola* indicated that it might be sufficient simply to urge the jury to be cautious when considering placing reliance upon the evidence of the relevant witness. Alternatively, their Lordships indicated that the judge may feel that it is necessary to advise the jury to look for evidence supporting that of the relevant witness before placing reliance upon it. It appears, however, that evidence which is not independent of the witness whose evidence requires support is not capable of amounting to supporting evidence (*R. v Islam* (1998)). Thus, if C tells W that she was indecently assaulted by D and C then testifies to this effect, W's repetition in court of C's statement to W is not independent evidence and thus is not capable of amounting to supporting evidence.

IDENTIFICATION EVIDENCE

KEY CASE

R. v TURNBULL

The Court of Appeal in *R. v Turnbull* (1977) laid down guidelines which are applicable when the prosecution's case against the accused is wholly or substantially based upon disputed identification evidence. Where the identification evidence is of good quality it is safe to leave the decision to the jury with a warning based on the *Turnbull* guidelines below. Where the evidence is of a poor quality the case should be removed from the jury (i.e. they should be directed to acquit the accused) unless there is other evidence capable of supporting the identification.

What are the "Turnbull guidelines"?

Essentially, the trial judge should warn the jury to be cautious when considering placing reliance upon the evidence of one or more witnesses who have identified the accused, explaining to them that such witnesses may be both convincing and mistaken. The judge should direct the jury to consider the circumstances in which an observation was made. Thus, they should be directed to consider factors such as:

- the duration of the period of observation;
- the distance between the witness and the person observed;
- the quality of the light;
- whether the observation was impeded in any way;
- whether the witness knew the accused and, if so, how many times they had met or how memorable their meetings had been;
- the length of time between the observation and the witness identifying the accused to the police; and
- any material discrepancies between the witness' description to the police of the person observed and the actual appearance of the accused.

Further, where the witness did know the accused at the time when the observation was made, the jury should be reminded that people do sometimes make mistakes in recognising friends and relatives.

Where identification evidence is of good quality (e.g. when the observation was made in good lighting by a friend of the accused who had a clear view of him a short distance away for several minutes) it is safe to leave the evidence to the jury provided that they have been given a warning in the terms outlined by the Court of Appeal (though no particular form of words is required). Where the quality of the identification evidence is poor, however (e.g. where the witness only had a fleeting glance of the person he observed or where the observation was made at a long distance and in bad light by a stranger), simply to warn the jury in the terms outlined by the Court of Appeal is not sufficient. Rather, in such circumstances, the judge should withdraw the case from the jury and direct them to acquit the accused unless there is other evidence which is capable of supporting the identification evidence. Where such evidence exists the judge should direct the jury's attention to it, but the judge should also direct them to ignore for this purpose any evidence which they might regard as providing support for an identification but which does not in fact do so. Examples of potentially supporting evidence are the evidence of other identification witnesses (though the jury should be warned that they all may be mistaken see *R. v Weeder* (1980) and *R. v Breslin* (1984)) and, in certain circumstances, lies told by the accused (see below).

If the court fails to comply with the *Turnbull* guidelines where they are applicable and the accused is convicted, the practical result (unless the identification evidence is of high quality) is likely to be that the accused's conviction will be quashed upon appeal.

Where a witness who attends an identification procedure makes a qualified identification (e.g. says that he is 90 per cent sure that it is the person), the court may still permit the witness to give identification evidence but it seems that a conviction should not solely be based on a single qualified identification and the judge should give the jury an appropriate warning if evidence of a qualified identification is admitted (*R. v George* (2002)).

Finally, where the issue before the court is not whether identification evidence was erroneous but, rather, is whether the identification witness was lying, a *Turnbull* warning is not required (*R. v Cape* (1996)). Similarly, a *Turnbull* warning is not required where a witness merely describes the person who the witness saw commit the offence with which the accused is charged (*R. v Gayle* (1999)).

Do the Turnbull guidelines apply to forms of identification other than identification of the accused by witnesses?

Where a witness identifies the accused from a photograph or video recording, the *Turnbull* guidelines are applicable (see, respectively, *R. v Blenkinsop* (1995) and *Taylor v Chief Constable of Cheshire* (1987)). Similarly, an appropriately modified version of the *Turnbull* guidelines is applicable in the context of voice identification by witnesses (*R. v Hersey* (1998)). Where, however, the jury themselves make an identification from a photograph or video recording without the assistance of a witness, it appears that the *Turnbull* guidelines are not applicable (*R. v Downey* (1995)). In such circumstances, however, the judge should, even so, direct the jury to consider factors such as the quality of the image and any change in the appearance of the accused between the time when the photograph or video recording was taken and the time of the trial (*R. v Dodson* (1984)). The jury may be entitled to rely upon a poor quality image if there is expert evidence (i.e. facial mapping evidence) to assist them or if a witness who knows the accused makes an identification of the accused from the image (*Att Gen's Reference (No. 2 of 2002)* (2003)).

Moreover, if there is strong evidence to the effect that the accused and another person were together at the time when the offence with which the accused is charged was committed and evidence identifying the other person is disputed, it appears that a *Turnbull* warning is required if the accused claims that he was not present (*R. v Bath* (1990)).

Further, it should be noted that where a witness identified not the accused but a car, whilst the *Turnbull* guidelines are not applicable, the jury should be directed to consider factors such as the opportunity which the witness had to identify the vehicle and the ability of the witness to distinguish between cars (*R. v Browning* (1991)). Similarly, the *Turnbull* guidelines do not apply where the issue of identification relates to the accused's clothes rather than to the accused's appearance (*R. v Hassan*).

Dock identifications and breaches of Code D

A dock identification is one which is made in court by a witness who has not previously identified the accused via an identification procedure (e.g. a video identification or an identification parade). Normally, the court will exercise its exclusionary discretion (i.e. its discretion under s.78 of **PACE**) so as to prevent a dock identification from taking place (*R. v Fergus* (1993)).

The court, in the exercise of its exclusionary discretion (i.e. under s.78 of **PACE**) is likely to exclude identification evidence in the context of serious or deliberate breaches of Code D (which regulates the conduct of identification procedures), the question for the court being whether, in the circumstances, the admission of the evidence would have such an adverse effect on the fairness of the proceedings that it ought not to be admitted (*R. v Quinn* (1990)). Where the court admits identification evidence in the context of breaches of Code D (i.e. in the context of less serious breaches) an appropriate direction to the jury will be required (*R. v Forbes* (2001)).

. . . .

THE ACCUSED'S LIES

A jury may be entitled to draw an inference of guilt from lies told by the accused either out of court or in court. It should be noted, however, that the jury should only draw such an inference if they are satisfied beyond reasonable doubt both that the accused did lie and that he did not lie for an innocent reason (see *R. v Burge*; *R. v Pegg* (1995)). Thus, for example, if the jury believe that D, charged with rape, may have lied to the police about having had intercourse with V not because he raped her but because he did not want his wife to find out that he had had intercourse with her, then the jury should not draw an inference of guilt from D's lie.

KEY CASES

R. v Lucas (1981)/R. v Burge; R. v Pegg (1996)

The Court of Appeal in *R. v Lucas* considered the evidential significance of lies told by the accused and formulated a warning which has become known as a "Lucas direction". The original version of the warning was formulated in terms of the law relating to corroboration, which now has little practical relevance, but the essence of the modern formulation of the Lucas direction, as laid down by the Court of Appeal in *R. v Burge*; *R. v Pegg*, is that where it is necessary to give a Lucas direction, the trial judge should warn the jury as to the significance of the accused's lies, and, in particular, to warn them that they should only draw an inference of guilt from them if sure both that he lied and that he did not lie for an innocent reason.

It appears that the giving of such a warning is usually necessary in four situations (*R. v Burge*; *R. v Pegg*):

(1) Where an alibi is raised by the defence.
(2) Where the judge advises the jury to look for evidence in support of the evidence of an unreliable witness (including evidence in support of poor-quality identification evidence) and identifies lies which the accused has or may have told as potential supporting evidence.
(3) Where the prosecution relies upon lies which the accused has or may have told as evidence of his guilt.
(4) Where there is a danger that the jury may rely upon lies which the accused may have told as evidence of his guilt.

Thus, for example, where the accused relies on an alibi, it should be made clear to the jury both that the prosecution must satisfy them beyond reasonable doubt that the alibi is false (i.e. that the accused is not required to prove his alibi) and that even if they are sure that the accused's alibi is false, this does not automatically mean that they are entitled to convict the accused because an innocent person may invent a false alibi to support his defence (*R. v Lesley*).

The giving of a *Lucas* direction is not required in every situation in which the accused has or may have told a lie. Thus, for example, a *Lucas* direction is not required where the alleged lie relates to a central issue of the case as, in such circumstances, the normal direction which the judge gives the jury concerning the burden and standard of proof will be adequate (*R. v Burge*; *R. v Pegg*). In general, a *Lucas* direction is not required in circumstances in which there is no danger that the jury may equate the fact that the accused has told a lie with his guilt (*R. v Middleton* (2001)) and it seems that a full *Lucas* direction need not be given where giving such a direction would work to the disadvantage of the accused (*R. v Nyanteh* (2005)).

Revision checklist

You should now know and understand:

- **what the term corroboration means and when corroboration may be required;**
- **the nature of the warning that may be given to the jury where there is an evidential basis for suggesting that a witness' evidence may be unreliable;**
- **the nature of the direction that should be given to the jury in relation to disputed identification evidence;**
- **the evidential significance of lies told by the accused and the nature of the warning that the jury should receive.**

QUESTION AND ANSWER

The Question

Bryn is charged with sexual assault. The prosecution allege that Bryn attacked Colleen in a multi-storey car park and fondled her breasts before running off. Bryn claims that at the time of the assault he was drinking in a pub five miles away. Amongst other things the prosecution intend to rely on the following pieces of evidence;
- CCTV footage appearing to show Bryn in the vicinity of the car park about five minutes before the alleged assault.
- The identification evidence of Kevin, an attendant on duty in the car park at the time of the assault. Kevin heard a woman scream and ran to investigate, as he arrived he saw a man run off towards the car park's rear exit. He made sure that the woman (Colleen)

was unharmed and then called the police. Kevin managed to pick Bryn out of an ID parade but told a police officer that he was only 80–90 per cent sure because "the car park is poorly lit and the man was running away".

- The identification evidence of Colleen who also picked Kevin out of an ID parade. Colleen said that she was "pretty certain" that it was Bryn despite the fact that she "only really got a glance at his face".

Five years ago Colleen falsely accused Craig, her ex-boyfriend, of sexually assaulting her.

Identify and discuss the nature of the warning, if any, that the judge should give to the jury in relation to any of the above pieces of evidence.

Model Answer

If the jury are satisfied that the CCTV footage does in fact show Bryn in the vicinity of the car park around five minutes before the alleged attack took place then this would tend to prove that Bryn's alibi is false and therefore that Bryn has lied. It would appear appropriate for the judge to give the jury a Lucas direction (*R. v Lucas*), as it is usually appropriate to give the direction where the accused has raised an alibi (*R. v Burge; R. v Pegg*). The judge should tell the jury that they may be entitled to draw an inference of guilt from the lie told by the accused, but only if they are sure that the accused lied and they are sure that he did not lie for an innocent reason. [Note: in practice the judge would be likely to give the jury the Judicial Studies Board's alibi specimen direction, which effectively incorporates the Lucas direction.]

The identification evidence of Kevin and Colleen would appear to require the judge to give the jury a *Turnbull* direction (*R. v Turnbull*). It would appear that a large part of the prosecution's case is based on the disputed identification evidence of one or more witnesses (in this case Kevin and Colleen) so it is appropriate for the judge to follow the *Turnbull* guidelines. The judge should warn the jury of the special need for caution before convicting on the basis of disputed identification evidence and should draw the jury's attention to the weaknesses in the identification evidence. In this case the weaknesses appear to be: the car park was poorly lit, the man was running away as Kevin made his identification, the fact that Colleen only got a glance at his face and the fact that neither witness claims to be certain of the identification that they have made (Kevin is 80—90 per cent sure and Colleen is <u>pretty</u> certain).

This does not appear to be a case where the judge should remove the evidence from the jury as it appears there is other evidence capable of supporting the identification evidence which the judge should draw the jury's attention to. In this case, the fact that more than one witness has identified the same person is capable of acting as supporting evidence, as is the failure of Bryn's alibi (see above).

Given that Colleen has made a false allegation of sexual assault in the past there may be an evidential basis for considering her to be an unreliable witness. The judge possess a discretion to give a *Makanjuola* warning to the jury. If the judge decides to give the warning it may be that simply warning the jury to exercise caution when considering Colleen's evidence is sufficient. Alternatively the jury may be asked to look for supporting evidence before relying on the evidence of the witness. In this case the identification evidence of Kevin and the failure of Bryn's alibi are capable of supporting Colleen's evidence. [Note: see Chapter 5, below, if there is an evidential basis for asserting that Colleen made a false sexual assault allegation in the past, leave will not be required under s.41 of the **Youth Justice and Criminal Evidence Act 1999** to cross-examine Colleen about it.]

The Accused's Right of Silence

Introduction

This chapter will consider the accused's right of silence and the limitations that can be placed upon it. Although at common law the accused has a right of silence there are common law principles and, more significantly, statutory provisions that allow the drawing of adverse "inferences" from the silence of the accused. This means that in some situations an evidential significance can be attached to the silence of the accused.

INFERENCES FROM SILENCE AT COMMON LAW

As is seen below, substantial inroads into the accused's common law right of silence were introduced by the Criminal Justice and Public Order Act 1994 which permits the drawing of adverse inferences from the accused's silence in certain situations. The common law itself also permits the drawing of adverse inferences from the accused's silence in limited circumstances. Basically, the court may be entitled to draw such an inference at common law in circumstances in which the accused, by his silence or other conduct, accepts a statement, such as an allegation, to which the accused could reasonably be expected to respond, the statement having been made in the accused's presence by a person with whom the accused was speaking on equal terms (i.e. it having been made by another member of the public rather than by a police officer) (*R. v Parkes* (1976)). Even where the court is entitled to conclude that the accused has adopted such a statement, however, the judge may still find it necessary to exclude such evidence either if it is irrelevant or if admitting it would have such an adverse effect on the proceedings that the court ought not to admit it (*R. v Osbourne* (2005)). Section 34(5) of the **Criminal Justice and Public Order Act 1994** specifically preserves the drawing of inferences at common law in such circumstances.

INFERENCES FROM SILENCE UNDER THE CRIMINAL JUSTICE AND PUBLIC ORDER ACT 1994

LEGISLATION HIGHLIGHTER

The Criminal Justice and Public Order Act 1994 ss.34, 35, 36 and 37

The Criminal Justice and Public Order Act 1994 introduced restrictions to the accused's right of silence both pre-trial and during the trial itself. Sections 34, 35, 36 and 37 (each dealt with in detail below) create specific situations in which adverse inferences from the accused's silence can be drawn.

The inferences drawn under the sections are inferences as to guilt and may be used as evidence supporting a conviction although, as discussed below, a conviction cannot be based solely or to a decisive extent on the silence of the accused.

Section 34 inferences from silence as to a fact later relied upon by the accused in his defence

When does s.34 apply?

In order for s.34 to apply, the accused must rely upon a fact in his defence that he did not mention when questioned under caution or charged and the fact must be one that the accused could reasonably have been expected to mention in the circumstances existing at the time when he was questioned under caution or charged. No inference may be drawn under s.34, however, if, when the accused failed to mention the relevant fact, the accused was at an authorised place of detention and had been denied the opportunity to consult a solicitor.

Section 34 CJ&PO Act 1994—Checklist

In order for an inference to be drawn under s.34 of the 1994 Act the following must be established:

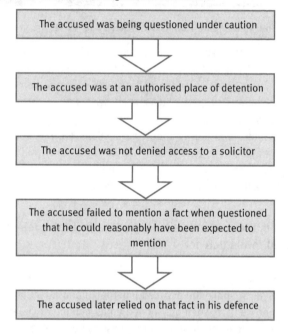

The accused was being questioned under caution

The accused was at an authorised place of detention

The accused was not denied access to a solicitor

The accused failed to mention a fact when questioned that he could reasonably have been expected to mention

The accused later relied on that fact in his defence

The accused relies upon a fact in his defence where he, or a defence witness, testifies as to the fact or even where it is revealed by a prosecution witness (*R. v Bowers* (1998)). The accused may rely on a fact in his defence even where the fact merely amounts to a positive suggestion which the defence puts to a witness as part of the defence case, and this is so even though the witness does not adopt the suggestion (*R. v Webber* (2004)). Section 34 will not apply, however, if the defence does not actually rely upon the fact that the accused failed to mention when questioned under caution or charged (*R. v Moshaid* (1998)). Moreover, where, at his trial, the accused merely proffers a theory or speculation (*R. v Nickolson* (1999)) or where the accused merely admits that a fact alleged by the prosecution is true (*R. v Betts* (2001)), s.34 will not be activated because, in both of these situations, the accused does not rely on a fact in his defence (though if a theory or speculation is based upon a fact that the accused could reasonably have been expected to mention when questioned or charged, s.34 will be activated (*R. v MB* (2000)).

Section 34 will not apply if the accused mentioned, when questioned or charged, a fact which he subsequently relies upon in his defence, and this may be so even if the accused gives a "no comment interview" if the fact was mentioned by the accused's solicitor in a prepared statement which the solicitor read out at the beginning of the accused's police station interview (*R. v Knight* (2004)). The court may be entitled to draw an inference, however, where the accused failed to mention a fact during a police station interview even though the accused does subsequently mention the fact during a subsequent police station interview (*R. v Betts and Hall* (2001)).

All relevant circumstances should be taken into account in assessing whether the accused could reasonably have been expected to mention the fact when questioned or charged. Thus, they can include, for example, the personal characteristics of the accused and any legal advice he received (*R. v Argent* (1997)), the complexity of the prosecution's case or how much of it has been disclosed to the accused (*R. v Roble* (1997)) and the nature of the questions put to him (*R. v Nickolson*).

What inferences can be drawn under s.34?

Where s.34 applies, the court may draw such inferences as appear proper from the failure to mention the relevant fact. Perhaps the most obvious inference which may be drawn is that the accused has fabricated the relevant fact since his police interview, but other possible inferences are that the accused had already begun to fabricate a defence when he was interviewed but was unwilling to mention it as he had not had the chance to think it through sufficiently to expose it to detailed questioning or that the accused tailored a fact in order to make it fit the defence case (*R. v Milford* (2001)).

Exclusionary discretion

The trial judge retains a discretion to prevent the drawing of an inference under s.34 (s.38(6)). This may be exercised where, for example, the accused's silence follows an unlawful arrest or breach of **PACE** or the Codes of Practice (*R. v Pointer* (1997)) or the prejudicial effect of the evidence outweighs its probative value (*R. v Argent*).

Remaining silent on solicitor's advice

The fact that the accused failed to mention a relevant fact because his solicitor advised him not to does not automatically render the failure reasonable, however good the advice in the circumstances (*R. v Condron* (1997)). What is relevant is not whether the advice was correct but whether it was reasonable for the accused to act upon it by remaining silent (*R. v Argent*). Where an accused genuinely acting on legal advice remains silent, inferences may still be drawn if the jury is satisfied that he had no explanation to give or none that would withstand questioning and investigation (*R. v Hoare* (2005)). The ultimate question which the jury must determine is whether the accused could reasonably have been expected to mention the relevant fact when he was questioned by the police and, thus, an inference should not be drawn where the jury consider that the accused genuinely and reasonably relied upon legal advice (*R. v Beckles* (2005)). Whether it was reasonable for the accused to rely on the advice that his solicitor gave him is a matter that the court must consider when determining the ultimate question (*R. v Essa* (2009)).

If the accused intends to rely upon the fact that he was advised by his solicitor to remain silent, he or his solicitor must reveal to the court the basis of the advice or the reasons for it (*R. v Condron*). This may lead to waiver of legal professional privilege. Waiver may also result if, during the course of a police interview, the accused, or his solicitor acting as his agent, revealed the reasons for the accused's silence (*R. v Fitzgerald* (1998)). There will be no waiver or privilege, however, where the accused or his solicitor testify that the accused mentioned a fact to his solicitor prior to being questioned by the police if they do so for the purpose of rebutting an allegation, made by the prosecution, that the accused fabricated the fact subsequent to the police station interview (*R. v Wishart* (2005)).

Can the accused be convicted solely upon his silence as to a relevant fact?

Such silence cannot form the sole or main basis of a conviction against him (s.38(3) and *Murray v UK* (1996)).

The trial judge's directions to the jury under s.34

The jury should be made aware that the accused was cautioned before being interviewed (*R. v Chenia* (2004)).The jury should be made aware of the inferences that they are potentially entitled to draw (*R. v Allan* (2004)). The judge should direct the jury only to draw an inference if they regard this as a fair and proper conclusion (*R. v Petkar* (2004)) and that they may not draw an inference unless they are satisfied that the requirements of s.34 have been met, that the accused's silence can only sensibly be attributed to his having no answer to the charges against him or none which would withstand questioning and investigation (*R. v Betts*) and that the case against the accused is so strong that, regardless of the accused's failure to mention the fact, it calls for an answer from the accused (*R. v Condron*). (Thus, where the jury is satisfied that there is a plausible explanation for the accused's silence other than that he had no answer to the charge or none which would withstand inquiry, they may not draw an inference.) Where the accused's solicitor advised the accused to give a no-comment interview, the jury should be directed to consider whether the accused genuinely and reasonably relied on the legal advice (*R. v Beckles*). The trial judge should also remind the jury that an accused cannot be convicted solely or mainly upon an inference drawn under the section (*Murray v UK*). Failure to direct the jury correctly on all these matters may result in a violation of the right to a fair trial under art.6 of the Convention (*Condron v UK* (2000)) and may result in the accused's conviction being quashed. Thus, in *R. v Betts*, a direction in terms which permitted the jury to draw an adverse inference even though they may have considered plausible the accused's explanation for his failure to mention a relevant fact was a breach of art.6.

█ DEFINITION CHECKPOINT

"Inference"

Where the jury are entitled to draw an inference from the silence of the accused, the inference that they are entitled to draw may, depending upon the circumstances, take a variety of forms. For example, in relation to s.34 of the 1994 Act, The Crown Court Bench Book (Judicial Studies Board March 2010 at p.261) recognises that the obvious inference under s.34 is that the fact that the accused failed to mention is not true and that if the jury draw this inference the drawing of a further inference may, but will not necessarily, be justified. Clearly, the most significant further inference would be that the accused is guilty, but the Bench Book makes clear that this inference will not automatically follow from an inference that the fact that the accused failed to mention is not true (e.g. the Bench Book recognises that the falsity of the fact might not undermine the accused's defence if the fact was merely "peripheral, secondary or irrelevant").

Sections 36 and 37 inferences from silence in response to a request to account for objects, substances, marks or one's presence at a particular place

LEGISLATION HIGHLIGHTER

Section 36 of the **Criminal Justice and Public Order Act 1994**

Section 36 permits inferences to be drawn at trial from the accused's silence or failure to account for the presence of objects, substances or marks where the following conditions are **all** satisfied:

(1) The accused was under arrest.

(2) An object, substance or mark was found at the place of the accused's arrest either in his possession, or on his person, clothing or footwear.

(3) The constable or Customs and Excise officer investigating the offence reasonably believed that the presence of the object, etc.

might be due to the participation of the accused in the commission of the offence he specified.

(4) The constable or Customs and Excise officer gave the accused the special warning (see Code C para.10.11), informed him of his belief and asked the accused to account for the presence of the object, etc.

(5) The accused failed so to account.

LEGISLATION HIGHLIGHTER

Section 37 **Criminal Justice and Public Order Act 1994**

Section 37 permits inferences to be drawn at trial from the accused's failure or refusal to account for his presence at the scene of the crime where the following conditions are **all** satisfied:

(1) The accused was under arrest.

(2) He was found at a place, at or about the time the offence was alleged to have occurred.

(3) The constable or Customs and Excise officer investigating the offence reasonably believed that the accused's presence at the scene at the time of his arrest might have been attributable to his participation in the offence.

(4) The constable or Customs and Excise officer gave the accused the special warning (see Code C para.10.11), informed him of his belief and asked the accused to account for the presence of the object.

(5) The accused failed so to account.

No inference may be drawn under s.36 or s.37 if, when the accused failed to account for the object, etc. or for his presence at the particular place, the accused was at an authorised place of detention and had been denied the opportunity to consult a solicitor.

The trial judge retains a discretion to prevent the drawing of an inference under s.36 or 37 (s.38(6)).

Can the accused be convicted solely or mainly upon his silence or failure to account for the presence of objects, etc. or his presence at a particular place?

As was seen above, silence cannot form the sole or main basis of a conviction (s.38(3) and *Murray v UK*).

The trial judge's directions to the jury under ss.36 and 37

Where the jury may be entitled to draw an inference under s.36 or s.37, it will be necessary for the judge to direct the jury in terms similar, though not identical, to those which apply where the judge directs the jury under s.34 (see above).

LEGISLATION HIGHLIGHTER

Section 35 of the **Criminal Justice and Public Order Act 1994**

Section 35 the drawing of inferences from the accused's silence at trial

Section 35 permits inferences to be drawn at trial, both where the accused fails to testify and where the accused refuses, without good cause, to answer a question whilst testifying.

An inference may not be drawn under s.35 if it appears to the court that the accused's physical or mental condition is such that it is undesirable for him to testify. This, it appears, may be the case where the accused's physical or mental health may be adversely affected if he testifies, but not merely because the accused has a mental condition which may affect the reliability of his evidence. Thus, for example, low IQ is not a mental condition which makes testifying "undesirable" for the purposes of s.35 (R. v Friend (1997)). Where the accused asserts that his physical or mental condition makes it undesirable for him to testify he will need to adduce evidence (i.e. expert medical evidence) of the physical or mental condition (R. v Friend).

Where the accused takes the stand but refuses to answer a question, an inference may not be drawn under s.35 where there is "good cause" for the refusal. This means that an inference may not be drawn from the accused's refusal to answer questions which he is not legally obliged to answer (e.g. where he is entitled to claim legal professional privilege).

Exclusionary discretion

The trial judge retains a discretion to prevent the drawing of an inference under s.35 (s.38(6)) but it ought only to be exercised if there is an evidential basis for doing so or in exceptional circumstances (R. v Cowan (1996)).

Can the accused be convicted solely upon his silence at trial?

Such silence cannot form the sole or main basis of a conviction or even contribute to a prima facie case against him (s.38(3) and Murray v UK).

The trial judge's direction to the jury under s.35

In *R. v Cowan* and *Condron v UK*, the court held that when directing the jury the trial judge must draw their attention to the following matters:

(1) The burden of proof remains on the prosecution and the standard of proof is beyond a reasonable doubt.

(2) The accused possesses a right of silence.

(3) An inference drawn from the accused's silence cannot on its own prove guilt and nor can a conviction be based mainly on silence.

(4) The jury cannot draw an inference from silence unless they find that the prosecution has established a case to answer.

(5) The jury may draw an adverse inference if they find that the accused's silence can only sensibly be attributed to his having no answer to the charges against him or none that would stand up to cross-examination, but they should not do so if they consider that there is another sensible explanation for his silence.

Failure to direct the jury correctly on these matters may result in a violation of the right to a fair trial under art.6 of the Convention (*Condron v UK*) and may result in the accused's conviction being quashed.

Revision checklist

You should now know and understand:

- that the accused has a right of silence at common law;
- common law restrictions on the right of silence;
- statutory restrictions on the accused's right of silence pre-trial;
- statutory restrictions on the accused's right of silence at trial;
- when the court will refuse to permit the drawing of an inference from the accused's silence.

QUESTION AND ANSWER

The Question

Stephanie is charged with arson. It is alleged that Stephanie set fire to a car belonging to Alan, her former employer, following a row about Stephanie being made redundant. Stephanie was arrested and questioned by police under caution. She refused the offer of a solicitor and gave a "no comment" interview throughout. At trial Stephanie intends to call her brother Mark to give evidence that Stephanie was with him all day on the day of the incident however Stephanie does not intend to testify

Advice and the Answer

Answer

If Stephanie relies upon her alibi at her trial, s.34 of the **Criminal Justice and Public Order Act 1994** will potentially entitle the jury to draw such inferences as appear proper from Stephanie's silence (since she was not prevented from consulting a solicitor but chose not to) on the basis that she is relying on facts in her defence (i.e. her alibi) that she failed to mention when questioned under caution or charged, though the jury may only draw a s.34 inference if they are satisfied that Stephanie could reasonably have been expected to mention the alibi when she was questioned or charged. The fact that Stephanie does not intend to testify will not prevent the drawing of an inference under s.34 as she is still relying upon a fact in her defence by calling Mark to give evidence of her alibi (*Bowers*).

The inference which the court may potentially be entitled to draw is either that Stephanie made up the alibi after she was questioned under caution or that she had already begun to fabricate this alibi when she was questioned under caution, but was unwilling to mention it as she had not had the chance to think it through sufficiently to expose it to detailed questioning (*R. v Randall*). [Note: as was made clear in Chapter 3 above, a Lucas Direction would be required in relation to this alibi.]

The fact that Stephanie may refuse to testify could result in the drawing of an inference under s.35 **Criminal Justice and Public Order Act 1994**. Stephanie does not appear to have "good cause" for her refusal to testify as there is no evidence that her physical or mental condition will make it undesirable for her to testify. It appears that Stephanie's decision not to testify is purely tactical and therefore it is likely that the judge will allow the drawing of an inference. The inference being that Stephanie has no explanation for the charges against her or none that would stand up to cross examination. [Note: it was made clear in Chapter 2, above, that the accused is not a competent witness for the prosecution and cannot be compelled to testify as a defence witness.]

When directing the jury on s.34, the judge should, amongst other matters, make clear to them that:

- they may not draw an inference unless they are satisfied that the requirements of s.34 have been met;
- they may not draw an inference unless they are satisfied that Stephanie's silence can only sensibly be attributed to her having no answer to the charges against her or none which would withstand questioning and investigation (*R. v Betts*); and
- Stephanie cannot be convicted solely or mainly upon an inference drawn under s.34 (*Murray v UK*).

When directing the jury on s.35, the judge should, amongst other matters, make clear to them that;

- The burden of proof remains on the prosecution and the standard of proof is beyond a reasonable doubt.
- The accused possesses a right of silence.
- an inference drawn from the accused's silence cannot on its own prove guilt and nor can a conviction be based mainly on silence.
- The jury may draw an adverse inference if they find that the accused's silence can only sensibly be attributed to her having no answer to the charges against her or none that would stand up to cross-examination, but they should not do so if they consider that there is another sensible explanation for her silence.

If the trial judge fails to direct the jury in relation to all of these matters (either in relation to s.34 or s.35), this may result in a violation of Stephanie's right to a fair trial under art.6 of the Convention (*Condron v UK*).

Examination, Cross-examination and Re-examination of Witnesses

Introduction

This chapter deals with rules of evidence relating to the three stages involved in questioning a witness in criminal and civil trials. These three stages are;

- examination in chief (conducted on behalf of the party who calls the witness),
- cross-examination (conducted on behalf of the other party or parties), and
- re-examination (conducted on behalf of the party who calls the witness).

EXAMINATION IN CHIEF

> **DEFINITION CHECKPOINT**
>
> Examination in chief is the first stage of the process of questioning a witness. Counsel for the party who has called the witness asks him questions in order to elicit from him evidence which is advantageous to that party's case.

The normal rules relating to the admissibility of evidence apply to examination in chief so that the party who has called the witness may not ask him to provide evidence which would be inadmissible at any stage of the trial (e.g. because it is hearsay evidence which is not admissible under an exception to the hearsay rule). In addition, there are rules particular to examination in chief which prevent the asking of certain types of question or preclude the admission of certain other types of evidence. Thus, leading questions should not normally be asked during examination in chief and, subject to exceptions, evidence of a witness' previous consistent statements is not admissible. A witness may be permitted to memory refresh whilst giving his or her evidence and special rules apply to hostile witnesses. Moreover, certain witnesses who are called to give evidence in criminal proceedings may have the benefit of a special measures direction.

Leading questions

> ### ■ DEFINITION CHECKPOINT
>
> Leading questions are questions which either imply that a certain answer is expected from the witness (e.g. "Was the car which knocked you over a blue Rolls Royce?", if asked after the witness testified that he had been knocked over by a car) or which presume certain disputed evidence has been accepted (e.g. "Did the defendant drive straight on after he had hit you?", if asked before the witness had testified that the defendant's car had hit the witness).

As a general rule, such questions should not be asked during examination in chief unless the other party does not object because it is not, in effect, the witness giving his own version of the events but, rather, it is counsel for the party who called the witness suggesting what he ought to say (*Ex p. Bottomley* (1909)). Strictly speaking, preliminary questions about a witness's name and address are leading questions but these are permitted for expediency.

Questions concerning a witness' previous consistent or self serving statements

Witnesses may frequently wish to bolster the credibility of their testimony by asserting that what they are now saying is consistent with oral or written statements they have made prior to trial, the hope being that the court is more likely to believe them if they have not wavered in their story. However, questions regarding such previous consistent or self serving statements are not normally permitted during examination in chief of their maker. This general rule also prevents other witnesses from testifying regarding such previous consistent statements (*R. v Roberts* (1942)). In addition to being inadmissible to show consistency, previous consistent statements, being hearsay statements, are also inadmissible as evidence of the matter stated. In practice, however, a variety of exceptions to this exclusionary rule exist both in the criminal and civil contexts.

Exceptions to the rule against previous consistent statements in criminal proceedings

As with many evidential rules, the rule against previous consistent statements has exceptions and the major exceptions are listed below.

Section 120 of the **Criminal Justice Act 2003**

All but one of the criminal exceptions to the rule against previous consistent statements, which are considered immediately below, have now been converted, by s.120 of the **Criminal Justice Act (CJA) 2003**, into exceptions to the hearsay rule. Where a previous consistent statement is admissible in criminal proceedings under a s.120 exception, it is not merely admissible as evidence of the witness's credibility (which was the position where such evidence was admitted at common law) but is also admissible as evidence of any matter stated of which the witness's oral evidence would be admissible.

The situations in which the exceptions created by s.120 of the **CJA 2003** apply are considered below.

Complaints made by victims

This exception to the rule against previous consistent statements, governed by s.120 of the **CJA 2003**, applies where the victim of an alleged offence testifies, and has previously made a complaint about the offence, the complaint being admissible as evidence of any matter stated of which the witness's oral evidence would be admissible.

If this exception is to apply, the following conditions must be satisfied:

(1) The witness must claim to be a person against whom an offence to which the proceedings relate has been committed.

(2) The statement must be a complaint about conduct which, if proved, constitutes all or part of the offence.

(3) The complaint must not have been made as a result of a threat or promise.

(4) The victim must give oral evidence in relation to the subject matter of the complaint before evidence of the complaint is adduced.

(5) Whilst testifying, the victim must indicate that to the best of his belief he made the statement and that it is true.

Where the above-mentioned conditions are satisfied, more than one previous consistent statement made by a victim may be admitted (*R. v Openshaw* (2006)).

Statements identifying or describing persons, places or objects

This exception to the rule against previous consistent statements, governed by s.120 of the CJA 2003, provides that, where a witness testifies and has previously made a statement identifying or describing a person, place or object, the witness' previous consistent statement is admissible as evidence of any matter stated of which the witness' oral evidence would be admissible, provided that the witness indicates whilst testifying that to the best of his belief he made the statement and that it is true.

Statements used to memory refresh
See below.

Statements relied on to rebut a suggestion during cross-examination that the witness has recently fabricated his testimony
If opposing counsel makes a specific suggestion to a witness during cross-examination that he has recently fabricated (i.e. made up) the evidence which he is giving in court, and the witness has previously made a statement which is consistent with his present testimony, that previous statement may be admitted to rebut the allegation of fabrication under s.120 of the **CJA 2003**. Where a previous consistent statement is admitted in such circumstances under s.120, it is admitted as evidence of any matter stated of which the witness's oral evidence would be admissible. Unlike the common law exception that it replaced, s.120 does explicitly refer to "recent" fabrication, but the Court of Appeal in *R. v Athwal* (2009) indicated that s.120 had not changed the nature of those circumstances in which such evidence is available. Rather, their Lordships in *Athwal* indicated that the court should not permit unjustified self corroboration but should only admit evidence of a previous consistent statement under this exception if the evidence, rationally and potentially cogently, assisted the court in determining where the truth lay.

Wholly exculpatory statements made by an accused during interviews with the police which become admissible at trial
Wholly exculpatory statements (i.e. total denials of guilt) made by the accused (e.g. made by the accused to the police when interviewed) are potentially admissible at common law as evidence of the accused's attitude at the time when the statement was made (*R. v Pearce* (1979)). Such statements do not fall with the new hearsay exceptions relating to previous consistent statements created by s.120 of the **CJA 2003** and, thus, statements admitted under this common law rule are not admitted as evidence of the matters stated.

Exceptions to the rule against previous consistent statements in civil proceedings

> **LEGISLATION HIGHLIGHTER**
>
> Section 6(2) of the **Civil Evidence Act 1995**
>
> Under s.6(2) of the **Civil Evidence Act (CEA) 1995,** a previous consistent statement may be admitted either with the leave (i.e. permission) of the court or (without the court's leave being required) in order to rebut a suggestion of recent fabrication (in relation to recent fabrication, see above). Where a previous consistent statement is admitted in civil proceedings it is admissible under s.1 of the **CEA 1995** as evidence of the matters stated under s.1 **CEA 1995** (**CEA 1995** s.6(5)). [Note: s.1 **CEA 1995,** which effectively abolished the hearsay rule as an exclusionary rule in civil proceedings, is considered in Chapter 10, below.]

Can a witness memory refresh outside the witness box?
Before going into court, a witness may read through a documentary statement he previously made at a time reasonably close to the events that the trial concerns in order to refresh his memory (*R. v Richardson* (1971)).

Can a witness memory refresh in the witness box?
The position here differs depending upon whether the proceedings are civil or criminal.

Criminal proceedings

> **LEGISLATION HIGHLIGHTER**
>
> Section 139 of the **Criminal Justice Act 2003**
>
> Section 139 of the **CJA 2003** provides that once a witness has begun to testify, he may refresh his memory from a document which he either made himself or which was made by another and verified by the witness provided that the following conditions are **both** satisfied:
>
> (1) The witness must testify that the document records his recollection of the matter at the time he made it.
> (2) The witness' recollection of the matter is likely to have been significantly better at the time the document was made or verified than it is at the time he testifies.

Basically, "verified" means that after the witness' statement was written down the witness either read the statement and confirmed that what it stated was correct or that the statement was read out to the witness who confirmed that it was correct (*R. v Kelsey* (1982)).

Civil proceedings

Once a witness has begun to testify he may, with leave, refresh his memory from a document which he either prepared himself or which was prepared by another and verified by the witness whilst the facts were still fresh in his memory (*R. v Mills* (1962)). The trial judge may grant leave for the witness to refresh his memory from such a document either if it was made contemporaneously with the events it described (i.e. at the time of the event or so soon afterwards that the facts were still fresh in the witness's memory (*R. v Richardson*)) or, if it was not made contemporaneously, in the exercise of his discretion (*R. v South Ribble Magistrates' Court Ex p. Cochrane* (1996)).

Are memory refreshing documents admissible in evidence?

Documents used to memory refresh in the witness box are not normally admissible, but may be admissible in the following circumstances:

(1) Where the witness's evidence and the memory refreshing document are not consistent (*R. v Sekhon* (1987)).

(2) Where it is suggested during cross-examination that the document was fabricated (*R. v Sekhon*).

(3) Where the jury will have problems following the cross-examination of the witness without copies of their memory refreshing document to read (*R. v Sekhon*).

(4) Where the party who called the witness wishes to admit the document and the witness is cross-examined on parts of it which the witness did not use for memory refreshing (*Senat v Senat* (1965)).

Under s.120(3) of the **CJA 2003**, if a witness is cross-examined on a memory refreshing document and it is received in evidence in criminal proceedings, the statement in the document will be admissible as evidence of a matter stated of which the witness' oral evidence would be admissible (i.e. the evidence is admissible under an exception to the hearsay rule created by s.120).

A memory refreshing document will not normally be admissible in civil proceedings, but will be admissible in the four situations outlined above, in which case it will be admissible under s.1 of the **CEA 1995** as evidence of the matter stated (s.6(4) and (5)) (i.e. the evidence is admissible under an exception to the hearsay rule created by s.1).

Witnesses in criminal proceedings who cannot remember the matters stated well enough to give oral evidence of them

Under a hearsay exception created by s.120(4) and (6) of the **CJA 2003**, a previous statement made by a witness will be admissible in criminal proceedings as evidence of a matter stated of which the witness' oral evidence would be admissible if the following conditions are **all** satisfied:

(1) The statement was made by the witness when the relevant matters were still fresh in his memory.

(2) The witness can no longer, and cannot reasonably be expected to, remember them sufficiently well to give oral evidence of them in the instant proceedings.

(3) The witness indicates whilst testifying that to the best of his belief he made the statement and that it is true.

What can be done if one's witness fails to give the evidence he had been called to give (i.e. "fails to come up to proof")?

A witness who fails to come up to proof (i.e. who fails to give the evidence that he has been called to give) may, depending upon the reason for his failure, either be treated by the court as merely an unfavourable witness or may be treated as actually hostile to the party who called him. The distinction between these two types of witness is important as the action which the party who called the witness may take to remedy the situation depends upon how the witness is treated by the court.

Unfavourable witnesses

> **DEFINITION CHECKPOINT**
>
> A witness who fails to come up to proof (e.g. due to memory loss) but who is not hostile to the party calling him is an unfavourable witness, not a hostile witness.

What action may be taken where an unfavourable witness is called?

If a witness proves to be unfavourable there is little that the party who called him can do other than to adduce further evidence to prove that which the witness has failed to prove, for example by calling other witnesses to counteract the evidence of the first (*Ewer v Ambrose* (1825) in which a second witness was called to prove the existence of a partnership, the first witness having failed to do so).

It is not permitted to discredit one's own witness by adducing "general evidence of his bad character" (**Criminal Procedure Act 1865** s.3). Nor is it permitted to put to an unfavourable witness a previous statement he has made which is inconsistent with his present testimony.

Hostile witnesses

> **DEFINITION CHECKPOINT**
>
> A witness is described as hostile if he clearly has no wish to tell the truth on behalf of the party who called him.

As a witness will not automatically be treated as hostile, the party who called him must first seek the judge's permission to have the witness declared hostile. The judge will take into account factors such as the witness' degree of co-operation and manner in assessing whether to declare him hostile. If the witness has made a previous inconsistent statement outside court, then, unless the witness is blatantly hostile, the judge and the party calling the witness ought to consider giving the witness the opportunity to refresh his memory from it. If the witness should refuse to do so and also to provide an explanation why his present testimony is inconsistent with his earlier statement, then the judge may consider that he should be declared hostile (*R. v Maw* (1994)).

What action may be taken once a witness has been declared hostile?
Where a witness is declared hostile, the following steps may be taken:

(1) Evidence may be adduced to contradict the witness.

(2) With the leave of the judge, the witness may be cross-examined and may be asked leading questions. He cannot, however, be treated in exactly the same way as a witness called by one party who is being cross-examined on behalf of another party (see below) in that, in accordance with s.3 of the **Criminal Procedure Act 1865 (CPA 1865)**, he cannot be discredited by adducing evidence of his bad character or previous convictions.

(3) With the leave of the judge, the party who called the witness may prove that the witness has made a previous inconsistent statement. Before doing so, details of the occasion on which the statement was made must be given to the witness so that he may remember making the statement and he must then be asked whether he made such a statement (**CPA 1865 s.3**).

Where a hostile witness admits making a previous inconsistent statement or it is proved under s.3 of the **CPA 1865**, it is admissible in criminal proceedings as evidence of any matter stated of which the witness' oral evidence would be admissible under a hearsay exception created by **CJA 2003** s.119. In such circumstances the jury have three options open to them, namely, to accept the truth of the previous inconsistent statement, to accept the truth of the witness' testimony in court or to reject both the previous inconsistent statement and the witness' testimony in court (*R. v Joyce* (2005)). Where a previous inconsistent statement is relied on by the defence it seems that the jury are entitled to rely on it if they consider that it might be true whereas it seems that they should only rely on one tendered by the prosecution if they are sure that it is true (*R. v Billingham* (2009)).

Where a hostile witness' previous inconsistent statement is admitted or is proved under s.3 of the **CPA 1865** in civil proceedings, it is admissible under s.1 of the **CEA 1995** as evidence of the matters stated (**CEA 1995** s.6(3) and (5)). It should be noted that, despite its title, the **CPA 1865** applies to civil proceedings as well as to criminal proceedings.

What action may be taken if a hostile witness refuses to testify?

Section 3 of the **CPA 1865** is inapplicable in this situation because the witness has not given any testimony with which his previous statement can be inconsistent. Thus, his previous statement may not be adduced under s.3. However, it may be adduced at common law with the leave of the judge. In *R. v Thompson* (1976), the Court of Appeal held that the judge has a common law discretion to permit cross-examination (including questions about a previous statement) of a hostile witness by the party who called him.

When can the court give a special measures direction?

LEGISLATION HIGHLIGHTER

Section 19 of the **Youth Justice and Criminal Evidence Act 1999**

Section 19 of the **YJ&CEA 1999** permits a criminal court to give special measures directions aimed at improving the quality of evidence given in court by witnesses who are eligible for assistance either because of age or incapacity or because of fear or distress about testifying. Either side may request such a direction and the court may also itself raise the issue.

A special measures direction may only be given where the court determines **both** that the witness is eligible for assistance (see below) **and** that one or more of the special measures would be likely to improve the quality of the witness' evidence. Where the court so determines, the court will then determine which measure(s) would be likely to maximise so far as practicable the quality of the evidence and will give a special measures direction providing that the measure or measures will apply to evidence given by the witness.

A special measure will not, however, be available, unless the Home

Secretary has notified the court that arrangements have been made for implementing the special measure in the area in which the court is located (s.18). Thus, for example, at the time of writing, video recorded cross-examination and re-examination are still not available.

Where the court has made a special measures direction, the court possesses the power (under s.20) to discharge or vary the direction in the interests of justice either on application by a party or of its own motion.

The procedure for making applications for special measures directions, applying to have such directions discharged or varied, etc. is governed by Pt 29 of the **Criminal Procedure Rules 2005** (**CrimPR** Pt 29).

DEFINITION CHECKPOINT

How is "eligible witness" defined?

An eligible witness is a witness other than the accused who is either eligible for assistance on grounds of age or incapacity (s.16) or is eligible for assistance on grounds of fear or distress about testifying (s.17). The former category includes child witnesses (i.e. witnesses under the age of 17) and witnesses the quality of whose evidence is likely to be diminished by mental disorder, significant impairment of intelligence and social functioning or physical disability or disorder. The latter category comprises witnesses the quality of whose evidence is likely to be reduced due to the fear or distress of testifying, and automatically includes sexual offence complainants unless they do not wish to be eligible.

Where a witness was a child witness at the date when he or she made video recorded statements to the police to be used as evidence in chief but has reached 17 years of age by the time the court has to determine whether to give a special measures direction, the witness is not an eligible witness but, rather, is a "qualifying" witness (see below) (s.22).

The special measures

The special measures available to the court are:

- screening the witness so that he cannot see the accused (s.23);
- giving evidence by live TV link (s.24);
- giving evidence in private (s.25);
- the removal of wigs and gowns whilst the witness testifies (s.26);
- video recording of evidence in chief (s.27);
- video recording of cross-examination or re-examination (s.28);
- giving evidence via an intermediary (s.29); and
- the use of devices to assist communication (s.30).

The latter two special measures are only available, however, where a witness is eligible for assistance on grounds of age or incapacity (s.18). Moreover, as was indicated above, video recorded cross-examination and re-examination had still not been made available by the Home Secretary at the time of writing.

Child witnesses (s.21)

> ### DEFINITION CHECKPOINT
> **The "primary rule" in relation to child witnesses**
> In relation to child witnesses, the "primary rule" is that a video recording of the witness' evidence should be admitted as evidence in chief and his or her cross-examination and re-examination should be given by live TV link unless the court directs that they ought to be video recorded.

However, s.27 provides that video recorded evidence should not be admitted if it is not in the interests of justice to do so and s.21 additionally provides that the primary rule does not apply where compliance with it would not be likely to maximise the quality of the witness' evidence so far as is practicable.

> ### DEFINITION CHECKPOINT
> **Child witnesses "in special need of protection"**
> A child witness is one who is in need of special protection if (i.e. where the proceedings involve one or more of the offences specified in s.35(3), namely certain sexual offences, kidnapping and any offence involving an assault on, or injury or threat of injury to, any person).

In respect of such a witness' evidence, the primary rule will still apply even if compliance with it would not be likely to maximise the quality of the witness' evidence so far as is practicable. Further, where the proceedings involve one of the sexual offences listed in s.35(3), and the court directs that a video recording of the witness' evidence is admitted as evidence in chief, it should also direct, unless the witness objects, that cross-examination and re-examination are also video recorded.

As was seen above, at the time of writing the Home Secretary had not yet made video recorded cross-examination and re-examination available.

Where a witness reaches the age of 17 after the witness has begun to give evidence in the proceedings the special measures direction will continue to have effect. Where a witness reaches the age of 17 before the witness begins to give evidence in the proceedings, the special measures direction will cease to have effect except that it will continue to have effect to the extent to which it provided for the admission of a video recording as evidence in chief and (if the video recording has already been made) to the extent to which it provided for the video recording of cross-examination and re-examination.

Qualifying witnesses (s.22)

The primary rule (see above) applies to a qualifying witness to the extent to which it requires the admission of a video recording as evidence in chief. Where a qualifying witness is in need of special protection, the video recording will be admissible as evidence in chief even if compliance with the primary rule would not be likely to maximise the quality of the witness' evidence so far as is practicable and, if the proceedings involve one of the sexual offences listed in s.35(3) and the court directs the admission of a video recording as evidence in chief, the court, unless the witness objects, will also be required to direct that cross-examination and re-examination are also video recorded. As was seen above, however, at the time of writing the Home Secretary had not yet made video recorded cross-examination and re-examination available.

Special measures directions and warnings to the jury

Where necessary, the judge must give the jury an appropriate warning to ensure that the accused is not prejudiced by virtue of the fact that a special measures direction was given in relation to a witness (s.32).

Special measures directions and human rights

The fact that a special measures direction cannot be made in relation to the accused does not mean that, in consequence of the principle of equality of arms (which forms an aspect of a fair trial under art.6 of the **European Convention on Human Rights**), a special measures direction cannot be made in relation to prosecution witnesses in circumstances in which the accused would, if not charged with an offence in the proceedings, be eligible for assistance. Rather, in such circumstances, the court should exercise its common law powers (e.g. to permit a child defendant to answer leading questions based on a written statement which the jury has seen) so as to ensure that the accused has a fair trial though, exceptionally, the court could discharge a special measures direction where its operation would be disadvantageous to the accused (*R. v Camberwell Green Youth Court* (2005)).

Section 33A of the 1999 Act (see below), which was inserted into the 1999 Act in 2007 and which concerns the making of live link directions will, presumably, reduce the potential for equality of arms issues to arise in the context of the making of special measures directions. Moreover, it appears that the court possesses the power at common law to exceptionally permit an accused who cannot be present during the trial to participate by live link (*R. v Ukpabio* (2007)).

Special measures directions and the Coroners and Justice Act 2009

The Coroners and Justice Act 2009 contains provisions which (when and if they are brought into force) will make a number of modifications to the special measures regime created by the 1999 Act. At the time of writing, however, none of these provisions had been brought into force.

Live link directions

LEGISLATION HIGHLIGHTER

Section 33 of the **Youth Justice and Criminal Evidence Act 1999**

Whilst the accused cannot be an eligible witness (see special measures directions above), s.33A of the **YJ&CEA 1999** empowers the court, upon application by the accused, to give a live link direction (i.e. a direction that the accused gives oral evidence through a live link) if the accused falls within either of two categories of accused specified by s.33A:

(1) The court may make a live link direction where the accused is below 18 years of age if the accused's level of intellectual or social functioning compromises his ability to participate effectively in the proceedings as a witness giving oral evidence in court, though the court may only give such a direction if the use of a live link would enable the accused to participate more effectively as a witness.

(2) The court may make a live link direction where the accused is 18 or over and is unable to participate effectively in the proceedings as a witness giving oral evidence in court either because he suffers from a mental disorder or because he has a significant impairment of intelligence and social function, though the court may only give such a direction if the use of a live link would enable the accused to participate more effectively as a witness.

Examination of the accused through an intermediary

The **Coroners and Justice Act 2009** contains provisions which (when and if they are brought into force) will insert a new s.33BA into the 1999 Act, permitting an accused who falls within the ambit of s.33A to be examined through an intermediary. At the time of writing, however, s.33BA had not been brought into force. In practice, however, it seems that the courts, in the exercise of their inherent common law powers, can already permit the accused to have the assistance of an intermediary (*R. (on the application of D) v Camberwell Green Youth Court* (2005)).

Other provisions permitting the giving of evidence in criminal proceedings via a live link

In the context of proceedings for certain offences, such as murder or manslaughter, witnesses outside the United Kingdom may be able to give their evidence via a live link under s.32 of the **Criminal Justice Act 1988**.

Witnesses inside the United Kingdom may be permitted to give their evidence via a live link under s.51 of the **Criminal Justice Act 2003** where this "is in the interests of the efficient or effective administration of justice".

Witness anonymity orders

LEGISLATION HIGHLIGHTER

Section 88 of the **Coroners and Justice Act 2009**

A criminal court may make a witness anonymity order under s.88 of the **C&JA 2009** if three conditions are all satisfied. First (Condition A) the order must either be necessary to prevent the safety of the witness or another person or to prevent serious damage to property or must be necessary to prevent real harm to the public interest (e.g. by disclosing the identity of an undercover police officer). Secondly (Condition B), the taking of the measures must be consistent with the accused receiving a fair trial. Thirdly (Condition C), the importance of the witness' testimony must be such that the witness ought to testify in the interests of justice and either the witness would not testify if the order was not made or there would be real harm to the public interest if the order was not made and the witness testified.

Essentially, a witness anonymity order may require the taking of measures (such as withholding the witness' name and identifying details, screening the witness and modulating the witness' voice) to prevent the identity of a witness being disclosed (**CAJA 2009** s.86).

In determining whether to make a witness anonymity order, s.89 of the 2009 Act requires the court, when determining whether the three conditions imposed by s.88 have been satisfied, to consider six specified considerations plus any other relevant matters. The six specified considerations are as follows. First, the accused's general right to know the identity of a witness. Secondly, the extent to which the witness' credibility would be relevant when the weight of the witness' evidence is assessed. Thirdly, Whether the witness' evidence may be the sole or decisive evidence against the accused. Fourthly, whether the witness' evidence could be properly tested without disclosing the witness' identity. Fifthly, whether there is reason to believe that the witness either tends to be dishonest or has a motive to be dishonest in the circumstances. Finally, whether it would be reasonably practicable to protect the witness by other means (e.g. a special measures direction).

Procedure re the making of an application for a witness anonymity order may be found in Part 29 of the **Criminal Procedure Rules 2010.**

Section 90 of the 2009 Act requires the judge to warn the jury such that the making of a witness anonymity order does not prejudice the accuse. Section 91 empowers the court to discharge or vary a witness anonymity order.

CROSS-EXAMINATION

> **DEFINITION CHECKPOINT**
>
> This is the second stage of the process of questioning a witness. It takes place after examination in chief and is the stage where a party may question his opponent's witness in an effort to gain favourable evidence, to undermine the witness' testimony or to discredit the witness. The general rule is that a party who fails to cross-examine a witness is taken to have accepted the witness' testimony and cannot later dispute it (*R. v Fenlon* 1980)).

As with examination in chief, the normal rules relating to the admissibility of evidence apply to cross-examination. Thus, for example, if the accused's confession is inadmissible, the prosecution cannot cross-examine the accused in relation to the confession (*R. v Treacy* (1944)). Unlike examination in chief, however, leading questions are usually allowed during cross-examination (*Ex p. Bottomley).*

Whilst cross-examination may be directed at discrediting a witness, it should be noted that the admissibility of evidence of bad character in criminal proceedings is now subject to provisions of the **CJA 2003** (which are considered in Chapter 13, below), and that cross-examination of sexual offence complainants is now restricted by s.41 of the **YJ&CEA 1999** (which is considered below).

Four rules relating specifically to cross-examination which are of particular importance are those relating to questions concerning collateral matters, cross-examination about previous inconsistent statements, cross-examination by the accused in person, and cross-examination of sexual offence complainants.

Questions concerning collateral matters

The rule of finality

The general rule with regard to questions concerning collateral matters is that whilst a witness may be asked questions about such matters during cross-examination for the purpose of discrediting the witness, subject to the exceptions which are listed below, a witness' answer to such questions will be treated as final so that the cross-examining party may not call evidence in rebuttal of the witness' answers (*R. v Edwards*).

What is a collateral matter?

■ DEFINITION CHECKPOINT

A collateral matter is one which is only relevant to the credit of the witness who is being cross-examined and is not relevant to any other issue in the proceedings. Unfortunately, whether a matter is relevant to credit only is not always easy to determine. Thus, in *Att Gen v Hitchcock* (1847), the court proposed a test to determine whether a matter is collateral. The test is basically as follows. If the party who is cross-examining the witness could not have called evidence on the matter if the witness had not been called, because the matter is not relevant to an issue in the proceedings, the matter is collateral only, and the witness' answer will be treated as final. If, on the other hand, the cross-examining party could have called evidence on the matter whether or not the witness had been called, because the matter is relevant to an issue in the proceedings, the matter is not collateral, and the witness' answer will not be treated as final.

An example of a case in which a matter was treated as collateral is *R. v Burke* (1858). A witness who had informed the court that he could not speak English was allowed to give his evidence through an interpreter. After he had done so, it was put to him in cross-examination that he had been heard speaking in English outside the court. This he denied and the court then had to determine whether his ability to speak English was a collateral matter, to which his answer would be treated as final. The court decided that, as the questioning related only to the witness' credit, it was collateral (the witness' knowledge of English not being an issue in the proceedings).

R. v NAGRECHA (1977)

This case provides an example of a matter which was held not to be collateral. The complainant in an indecent assault trial denied that she had previously made indecent assault allegations to former work colleagues and the Court of Appeal held that the trial judge should have permitted a former work colleague to give evidence in rebuttal because the evidence did not merely go to the complainant's credit but went to the issue of whether an indecent assault had taken place (the only evidence that an indecent assault had taken place being the complainant's evidence). If, however, the complainant had admitted making the previous allegations but had claimed that they were true, it appears that questions concerning the truth or falsehood of the allegations would have been collateral, as admitting evidence in rebuttal would have required the court to undertake a lengthy exploration of irrelevant and peripheral issues.

The exceptions to the rule regarding the finality of questions relating to collateral matters

Bias or partiality

If a witness denies an allegation put to him during cross-examination that he is biased, although bias is a collateral matter, the cross-examining party may call evidence to prove the witness' bias. The following cases illustrate this exception.

R. v MENDY (1976), R. v PHILLIPS (1936) AND R. v BUSBY (1982)

In *R. v Mendy* (1976), the accused's husband was asked during cross-examination whether he had, prior to testifying, and in an attempt to adapt his evidence, spoken to someone who had heard the testimony of the prosecution witnesses. The husband denied this allegation. The Court of Appeal upheld the trial judge's decision to allow the prosecution to call evidence in rebuttal.

In *R. v Phillips* (1936), the accused was charged with incest. During cross-examination, his daughter (the alleged victim) and another daughter denied having been schooled by their mother into putting forward the allegation of incest. On appeal, the court held that the trial judge had been wrong in refusing to allow the defence to call evidence to rebut the daughters' denial.

In *R. v Busby* (1982), an allegation was put during cross-examination that police officers were prepared to cheat in order to obtain a conviction by fabricating evidence and threatening a defence witness. Although the Court of Appeal ruled that the questions were not collateral but rather were relevant to an issue in the trial, the case has subsequently been interpreted (in *R. v Edwards*, below) as possibly being one involving collateral questions which fell within the bias exception. If the latter view of *Busby* is correct then (as the Court of Appeal in *Busby* had in fact held), the trial judge ought to have allowed the defence to call evidence from the defence witness who had been threatened to rebut the officers' denials. Alternatively, if the bias exception did not apply, the Court of Appeal in *Edwards* indicated that, the questions being collateral, evidence in rebuttal should not have been admitted.

A similar case to *Busby*, but one which fell outside the exception, is *R. v Edwards*. The Court of Appeal held that questions concerning the conduct of police officers during other investigations were collateral and that since no exception to the rule of finality was applicable, evidence in rebuttal was not admissible.

It should be noted that the admissibility of evidence of bad character in criminal proceedings is now subject to provisions of the **CJA 2003** which are considered in Chapter 13, below.

Previous inconsistent statements

Where questions are put to a witness during cross-examination concerning previous inconsistent statements made by the witness, the witness' answers to such questions are not final, and evidence of the previous inconsistent statements can be adduced in rebuttal (see below).

The previous convictions of a witness, other than the accused

LEGISLATION HIGHLIGHTER

Section 6 of the **Criminal Procedure Act 1865**

The effect of s.6 of the **CPA 1865** is that should a witness in either civil or criminal proceedings, on being lawfully questioned about their previous convictions, deny during cross-examination the existence of their previous convictions, fail to admit the existence of the convictions or refuse to answer, cross-examining counsel may adduce evidence of those convictions in rebuttal.

It should be noted that the admissibility of evidence of bad character in criminal proceedings is now subject to provisions of the **CJA 2003**, which are considered in Chapter 13, below.

Witness' reputation for untruthfulness

A witness may be called to state that the other side's witness is generally known to be untruthful (*R. v Longman* (1968)). The admissibility of evidence of bad character in criminal proceedings is now subject to provisions of the **CJA 2003** which are considered in Chapter 13, below.

Disability of witness

A medical witness may be called to attack a witness' credibility on the basis of their inability to give reliable testimony due to their physical or mental disability (*Toohey v Metropolitan Police Commissioner* (1965)).

Cross-examination about a previous inconsistent statement

A witness may be cross-examined about a previous inconsistent statement made by the witness. If the witness does not admit making the statement, the statement may be proved under s.4 of the **CPA 1865** (applicable both in civil and criminal proceedings), but before the statement is proved, details of the occasion on which the statement was made must be given to the witness so that he may remember making the statement, and he must then be asked whether he made such a statement. If the inconsistent statement is a written statement and it is intended to prove the written statement to contradict the witness, s.5 of the **CPA 1865** requires that the witness' attention must first be drawn to the parts of the written statement that are to be used to contradict the witness.

Relevance of a previous inconsistent statement

In **criminal proceedings**, where a witness admits making a previous inconsistent statement or where such a statement is proved under s.4 or s.5 of the CPA 1865, the witness' previous inconsistent statement is relevant both to the credit of the witness and also (under s.119 of the **CJA 2003**) as evidence of any matter stated of which the witness's oral evidence would be admissible. Thus, as was seen above in relation to hostile witnesses, the three options open to the jury will be to accept the truth of the previous inconsistent statement, to accept the truth of the witness' testimony in court or to reject both the previous inconsistent statement and the witness's testimony in court (*R. v Joyce*). Where a previous inconsistent statement is relied on by the defence it seems that the jury are entitled to rely on it if they consider that it might be true whereas it seems that they should only rely on one tendered by the prosecution if they are sure that it is true (*R. v Billingham* (2009)).

In **civil proceedings,** a witness' previous inconsistent statement is also relevant both to the credit of the witness and (under s.1 and s.6(5) of the **CEA 1995**) as evidence of the matters stated.

What restrictions are imposed on the right of an accused to cross-examine a witness in person?

Sexual offence complainants

LEGISLATION HIGHLIGHTER
Section 34 of the **YJ&CEA 1999** prevents the accused from personally cross-examining a sexual offence complainant.

Protected witnesses

If the accused is charged with a sexual offence, with kidnapping or with an offence involving an injury or threat of injury, s.35 of the **YJ&CEA 1999** prevents the accused from personally cross-examining a "protected witness".

DEFINITION CHECKPOINT
A protected witness is one who is either the complainant or someone who witnessed the commission of the offence **and** who was a child either when he gave his evidence or when he made a video recording which stood as his evidence in chief. Where the accused is charged with a sexual offence, a child is a person under 17 years of age but, otherwise, a child is a person under 14 years of age.

Discretion

The trial judge also possesses a discretionary power under s.36 of the **YJ&CEA 1999** to prevent the accused from personally conducting the cross-examination of any other witness (except a co-accused). The discretionary power may only be exercised if the court is satisfied that the quality of the witness' evidence is likely to be diminished if the accused conducts the cross-examination **and** that it would be likely to be improved if he were prevented from doing so **and** that preventing the accused from cross-examining the witness would not be contrary to the interests of justice.

The court may exercise the s.36 discretion either upon an application by the prosecution or of its own motion.

The procedure re the making of applications by the prosecution for directions under s.36 is governed by **CrimPR** Pt 31.

Who may conduct cross-examination of a witness where the accused is prevented from doing so in person?

Where the accused is prevented from personally cross-examining a witness by virtue of s.34, 35 or 36, the court must give the accused the opportunity to appoint a legal representative to conduct the cross-examination. If the accused chooses not to do so, the court must appoint a qualified legal representative to conduct the cross-examination of the witness if it considers it to be in the interests of justice to do so (s.38).

Is the judge required to direct the jury where he prevents the accused cross-examining a witness in person?

Where the accused is prevented from personally cross-examining a witness by virtue of s.34, 35 or 36, the judge may, if he considers it necessary, give the jury an appropriate warning to ensure that the accused is not prejudiced either by inferences that might be drawn from the fact that he was not permitted to personally cross-examine the witness or by the fact that the witness was cross-examined by a qualified legal representative rather than by a legal representative acting for the accused.

Can a sexual offence complainant be cross-examined about his or her sexual behaviour?

LEGISLATION HIGHLIGHTER

Section 41 of the Youth Justice and Criminal Evidence Act 1999

Section 41 of the YJ&CEA 1999 provides that where the accused is tried for a sexual offence, no evidence may be adduced or question asked in cross-examination by or on behalf of the accused about any sexual behaviour of the complainant except with the leave of the court.

DEFINITION CHECKPOINT

What does the term "sexual behaviour" mean?

Sexual behaviour is defined in s.42 as being "any sexual behaviour or other sexual experience, whether or not involving the accused or other person, but excluding (except in s.41(3)(c)(i) and 5(a)) anything alleged to have taken place as part of the event which is the subject matter of the charge against the accused".

Questions or evidence about false sexual offence allegations

Where the accused has an evidential basis for suggesting that the complainant has made false sexual offence complaints in the past, questions or evidence concerning the false complaints will not be questions or evidence about the complainant's sexual behaviour and leave under s.41 will not be requited (*R. v T; R. v H* (2002)).

When may leave be granted?

Section 41(2) provides that leave may only be granted on an application by the accused and that leave may only be given if the evidence or question falls within one of the five situations set out in s.41(3) and s.41(5) **and** refusing to give leave might render unsafe a conclusion of the jury or of the court.

The procedure to be followed where the defence wish to adduce evidence or ask a question under s.41 is governed by **CrimPR** Pt 36.

What are the five situations in which leave may be given if refusing to give leave might render unsafe a conclusion of the jury or of the court?

Leave may be given in any of the following five situations:

(1) Leave may be given if the evidence or question goes no further than is necessary to rebut or explain prosecution evidence of the complainant's sexual behaviour (s.41(5)). For this purpose, sexual behaviour includes behaviour which is alleged to have occurred as part of the offence (s.42). Section 41(5) would apply where, for example, the prosecution gave evidence that the complainant was a virgin prior to being raped (see, for example, *R. v Rooney* (2001)).

(2) Leave may be given if the evidence or question relates to a relevant issue in the case other than whether the complainant consented (s.41(3)(a)). Section 41(3)(a) is, for example, wide enough to encompass the situation in which the accused's defence is that he reasonably believed the complainant consented (*R. v A* (2001)).

(3) Leave may be given if the evidence or question relates to a relevant issue of consent and the sexual behaviour to which the evidence or question relates is alleged to have taken place at or about the same time as that on which the alleged offence occurred (s.41(3)(b)). The term "at or about the same time" may be capable of encompassing hours or days but not it appears weeks before or after the offence (*R. v A*).

(4) Leave may be given if the evidence or question relates to a relevant issue of consent and the sexual behaviour to which the evidence or question relates is allegedly so similar to the accused's version of the sexual behaviour of the complainant during the commission of the alleged offence that the similarity cannot reasonably be explained as a coincidence (s.41(3)(c)(i)). For the purposes of this condition, sexual

behaviour includes behaviour which is alleged to have occurred as part of the alleged offence (s.42). In *R. v Tahed* (2004), where the accused was charged with raping the complainant in a climbing frame in a public park, the trial judge would have been entitled to admit evidence that the accused and the complainant had had consensual intercourse in the climbing frame on an earlier occasion under s.41(3)(c)(i).

(5) Leave may be given if the evidence or question relates to a relevant issue of consent and the sexual behaviour to which the evidence or question relates is allegedly so similar to any other sexual behaviour of the complainant which (according to the accused) occurred at or about the same time as the alleged offence that the similarity cannot reasonably be explained as a coincidence (s.41(3)(c)(ii)).

Evidence or a question does not relate to a relevant issue in the case for the purposes of s.41(3) if its purpose or main purpose was to attack the complainant's credibility (s.41(4)), though credibility may be attacked under s.41(5). Moreover, s.41(3) and s.41(5) only apply where the evidence or question relates to a specific instance or specific instances of the complainant's sexual behaviour (s.41(6)).

Human rights

A literal interpretation of s.41 of the **YJ&CEA 1999** may, in certain circumstances, potentially result in a violation of art.6 of the European Convention on Human Rights by preventing the accused from having a fair trial (e.g. where s.41 prevents the defence asking questions concerning, or adducing evidence of, a sexual relationship between the accused and the complainant (*R. v A*)). Thus, where the fairness of the trial would otherwise be endangered, it may be necessary to read s.41 down under s.3 of the **Human Rights Act 1998** such that questions may be asked or evidence may be adduced in relation to a logically relevant sexual relationship between the accused and the complainant under s.41(3)(c) even though, on a literal interpretation of s.41(3)(c), the strict requirements of s.41(3)(c) would not be satisfied (*R. v A*).

Equally, whilst, as was seen above, s.41(4) provides that evidence or a question does not relate to a relevant issue in the case for the purposes of s.41(3) if its purpose or main purpose was to attack the complainant's credibility, it seems that it may be necessary to adopt a narrow interpretation of s.41(4) where excluding evidence of the complainant's sexual behaviour would endanger the fairness of the accused's trial (*R. v T; R. v H*).

Similarly, again for the purpose of ensuring the fairness of the trial, it seems that it may be necessary to permit the accused to adduce evidence under s.41(5) in order to rebut evidence given by a prosecution witness even though counsel for the prosecution had not intended to adduce the relevant evidence (*R. v Hamadi* (2007)).

RE-EXAMINATION

This, the third and final stage of the examination of a witness, is the stage at which a witness who has been cross-examined may be re-examined by the party who called him. Re-examination gives the party who called a witness an opportunity to ask the witness about matters raised in cross-examination. A re-examining party will not normally be permitted to raise new matters which are unconnected with the subject matter of cross-examination, the leave of the court being required if such matters are to be raised during re-examination (*Prince v Samo* (1838)). As with examination in chief, leading questions may not normally be asked (*Ex p. Bottomley*).

Revision checklist

You should now know and understand:

- the general rules regarding the examination in chief of a witness;
- the rules relating to the use of previous consistent statements in criminal and civil proceedings;
- when a witness may be permitted to memory refresh from a document in criminal and civil proceedings;
- the distinction between an unfavourable and a hostile witness and the measures that can be taken to deal with situations where a witness is hostile;
- when a witness will be eligible for a special measures direction;
- the exceptional circumstances in which a witness anonymity order may be made;
- the general rules regarding the cross examination of witnesses;
- how to identify when a matter will be regarded as "collateral" and the rule of finality relating to collateral matters and its exceptions;
- restrictions on the cross examination of sexual offence complainants and "protected witnesses" by the accused in person;
- when a sexual offence complainant may be cross-examined about their previous sexual behaviour;
- the general rules relating to the re-examination of witnesses.

QUESTION AND ANSWER

William is charged with two counts of rape. Specifically, he is charged with raping his two daughters, Barbara, aged 16, and Julie, aged 13. The girls allege that, during the year before their father left home to live with his girlfriend, Sonya, he had, on different occasions, raped both of them. Both daughters claim that they did not dare inform the police of their father's conduct because he had threatened to kill them both if they did so. William claims that the allegations are totally false and claims that Barbara and Julie have fabricated them to punish him for leaving his wife to move in with Sonya.

The counts relating to Barbara and Julie are being jointly tried in Oxgate Crown Court. Consider whether:

(a) William will be entitled to personally cross-examine Barbara and Julie;

(b) evidence of Barbara's sexual experience with other men will be admissible in William's defence;

(c) if William is called as a witness he will be cross-examined and if so by whom;

(d) either Barbara or Julie (or both) will be eligible for a special measures direction?

Advice and the Answer

General guidance

The testimony of witnesses is an essential component of most court proceedings. In particular in criminal proceedings where the rule against hearsay (see Chapter 9 below) tends to prevent the admission of out of court statements evidence will, wherever possible, be given orally by witnesses in the witness box. [Note: as is seen in Chapter 10, below, evidence in chief in civil proceedings will normally be given by written witness statement.]

Some key points to remember include:

- The party who calls a witness will examine that witness in chief. This means that the examining party cannot ask leading questions and must allow the witness to tell their own story. Where a witness is vulnerable or may find it difficult to testify due to age or incapacity special measures may be put in place to assist the witness in giving evidence. Witnesses may be entitled to refresh their memories from documents that they made or verified and which record the witnesses' recollection of events provided that their recollection at the time is likely to have been significantly better than when the witness gives evidence. If the judge considers the witness to be hostile, then the judge may permit the party who called the witness to cross-examine them about their previous inconsistent statements. Note however that if the witness is simply unfavourable then there is little that the examining party can do; they cannot impeach the witness' credibility though the party could adduce other evidence which is of relevance in relation to the issue that the unfavourable witness' evidence concerned.

- Witnesses will be cross-examined by the opposing party (i.e. the defence will cross-examine prosecution witnesses (or witnesses called by the claimant in civil proceedings) and vice versa). Cross-examination is the primary mechanism for challenging the evidence in chief given by a witness and so in cross-examination the cross-examining party is entitled to ask leading questions. Note that if a witness is cross-examined about a collateral matter then (subject to exceptions) their answer to the question will be final. Special rules relate to cross-examination by the accused in person and to cross-examination of sexual offence complainants.
- Re-examination is the final stage in the examination of the witness where the party who called the witness can question the witness about matters raised in cross-examination. Note it is generally not permitted for the examining party to raise new matters in re-examination.

Model answer

(a) Under s.34 of the **YJ&CEA 1999**, an accused charged with a sexual offence is not permitted to personally cross-examine the complainant. William will, however, be permitted to instruct counsel to cross-examine Julie on his behalf and, if he fails or refuses to do so, the court may, in the interests of justice, appoint a qualified legal representative (under s.38) to cross-examine Barbara and Julie.

(b) Under s.41 of the **YJ&CEA 1999**, evidence of Barbara's sexual behaviour (which does not include the facts of the alleged rape itself) will not be admissible (and questions concerning her sexual behaviour may not be asked during cross-examination) without the leave of the court. Leave can only be given if the evidence (or question) is relevant to an issue other than consent or, in certain circumstances specified by s.41, if the evidence (or question) is relevant to consent or if the evidence (or question) is given in rebuttal of (or in order to explain) evidence of the complainant's sexual behaviour that was adduced by the prosecution and goes no further than is necessary to do so. Moreover, leave can only be given if failing to give it might render a conclusion of the jury unsafe. Here, so far as we can tell, evidence of Barbara's sexual experience with other men does not appear to be relevant to any issue in the proceedings, whether or not one of consent, and does not appear to relate to any evidence adduced by the prosecution in relation to her sexual behaviour. Moreover, so far as we are aware, the prosecution have not adduced evidence of Barbara's sexual behaviour. Thus, so far as we can tell, it appears that evidence of Barbara's sexual experience with other men will not be admissible. It should be noted that when determining whether evidence of a complainant's sexual behaviour (or a question relating thereto) is relevant to an issue in the proceedings for the purposes of s.41, evidence of the complainant's sexual behaviour will not relate to such an issue if the sole or main purpose for adducing it is merely to discredit Barbara (though evidence of sexual behaviour may be adduced for the sole or main purpose of impugning the complainant's credibility where adduced in rebuttal of explanation of evidence of her sexual behaviour that was adduced by the prosecution). It should also be noted that evidence of the complainant's sexual behaviour can only be admissible under s.41 (and questions relating thereto may only be asked) if it relates to specific instances of sexual behaviour. The procedure to be followed where the defence wish to adduce evidence (or ask a question) under s.41 is laid down by **CrimPR** Pt 36. If the application of s.41 made William's trial unfair, the court might have been required to "read down" s.41 under s.3(1) of the **HRA 1998** (R. v A), but that does not seem to be the case here.

(c) As was seen in Chapter 2, above, the accused is neither a competent nor compellable prosecution witness. If William chooses to testify he will be a defence witness. [Note: if he does not testify then, as was seen in Chapter 4, above, the court may be entitled to draw an inference in respect of his silence.] A witness is examined in chief by the party calling witness (in William's case the defence) and he will therefore be cross examined by the prosecution.

(d) Both Barbara and Julie, being under 17, will be eligible for a special measures direction under the 1999 Act. Since William is charged with sexual offences, both Barbara and Julie will be child witnesses who are in need of special protection. Thus, the primary rule will apply even if applying special measures would not be likely to maximise the quality of their evidence and it is, thus, likely that their evidence in chief will be video recorded and that their cross-examination and re-examination will be by live link. Video recorded evidence will not be admitted, however, if this is not in the interests of justice.

Evidence of Opinion

Introduction

In this chapter we will consider when a witness may be entitled to give evidence of opinion in criminal and civil proceedings. Primarily, witnesses are called to give evidence of facts which they have perceived. Thus, the basic rule is that evidence of opinions that witnesses have formed upon the basis of facts that they have perceived is not admissible, it being the role of the court, not that of the witnesses, to form such opinions. At times, however, the opinion evidence of a witness may be admissible because the opinion of that witness forms an issue before the court (e.g. the opinion of a person charged with handling stolen goods is admissible to prove that the accused believed the goods to be stolen (*R. v Hulbert* (1979)). Moreover, for a variety of purposes, witnesses are permitted to give evidence of general reputation (e.g. a character witness may give evidence of the general reputation of the accused in the neighbourhood where he lives (see *R. v Rowton* (1865) and **Criminal Justice Act (CJA) 2003** s.118 in Chapter 13, below)). The two major situations in which opinion evidence is commonly admitted, however, are:

(1) When a non-expert witness conveys evidence of facts which he has perceived to the court in terms of his opinion.

(2) Where an expert witness gives the court the benefit of his expert opinion in relation to a matter falling outside the knowledge and experience of the court.

NON-EXPERT WITNESSES

In civil proceedings, where a non-expert witness conveys relevant facts which he has personally perceived to the court in terms of his opinion on a relevant matter, his statement of opinion is admissible as evidence of what the witness perceived (**Civil Evidence Act (CEA) 1972** s.3(2)). It appears that the (common law) position in criminal cases is largely identical.

R. V DAVIES (1962)

In *R. v Davies* (1962), it was proper for a witness to state his opinion to the effect that when he and the accused met, "the accused was under the influence of drink". In order for such opinion evidence to be admissible, however, the witness must be able to give evidence of the primary facts, perceived by the witness, upon which the witness's opinion is based.

Further, a non-expert witness cannot state his opinion upon a matter if the formation of a proper opinion in respect of the matter requires expertise (*R. v Loake* (1911)). Moreover, a confession in the form of a statement of opinion may be worthless if its maker does not possess sufficient knowledge or expertise to make his opinion of some value (*Bird v Adams* (1972)).

Is there any difference between the position of the non-expert witness in civil and in criminal proceedings?

If there is a significant distinction between the position of the non-expert in civil and in criminal proceedings it is that in criminal proceedings it may be that the non-expert should not be permitted to state his opinion upon an ultimate issue (i.e. one which the court is required to determine). Thus, for example, in *R. v Davies*, in which the accused was charged with being unfit to drive through drink, the Court of Appeal held that a non-expert witness should not have been permitted to state that in his opinion the accused was "in no condition to handle a motor vehicle". It may be, however, that the "ultimate issue rule" is no longer strictly applied by the criminal courts in relation to non-expert opinion evidence, though if non-expert opinion evidence is admitted in relation to an ultimate issue, the judge should direct the jury to the effect that it is the opinion of the jury which determines the ultimate issue (*R. v Tagg* (2001)).

Section 3(2),(3) of the **Civil Evidence Act 1972**

In civil proceedings, the "ultimate issue rule" was abolished by **CEA 1972** s.3(2),(3). Consequently, where non-expert evidence is otherwise admissible in civil proceedings, the fact that it relates to an ultimate issue will not prevent its admission.

EXPERT WITNESSES

Essentially, as is seen below, the opinion evidence of an expert witness is admissible at common law in criminal proceedings and under the **Civil Evidence Act 1972** in civil proceedings if it relates to a matter which falls outside the knowledge and experience of the court, though expert evidence may only be adduced in civil proceedings if permission is given under the **Civil Procedure Rules 1998** (CPR) and where a party to criminal proceedings fails to comply with service or pre-hearing discussion requirements imposed by the **Criminal Procedure Rules 2010 (CrimPR)**, the court's permission may be required if the expert evidence is to be adduced.

DEFINITION CHECKPOINT

In order for a witness to give expert testimony in criminal or civil proceedings it must first be established that;
- the expert is competent (i.e. is expert in a relevant field), and
- the expert's evidence relates to a matter which falls outside of the knowledge and experience of the court.

The expert witness in criminal proceedings and CrimPR Pt 33

Where expert evidence is admissible in criminal proceedings (see below), **CrimPR** Pt 33 makes provision concerning the duties of experts, the service of expert evidence, the contents of experts' reports, pre-hearing discussions between experts and the use of single joint experts. **CrimPR** Pt 33 applies to experts who are required either to give or to prepare expert evidence for criminal proceedings (i.e. it does not apply either where an expert whose evidence is not to be adduced in the proceedings merely advises a party or where a person who is competent to give expert evidence is called to give evidence as a witness of fact).

CrimPR 33.2 provides that the duty of an expert to give objective unbiased opinion on matters falling within the expert's expertise overrides the expert's obligations to the party who instructed/paid the expert and includes a duty to inform the parties and the court if the expert's opinion changes from that in the expert's report. In addition, case law makes clear that, amongst other matters, experts should consider facts that detract from their opinions and should make clear when matters fall outside their expertise (*R. v Harris* (2005)). Moreover, guidance issued by the Crown Prosecution Service in 2006 makes clear that prosecution experts must retain all material until instructed to do otherwise, should record all the work they have done and should reveal all that they have recorded to the prosecution. The prosecution are under a duty (under the Criminal Procedure and Investigations Act 1996) to disclose to the defence all material that might reasonably be considered capable of undermining the prosecution case or assisting the defence case.

LEGISLATION HIGHLIGHTER

Criminal Procedure Rules 2010 Part 33.3

In accordance with **CrimPR** 33.3, an expert's report must:
- detail the expert's qualifications, experience and accreditation;
- detail literature or information on which the expert relied;
- state the substance of the material facts upon which the expert's opinions are based;
- indicate which of these facts are in the expert's personal knowledge;
- state who carried out examinations, tests, experiments, etc. upon which the expert relied, giving their qualifications, experience and accreditation, indicating whether the expert supervised and summarising the findings that the expert relies upon;
- where there is a range of opinion in the relevant area, summarise the range of opinion and give reasons for the expert's opinion;
- if the expert's opinion is qualified, state any qualifications;
- summarise the expert's conclusions;
- contain a statement that the expert understands, has complied with and will continue to comply with the expert's duty to the court; and
- contain a declaration of truth.

It should be noted that an expert's report is admissible in criminal proceedings under s.30 of the **CJA 1988**, but if the expert is not called to give oral evidence his report is only admissible under s.30 with the leave of the court. Alternatively, an expert's report may be admissible under s.9 of the **Criminal Justice Act 1967** where none of the other parties object to its admission.

If a party to criminal proceedings who wants to adduce expert evidence fails to comply with the service requirements laid down by **CrimPR** 33.4, the party must either obtain the agreement of the other parties or the permission of the court if the expert evidence is to be adduced. **CrimPR** 33.4 requires a party to criminal proceedings who wishes to adduce expert evidence to serve it on the court and the other party(ies) as soon as is practicable (and in any event with any application in support of which the expert evidence is relied). Any party(ies) who so require must be given a copy of /a reasonable opportunity to inspect both the records of examinations, measurements, tests or experiments on which the findings or opinions of the expert are based/which were carried out in the course of reaching the expert's findings and opinions and anything on which those examinations, measurements tests or experiments were carried out. Where expert evidence is served on the court or a party, **CrimPR** 33.5 requires the party who served the expert evidence to inform the expert that service has taken place.

Where more than one party to criminal proceedings wishes to adduce expert evidence, **CrimPR** 33.6 empowers the court to direct the experts to discuss the expert issues and to prepare a statement of the matters on which they agree and disagree. Where a party fails to comply with a direction under **CrimPR** 33.6, the court's permission will be required if the party is to adduce expert evidence. Where such discussions have taken place, the statement prepared by the experts may be referred to in court but the content of the discussion may only be referred to with the court's permission.

Where two or more defendants to criminal proceedings wish to adduce expert evidence in relation to an issue, the court may direct that expert evidence in relation to the issue be given by a single joint expert (**CrimPR** 33.7). If the defendants cannot agree the identity of the expert, the court may either select the single joint expert from a list that the defendants have agreed or identified or may direct some other method of selecting the single joint expert. Where expert evidence in criminal proceedings is to be given by a single joint expert, **CrimPR** 33.8 provides that each of the defendants may give the expert instructions and requires a defendant who gives instructions to the expert to send a copy to the other defendant(s).

CrimPR 33.9 empowers the court to extend time limits imposed by **CrimPR** Pt 33 and to admit expert evidence even though the evidence omits details required by **CrimPR** Pt 33.

The expert witness in civil proceedings and CPR Pt 35

As is seen below, expert evidence is only admissible in relation to matters which fall outside the court's knowledge and experience (admissibility in civil proceedings being governed by **CEA 1972** s.3(1)).

LEGISLATION HIGHLIGHTER

Civil Procedure Rules 1998 Part 35

In civil proceedings even where a matter does fall outside the court's knowledge and experience, the parties still require the leave of the court, under **CPR** Pt 35, to adduce expert evidence. **CPR** Pt 35 also makes provision concerning the use of single joint experts, the duties of expert witnesses, the contents of experts' reports, the putting of written questions to experts and discussions between experts. **CPR** Pt 35 applies to experts who are instructed to give or prepare evidence for the purposes of proceedings (i.e. it does not apply either where an expert whose evidence is not to be adduced in the proceedings merely advises a party or where a person who is competent to give expert evidence is called to give evidence as a witness of fact).

Under **CPR** Pt 35, the court's permission is required either to call an expert witness or to put an expert's report in evidence (**CPR** 35.4(1)), the court being required to restrict expert evidence to that which is reasonably required to resolve the proceedings (**CPR** 35.1). Even where the court gives a party permission to adduce expert evidence in civil proceedings, such evidence will be given by written report unless the court directs otherwise (indeed where a claim has been allocated to the small claims track or the fast track the court will not direct an expert to attend a hearing unless this is necessary in the interests of justice) (**CPR** 35.5). In other words, a civil court will not normally permit an expert witness to be called to give oral evidence, expert evidence in civil proceedings normally taking the form of the expert's written report. Moreover, where the parties to civil proceedings wish to adduce expert evidence in relation to an issue, the court may direct that the expert evidence will be given by a single joint expert (**CPR** 35.7). In such circumstances, if the parties fail to agree a single joint expert, the court may select a single joint expert from a list which the parties have prepared or identified or may direct another method of selecting a single joint expert. Where a party instructs a single joint expert, the party must send a copy of the instructions to the other party(ies) who are instructing the single joint expert (**CPR** 35.8). Where the court does direct that expert evidence in relation to an issue be given by a single joint expert, the court may, in appropriate circumstances, subsequently permit one of the parties to instruct his own expert (*Daniels v Walker* (2000)).

 CPR 35.3 provides that the expert is under a duty to help the court which overrides the expert's duty to the party who instructed or is paying the expert. The Practice Direction that supplements **CPR** Pt 35 makes clear that the expert's evidence should be independent and unbiased and he should take all material facts into account, even those which detract from his opinion. If a matter falls outside his expertise or if he cannot reach a definite opinion he should make this clear, and if he changes his view after producing his report he should communicate this to the parties.

 In his report, the expert is required to state that he understands this duty, has complied with it and will continue to do so.

What should an experts report contain?

As required by **CPR** 35.10 and the associated Practice Direction, an expert's report must, amongst other matters, specify the expert's qualifications, the literature, etc, which the expert relied upon when making the report, and the expert's conclusions. It must set out the substance of the facts and instructions which are material to the expert's opinions or on which those opinions are based. It must contain a statement that the expert understands his duty to the court, has complied with it and will continue to do so and is aware of the requirements imposed by **CPR** Pt 35, the Practice Direction and the associated Protocol and it must be verified by a "statement of truth". If a range of expert opinions exist in relation to the matter which the report concerns, the report must summarise these and must indicate why the expert formed his opinion. It must indicate which of the facts stated are within the expert's knowledge and must identify and state the qualifications of persons who carried out tests, experiments, etc. It must summarise the expert's conclusions and, if the expert's opinion is qualified, the nature of the qualification must be stated. If there are reasonable grounds to consider that the statement of instructions which the expert's report contains is inaccurate or incomplete, the court may order disclosure of documents or questioning of witnesses in relation to the instructions. If an expert's report does not comply with the requirements of **CPR** Pt 35 and/or the expert witness does not appear to have complied with his duty to the court, the court may, in appropriate circumstances, be prepared to exclude the expert's evidence in the exercise of its exclusionary discretion (*Stevens v Gullis* (1999)). If there are reasonable grounds to believe that the statement of instructions in an expert's report is inaccurate or incomplete, the court may order disclosure of documents or questioning in court concerning the instructions (**CPR** 35.10(4)).

Under **CPR** Pt 35, where the court does not direct the use of a single joint expert, it will normally direct the parties to exchange expert reports simultaneously on a specified day. If a party fails to disclose an expert's report, the party will only be able to rely upon the report or call the expert with the court's permission (**CPR** 35.13). Once an expert's report has been disclosed, however, any party may use the report at the trial (**CPR** 35.11). Moreover, where an expert's report (including a single joint expert's report) is served on a party, the party is, within 28 days, entitled to put written questions about the report to the expert for the purpose of clarifying it (**CPR** 35.6). The expert's answers are treated as part of the report. If the expert does not provide answers, the court may direct that the party who instructed the expert cannot rely on his evidence.

CPR Pt 35 empowers the court to direct a party to provide another party with information (e.g. concerning tests or experiments) which is accessible to the former but which is not reasonably accessible to the latter (**CPR** 35.9). Moreover, where the parties have their own experts, the court, in an attempt to identify and agree the expert issues, is empowered to direct discussions between the experts and to direct them to prepare a statement for the court of the issues on which they agree and disagree (**CPR** 35.12). The content of the discussion itself cannot be referred to at the trial without the agreement of the parties. Moreover, the parties are not bound by an agreement reached by their experts unless the parties agree to be so bound, but even where the parties do not agree to be bound the court may well be likely to accept the agreed opinion (*Stallwood v David* (2007)).

Can an employee be an expert witness on behalf of the party employing him?

An expert may be permitted to appear in civil proceedings as an expert witness on behalf of the party employing him (though not as a single joint expert), though the weight of the expert's evidence may be reduced (*Field v Leeds City Council* (2001)). Where an expert witness has a conflict of interest, this should be disclosed to the other party(ies) to the civil proceedings (*Toth v Jarman* (2006)). Similarly, where an expert was employed by the victim of an alleged criminal offence, whilst the expert was properly permitted to give evidence for the prosecution, this was a matter that went to the weight of his evidence (*R. v Stubbs* (2006)).

Who is an expert?

> **DEFINITION CHECKPOINT**
>
> Only an expert is competent (or, in the words of s.3(1) of the **CEA 1972** "qualified") to give expert evidence. It is for the judge, at common law in criminal proceedings or under s.3(1) in civil proceedings, to determine the competence of a witness to give expert evidence. Clearly, factors such as qualifications, training and experience will all be relevant but, fundamentally, if, by virtue of his experiences, the witness has acquired the necessary expertise, the fact that he lacks formal qualifications and training does not prevent him from being competent to give expert evidence (*R. v Stockwell* (1993)).

Where a witness is not an expert, however, then, as was noted above, the witness cannot state his opinion upon a matter the formation of a proper opinion in respect of which requires expertise. Moreover, even where a witness is an expert, an expert will only be competent to give expert evidence in the witness' own field of expertise. Thus, for example, in *R. v Barnes* (2005), the Court of Appeal held that an expert in wood grain was not qualified to give expert evidence in relation to the issue whether a particular fingerprint had been lifted from a particular door.

Must the expert have personally perceived the facts upon which his opinion is based?

Essentially, the facts upon which the opinion evidence of an expert is based must be proved by admissible evidence. It may be that the expert perceived the relevant facts himself and can give evidence of them, in which case they may be proved by his evidence. Alternatively, where the expert did not perceive the relevant facts himself, it may be necessary to call another witness to prove them, the expert stating his opinion based upon the facts so proved. Thus, in *R. v Abadom* (1983), an expert witness was by his own testimony able to prove that the refractive indices of two samples of glass were the same because he had personally analysed the samples. In contrast, in *R. v Mason* (1911), an expert was only entitled to state his opinion as to whether wounds on a body which the expert had not examined were self-inflicted, a witness who had examined the body having been called to prove the relevant facts.

Where the expert did not personally perceive the facts upon which the opinion is based, it may be possible to prove those facts by relying upon hearsay evidence, though the weight of the hearsay evidence may be less than that of the evidence of a witness who personally perceived the relevant fact (the nature of hearsay evidence is considered in Chapter 9, below). As is seen in Chapters 9 and 12 below, under the hearsay provisions of the **CJA 2003**, hearsay evidence is only admissible in criminal proceedings where it falls within a statutory or preserved common law exception to the hearsay rule, where the court admits it under the inclusionary discretion conferred by s.114(1)(d) of the 2003 Act or by agreement of the parties. Conversely, hearsay evidence is now generally admissible in civil proceedings under s.1 of the **CEA 1995** (see Chapter 10, below).

LEGISLATION HIGHLIGHTER

Section 127 of the **Criminal Justice Act 2003**

Section 127 of the **CJA 2003** created a new exception to the hearsay rule which relates to the evidence of expert witnesses. Under this hearsay exception, an expert may base an opinion or an inference on a statement which was prepared for the purposes of criminal proceedings (or for those of a criminal investigation) by a person who had or may reasonably be supposed to have had personal knowledge of the matters stated if notice is given that the expert will base an opinion or an inference thereupon. Where an expert's evidence is based upon such a statement, the statement is treated as evidence of what it states. The court may, however, upon application by a party, order that it is not in the interests of justice for s.127 to apply. In deciding whether to so order, the matters the court should consider include the expense of calling the person who prepared the statement, whether the person could give relevant evidence that the expert could not give and whether the person can reasonably be expected to remember the matters stated well enough to give oral evidence thereof.

In forming his opinion, it may be that an expert does not merely consider the facts of the case with which he is concerned but also takes into account other information, such as that contained in specialist text books and articles. The expert may well have no personal knowledge of some or all of the information contained in these books or articles because, for example, they relate to scientific tests which he has not himself conducted or to phenomena which he has not personally perceived. Even so, the expert is entitled to take this information into account in forming his opinion (see *R. v Abadom*).

KEY CASE

R. v ABADOM (1982)

In *R. v Abadom*, a scientist was required to determine whether broken glass found in the accused's shoe had come from a particular window. He determined and compared the refractive indices of the glass in the shoe and of glass from the window and found that they were the same. He also relied upon Home Office statistics which showed that only a small percentage of glass samples shared this refractive index. Thus, he concluded that there was strong evidence that the glass in the shoe had come from the window. The Court of Appeal held that the expert was entitled to rely upon the Home Office data. The common law rule under which such evidence is admitted is preserved in criminal proceedings by s.118 of the CJA 2003.

When does a matter fall outside the court's knowledge and experience?

Expert evidence is admissible in criminal proceedings (at common law) if the court is required to determine an issue which falls outside its knowledge and experience (*R. v Turner* (1975)).

R. v SMITH (1979)

The defendant was charged with murder following an incident in which he stabbed the victim some 26 times. As part of his defence the defendant plead automatism on the basis that he was sleepwalking at the time that he stabbed the victim. The jury was required to consider whether the accused could have killed the victim whilst the accused was sleepwalking, as a result the jury was entitled to expert assistance, the capabilities of a sleepwalker being outside the experience of the average juror.

Equally, where a jury in reaching its verdict is required to take into account the characteristics of an accused who is said to be mentally ill or of subnormal IQ, the evidence of psychiatrists or psychologists may be admissible (*R. v Masih* (1986)). Equally, expert evidence is admissible in civil proceedings (under CEA 1972 s.3(1)) if it is relevant to a matter on which the expert is qualified to give expert evidence (i.e. if the court requires such evidence in order to make a properly informed decision (*M & R (Minors), Re* (1996)). As was seen above, however, admissibility in civil proceedings is subject to the permission of the court to adduce expert evidence being obtained, as required by CPR Pt 35.

Expert evidence is not admissible in criminal or civil proceedings where the issue before the court is one which falls within the court's experience. Thus, for example, if a jury is required to consider whether it is likely that a normal person (i.e. one who is not mentally ill or of sub-normal IQ) would have been provoked in given circumstances, psychiatric advice is not required, and, consequently, is not admissible, the issue falling within the experience of the jury (*R. v Turner* (1975)). Equally, it has been held that a jury does not require expert advice in order to determine whether a publication is obscene (see *R. v Calder & Boyars* (1969)). Similarly, in civil proceedings, whilst the court, in the context of a case concerning a road traffic accident, may need the assistance of an expert witness to determine the speed of a car from evidence such as marks on the road or damage to cars, the court does not require the evidence of an expert witness to draw conclusions concerning matters such as the speed of a car from the evidence of eyewitnesses, evidence of the latter type being, for the purposes of s.3(1) of the **CEA 1972**, irrelevant and inadmissible (*Liddell v Middleton* (1995)).

█ DEFINITION CHECKPOINT

When will the court require the assistance of an expert?
Fundamentally, whether a court requires the assistance of an expert will vary with the specific facts of the specific case before it. Thus, for example, whether a jury requires the assistance of a facial mapping expert in order to determine whether the man whose image was captured in a photograph is the man in the dock before them may depend upon factors such as whether the man in the photograph was wearing a disguise (*R. v Stockwell*).

It seems that expert evidence may potentially be admissible even though it is based upon a scientific technique that has not been generally accepted by the expert's profession (*R. v Dallagher* (2003)). It also seems, however, that the court may at times find it necessary to exclude such evidence either upon the basis that the technique is so little recognised that the expert is not competent to give expert evidence in the relevant field or that the technique is so unreliable that the expert evidence possesses no weight (*R. v Luttrell* (2004)). Exceptionally in criminal proceedings it may be that a case should be withdrawn from the jury if it is mainly based upon disputed expert evidence in a newly developing field of expertise (*R. v Cannings* (2004)), but normally (as is seen below) it will be for the jury to decide which expert evidence to accept and which to reject (*R. v Kai-Whitewind* (2005)), so the reliability of expert evidence will normally go to its weight rather than to its admissibility. [Note: The Law Commission has recently engaged in consultation concerning whether the reliability of expert evidence should be a condition of its admissibility in criminal proceedings.]

Where the jury may not be aware that an expert technique is subject to a risk of error, it may be necessary to give the jury a special warning if expert evidence based upon the technique is admitted (*R. v Luttrell*).

Whose opinion is decisive, the court's or the expert's?

Where expert evidence is admissible, the opinion of the expert should not be permitted to replace that of the tribunal of fact. Thus, for example, in a jury trial it should be the opinion of the jury, not the opinion of the expert, which determines the issues before the court. Equally, in a civil trial, it is the opinion of the judge, not that of the expert witnesses, which determines the issues. It is for the jury (or the judge in a civil trial) to determine the weight (i.e. the probative value) of an expert's evidence. Consequently, a jury should not normally be directed to accept the evidence of an expert (*R. v Lanfear* (1968)). Indeed, it will often be that the jury are required to choose between the opinions of two or more experts, prosecution and defence. Exceptionally, however, it may be that in the absence of other evidence a jury should be directed to accept "unequivocal, uncontradicted" expert evidence (*R. v Sanders* (1991)). Similarly, whilst in civil proceedings, the judge is not inherently required to accept even the opinion of a single joint expert (*Fuller v Strum* (2001)), there may be circumstances in which the judge will effectively be required to accept cogent expert evidence which is uncontradicted. A civil judge might, however, prefer the evidence of witnesses of fact to that of a single joint expert (*Armstrong v First York* (2005)). Equally, where a judge is required to choose between the opinions of two or more experts called by different parties, factors such as the performance of the various experts under cross-examination may assist the court in determining which expert evidence to accept (*Davis v Stena Line* (2005)).

Whilst it is for the tribunal of fact and not for the expert to determine the issues before the court, this does not prevent the expert from stating his opinion upon an ultimate issue (i.e. the very issue the court is required to determine) provided that expert assistance is required. That this is so in civil proceedings is made clear by s.3(3) of the **CEA 1972** (*M & R (Minors), Re* (1996)). So far as criminal proceedings are concerned, the common law "ultimate issue rule" has not been abolished by statute and thus, technically, an expert witness should not give his opinion on an ultimate issue in criminal proceedings. In practice, it appears that experts are often permitted to give such evidence in criminal proceedings, though the jury must be reminded that it is for them, and not for the expert, to determine the relevant issue (*R. v Stockwell*), and the criminal courts do still appear to apply the ultimate issue rule in some contexts, such as that of DNA evidence (*R. v Doheny* (1997)).

Revision checklist

You should now know and understand:

- when a non-expert witness may be able to give evidence of opinion in civil and criminal proceedings;

- when an expert witness may be competent to give opinion evidence in civil and criminal proceedings;

- when an issue will fall outside of the knowledge and experience of the court;

- the operation of Pt 33 of the Criminal Procedure Rules;

- the operation of Pt 35 of the Civil Procedure Rules;
- the operation of the rule against hearsay in the context of expert evidence;
- the duties of expert witnesses;
- that the issues before the court are determined by the opinion of tribunal of fact and not by the opinions of expert or non-expert witnesses.

QUESTION AND ANSWER

The Question

Paul is bringing an action in negligence against Amanda as a result of an accident in which he was hit by Amanda's car. Amanda denies negligence and claims that the steering on her car failed at the time of the accident. In her defence Amanda wishes to call Mr Smith, the mechanic who maintains her car, to state in court that he examined the car after the accident and that, in his opinion, the steering had probably failed before she crashed into Jack.

Advice and the Answer

General guidance

If a question relates to opinion evidence you first need to establish whether the witness is being called to give expert or non-expert opinion evidence. Next you must establish whether the witness is being called to give evidence in criminal or civil proceedings. In civil proceedings the admissibility of opinion evidence (both non-expert and expert) is governed by statute, namely s.3 of the **Civil Evidence Act 1972** and by Pt 35 of the Civil Procedure Rules. In criminal proceedings the admissibility of opinion evidence is governed by the common law, though there are relevant statutory provisions (e.g. s.127 of the **Criminal Justice Act 2003**) and relevant rules of court (under Pt 33 of the Criminal Procedure Rules).

Generally a non-expert witness can only give opinion evidence about relevant facts which they have personally perceived. Technically in criminal proceedings an expert or non-expert witness should not give opinion evidence about an ultimate issue (an issue which the court must decide) although this rule is not always strictly applied (*R. v Stockwell*). The ultimate issue rule was abolished in civil proceedings by s.3(3) of the Civil Evidence Act 1995.

When determining whether expert evidence is admissible in either criminal or civil proceedings there are always two things that must be established. The first is that the witness must be competent. To be competent the witness must possess sufficient expertise in the area in which they will be testifying. The second thing that must be established is whether the matter upon which the expert is to testify falls outside the knowledge and experience of the court. If the court can determine the issue without the need for expert evidence then the expert evidence will not be admissible. It is important to note, however, that in the civil context even where both of these requirements are satisfied the permission of the court under **CPR** Pt 35 will be required if the evidence is to be adduced, and the court may give direction in relation to the way in which the evidence may be adduced (e.g. by directing that it will be given by a single joint expert).

Model Answer

The admissibility of expert opinion evidence in civil proceedings is governed by s.3(1) of the **CEA 1972** and **CPR** Pt 35. Under s.3(1), the expert evidence must relate to a relevant matter on which the expert is qualified to give expert evidence. In other words, the matter must be a matter which the court requires the assistance of an expert in order to resolve (see, for example, *Liddell v Middleton*) and the expert must be competent to give expert evidence in the relevant field. A witness is only competent (or "qualified") to give expert evidence if he is an expert. Formal training and/or qualifications are not required provided that the witness has obtained the necessary expertise (see, for example, *R. v Stockwell*).

It would appear that a judge would require the opinion of an expert witness in order to determine whether Amanda's steering had failed prior to the accident. Thus, it appears that expert evidence is admissible in this context.

If the judge is satisfied that Mr Smith is competent (i.e. qualified) to give expert evidence on this issue then he may receive Mr Smiths' evidence under s.3(1).

Even though the evidence of Mr Smith is technically admissible under s.3(1) of the 1972 Act, it should be noted that **CPR** Pt 35 gives a judge in civil proceedings the powers to exclude, limit or determine the nature of expert evidence. Thus, the court's permission will be required either to call Mr Smith as an expert witness or to put his report in evidence, the court being required by CPR Pt 35 to restrict expert evidence to that which is reasonably required to resolve the proceedings. Further, if the court gives Amanda permission to adduce Mr Smith's evidence, it is probable that his evidence will be given by written report and that Amanda will not be permitted to call Mr Smith to give oral evidence. Moreover, again under **CPR** Pt 35, the court may direct that the expert evidence in relation to the issue be given by a single joint expert, in which case the claimant may not be prepared to agree Mr Smith as a suitable single joint expert.

If Amanda is permitted to adduce Mr Smith's evidence, he must be aware of the fact that, under the **CPR**, his duty to the court over-rides his duty to Amanda. His report must state that he understands this duty, has complied with it and will continue to do so. The report must, as required by **CPR** Pt 35, amongst other things, specify Mr Smith's qualifications, the literature etc., which he relied upon when making the report, and his conclusions; it must summarise his instructions and must be verified by a "statement of truth". If a range of expert opinions exist in relation to the matter which the report concerns, the report must summarise these and must indicate why Mr Smith formed his opinion. The report must summarise Mr Smith's conclusions and, if his opinion is a qualified opinion, it must state the nature of the qualification.

If the court does not direct the use of a single joint expert, it will probably direct the parties to exchange expert reports simultaneously on a specified day. If Amanda fails to disclose Mr Smith's report then, under **CPR** Pt 35, Amanda will only be able to rely upon the report or to call Mr Smith at the trial with the court's permission. If both parties are permitted to instruct their own experts, the court may direct that discussions between the experts take place and that the experts produce a statement of the issues on which they agree and disagree.

Finally, when Mr Smith's report is served on Paul, Paul will, within 28 days, again under **CPR** Pt 35, be entitled to put written questions about the report to Mr Smith for the purpose of clarifying it. Mr Smith's answers will be treated as part of the report. If Mr Smith does not provide answers, the court may direct that Amanda cannot rely on his evidence. If Mr Smith is a single joint expert then both parties can send him written questions on the report.

Privilege and Public Interest Immunity

7

Introduction

In this chapter we will consider the nature of three forms of privilege, namely, the privilege which attaches to communications made "without prejudice", the privilege against self-incrimination and legal professional privilege. We will also consider the nature of public interest immunity. Essentially, where a party is entitled to claim privilege and does so, he may be entitled to refuse to answer questions in court or to withhold inspection of documents and may also be entitled to require another person (e.g. his legal adviser or an expert witness) to do the same. A party entitled to claim privilege may, however, waive it (i.e. relinquish the right to claim it). Public interest immunity is not a form of privilege though, like privilege, a successful public interest immunity claim may entitle a party to refuse to disclose documents or answer questions.

COMMUNICATIONS MADE "WITHOUT PREJUDICE"

When does the privilege arise?

> **DEFINITION CHECKPOINT**
>
> Essentially, a communication is privileged as a "without prejudice communication" if made in the course of a genuine attempt to negotiate the settlement of a dispute (*Rush and Tompkins v GLC* (1989)).

This will be so unless the communication is made upon an "open" basis. Thus, during a genuine attempt to negotiate a settlement, a party may make an admission of liability safe in the knowledge that, should the negotiations be unsuccessful and the matter end up in court, the admission will be inadmissible and cannot be put in evidence against him unless privilege is waived. Indeed, the privilege may be claimed even though the proceedings in relation to which it is claimed are not those which the negotiations were intended to settle but are subsequent proceedings between the parties to the negotiations (*Ofulue v Bossert* (2009)). Whilst it is normal and correct practice to head a letter written in the course of such negotiations "without pre-judice", and the presence or absence of such a heading will be taken into account by the court in determining whether the privilege arises (*Prudential Assurance Company Ltd v Prudential Assurance Company of America (No.2)* (2003)), the presence or absence of such a heading is not decisive. Conse-quently, the fact that a letter is headed "without prejudice" does not, in itself, give rise to the privilege and, conversely, a letter written in the course of genuine negotiations aimed at settlement may be privileged even though the "without prejudice" heading is missing and even though it is headed "open letter" (*Dixons Stores Group Ltd v Thames Television Plc* (1993)).

Without Prejudice privilege

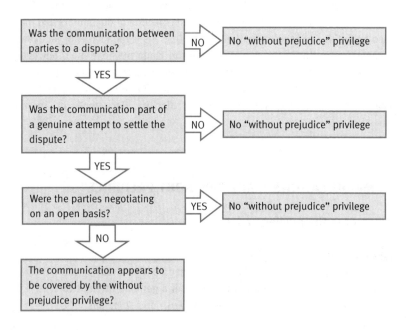

Does the privilege come to an end when settlement is reached and can it be claimed against a third party?

The privilege subsists even after a settlement has been reached between the negotiating parties and not only prevents the party to whom the privileged communication was made from making use of admissions contained therein against its maker but also prevents third parties from so doing and, indeed, may be claimed so as to prevent a third party from inspecting the privileged documents (*Rush & Tompkins v GLC*). Thus, where A makes an admission in the course of negotiations with B which are aimed at the settlement of a dispute between them, the communication is privileged whether or not a settlement was eventually reached and, consequently, neither B nor C (a third party who is also bringing proceedings against A) can make use of the admission in litigation concerning its subject-matter and, moreover, A will be able to claim the privilege so as to prevent C from inspecting correspondence between A and B which formed part of the negotiations. The parties to "without prejudice negotiations" may, however, jointly waive the privilege (*Walker v Wilsher* (1889)). Moreover, it appears that, in the context of litigation by a third party against one of the parties to the negotiations, the privilege may be waived by that party alone (*Muller v Linsley & Mortimer (A Firm)* (1994)).

▌ DEFINITION CHECKPOINT

What is the rationale for the existence of the privilege?
The rationale for the existence of the without prejudice privilege has two limbs, namely, the public interest in encouraging the settlement of disputes and the existence of an express or implied agreement between the negotiating parties (*Unilever Plc v Procter and Gamble* (1999)).

Does the privilege only apply to admissions?

Whilst the position is not totally clear, it is submitted that the better view is that the privilege applies to all communications between the negotiating parties, not merely to admissions (*Unilever Plc v Procter and Gamble*). Whilst Lord Hoffmann has suggested on more than one occasion (most recently in *Bradford and Bingley Plc v Rashid* (2006)) that the privilege's public policy rationale only encompasses admissions, it is submitted that the decision of the House of Lords in *Rashid* does not provide authority for this proposition.

Are there any exceptions to the operation of the privilege?

The operation of the privilege is subject to a number of exceptions. For example, it does not prevent the admission of communications where the issue before the court is whether a settlement was reached (*Tomlin v Standard Telephones and Cables Ltd* (1969)). Equally, privileged communications may be relied upon in relation to the issue of costs (but not when the court is determining liability or quantum) where an offer is made "without prejudice except as to costs" (*Cutts v Head* (1984)).

SELF-INCRIMINATION

DEFINITION CHECKPOINT
When does the privilege arise?
Basically, a person is not required to answer a question in court, and is entitled to withhold inspection of a document sought by another party, if answering the question or permitting inspection of the document would tend to expose him to a criminal charge which is reasonably likely to be preferred or to proceedings in respect of a penalty or forfeiture which are reasonably likely to be brought (*Blunt v Park Lane Hotel Ltd* (1942)). A person entitled to claim the privilege against self-incrimination may, however, waive the right to do so.

An example of a penalty is one imposed by HM Revenue and Customs. An example of forfeiture is forfeiture of property under a lease.

Why does the privilege exist?
It seems that the privilege exists in English law in order to discourage the ill-treatment of suspects and the production of dubious confessions (*Istel v Tully* (1993)). Moreover, the European Court of Human Rights has recognised that the rights of silence and self-incrimination, in protecting the accused from improper coercion, form central aspects of an art.6 fair trial (*Saunders v UK* (1996)).

Statutory removal of the privilege
The right to claim the privilege against self-incrimination has been removed by statute in a variety of contexts, both expressly and by necessary implication. Thus, for example, where the accused chooses to testify in criminal proceedings, statute expressly provides that he may be asked questions tending to criminate him (**CEA 1898** s.1(e)). Where the accused, being asked an incriminating question, refuses to answer, then (as was seen in Chapter 4, above), the court may be entitled to draw an inference under the **Criminal Justice and Public Order Act 1994** s.35.

Equally, statute expressly provides that a person may be asked questions which may incriminate that person or his or her spouse or civil partner (or may be required to comply with an order of the court which is of the like effect) in proceedings for the recovery or administration of property, for the execution of a trust or for an account of property or dealings therewith (**Theft Act 1968** s.31). Where a person answers such a question or complies with such an order as required by s.31, however, the statements or admissions which the person makes are not admissible in evidence against the person or the spouse/civil partner in subsequent proceedings for an offence under the

Theft Act 1968 unless, in the case of the spouse/civil partner, the marriage took place/the civil partnership commenced after the statements or admissions were made.

An example of the implied removal of the privilege by statute is provided by the examination of persons by inspectors appointed by the Department for Business, Innovation and Skills under the authority of the **Companies Act 1985**. Whilst the relevant statutory provisions do not expressly remove the privilege, if the privilege could be claimed by persons so examined this would prevent the attainment of the relevant statutory purpose (namely, the investigation of fraud: *London United Investments Plc, Re* (1992)).

Human rights

Where statute expressly or impliedly removes the privilege against self-incrimination and does not provide an alternative protection, thus compelling a person, upon pain of a possible fine or imprisonment, to provide evidence which is later used in subsequent criminal proceedings against him, this is likely to result in a violation of art.6 of the **European Convention on Human Rights** (*Saunders v UK*). Consequently, a number of statutory provisions, which removed the privilege against self-incrimination and did not prevent the use of evidence obtained by compulsion from being used in subsequent criminal proceedings against the person from whom the evidence was obtained, were amended by the **YJ&CEA 1999** in order to avoid future violations of art.6. An example is provided by the provisions concerning examination of persons by Department for Business, Innovation and Skills inspectors which were referred to above. The effect of the amendments to these provisions is, essentially, that, in subsequent criminal proceedings, the prosecution cannot adduce evidence concerning the accused's answers to the inspectors' questions and cannot ask questions concerning those answers.

It should be noted that the relevant amendments do not prevent the use in evidence of pre-existing documents or other pre-existing evidence which the accused was compelled to produce. This is so because the art.6 right not to incriminate oneself does not encompass such evidence but, rather, only encompasses answers that the accused has been compelled to give against his will to remain silent (*Saunders v UK*).

Does the English Law privilege apply to pre-existing incriminating documents?

Currently, it appears to be unclear whether the privilege against self-incrimination may be claimed in English Law so as to prevent a person from being required to disclose pre-existing incriminating documents or whether it may only be claimed so as to prevent a person from being required to answer incriminating questions. Thus, the Court of Appeal has indicated that until this issue has been determined by the Supreme Court, the courts should take the privilege against self-incrimination into account when considering whether to order the production of pre-existing incrimination documents (*Malik v Manchester Crown Court* (2008)).

Judicial alternatives to the privilege

A civil court may be prepared to order a person to disclose information, the production of which might ordinarily expose him to a criminal charge, in circumstances in which the court is able to ensure that the relevant information will not be used against that person in subsequent criminal proceedings. Thus, for example, disclosure has properly been ordered in civil proceedings subject to a condition that the information disclosed would not be used in criminal proceedings against the person required to disclose the relevant information. It appears, however, that such an order should only be made where the prosecuting authority agrees not to use the information so disclosed in criminal proceedings against the person required to disclose it (*Istel v Tully*).

When will a judge uphold a claim of privilege?

As was indicated above, the privilege against self-incrimination arises if answering a question or permitting inspection of a document would tend to expose the party entitled to claim the privilege to a criminal charge which is reasonably likely to be preferred or to proceedings in respect of a penalty or forfeiture which are reasonably likely to be brought (*Blunt v Park Lane Hotel Ltd*). In determining whether the privilege against self-incrimination arises, the judge must consider not merely whether the answer to a question or the production of a document would directly criminate the person answering the question or producing the document but also whether it would provide evidence which, in combination with other evidence, might form the basis of a charge against that person (*R. v Slaney* (1832); *R. v Boyes* (1861)). Conversely, even if answering a question or producing a document would either incriminate the person answering the question or producing the document or provide evidence against that person, the judge will not uphold a claim of privilege if the possibility that a charge will be preferred is a remote one such as would not influence the conduct of a reasonable man (*R. v Boyes*). Further, it appears that where the person claiming privilege is already exposed to the risk that criminal charges will be preferred and that answering a question or producing a document will not increase that risk, the claim will not be upheld (*Khan v Khan* (1982)).

Where the privilege has not been removed by statute, is its application in civil and in criminal proceedings identical?

A person can no longer claim the privilege against self-incrimination in civil proceedings upon the basis that answering a question or producing a document would tend to expose that person to a forfeiture (**CEA 1968** s.16(1)(a)). Moreover, in civil proceedings, a spouse or civil partner may refuse to answer a question or to produce a document if answering the question or producing the document would tend to expose his or her spouse or civil partner to a charge or penalty (**CEA 1968** s.14(1)(b)). Further, in civil proceedings a person cannot claim the privilege merely because answering a question or producing a document would expose that person to a charge or penalty under the law of a foreign country (**CEA 1968** s.14(1)(a)).

It may well be that in context of criminal proceedings (unlike the civil position), a spouse or civil partner cannot claim the privilege against self-incrimination so as to prevent the incrimination of his or her spouse or civil partner, though the position in criminal proceedings has not been conclusively determined (*Rio Tinto Zinc Corp v Westinghouse Electric Corp* (1978)). It seems that exposure to a criminal charge or a penalty under foreign law does not give rise to the privilege in the context of criminal proceedings (*Brannigan v Davison* (1997)), the position thus equating with that encountered in the civil context. It should be noted, however, that, a penalty imposed under the law of the European Community is imposed under domestic law, not under foreign law (*Rio Tinto Zinc Corp v Westinghouse Electric Corp*).

. . . .

LEGAL PROFESSIONAL PRIVILEGE

When does the privilege arise?

Legal professional privilege had two forms, namely, legal advice privilege and litigation privilege.

DEFINITION CHECKPOINT
Basically, the effect of legal advice privilege is that a client is entitled to refuse to answer questions in court or to withhold inspection of documents sought by another party where the questions concern or the documents comprise confidential communications between the client and the client's legal adviser which were made for the purposes of obtaining or giving legal advice (*Balabel v Air India* (1988)). Legal advice privilege also entitles the client to require his legal adviser to refuse to answer such questions and to withhold inspection of such documents (*Greenough v Gaskell* (1833)).

Legal Advice Privilege

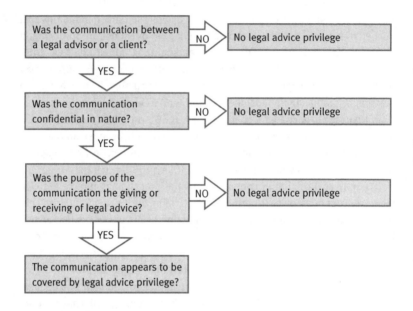

DEFINITION CHECKPOINT

Litigation privilege entitles the client to refuse to answer questions and to withhold the inspection of documents where the questions or documents concern confidential communications between the client or his legal adviser and third parties (i.e. expert or non-expert witnesses) if the dominant purpose of the relevant communications was that of preparing for adversarial litigation which had commenced or was contemplated (*Wheeler v Le Marchant* (1881); *Waugh v British Railways Board* (1980); *L (a minor) (police investigation: privilege), Re* (1996)). The privilege also entitles the client to require the legal adviser and the third party to refuse to answer the relevant question or produce the relevant document (*Harmony Shipping Co v Saudi Europe* (1979)). Further, litigation privilege entitles the client to refuse to reveal the identity and personal details of the witnesses that the party intends to call in adversarial litigation (*R. (on the application of Kelly) v Warley Magistrates' Court* (2007)).

Litigation Privilege

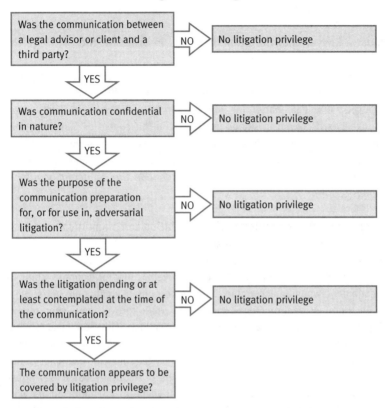

What is the rationale for the existence of the privilege?

Basically, the rationale for the existence of legal advice privilege is that it is in the public interest that clients can obtain legal advice in order to arrange their affairs, that this can only be achieved if clients puts the facts before their legal advisers and that clients may not be willing to do so unless they are sure that what they tell their legal advisers will not be disclosed in the absence of the clients' consent (*Three Rivers DC v Governor and Company of the Bank of England (No.4)* (2004)). Legal advice privilege is not merely a rule of evidence but is a fundamental human right which is both recognised by the common law and protected by the European Convention on Human Rights (*R. (on the application of Morgan Grenfell & Co Ltd) v Special Commissioners of Income Tax* (2003)).

To the extent to which litigation privilege may arise in circumstances in which disclosing a communication would not violate the confidentiality of communications between legal adviser and client, its sole rationale appears to be that in the context of adversarial proceedings, the parties are not entitled to see each other's materials (*L (a minor) (police investigation: privilege), Re* (1996)).

Must a lawyer-client relationship exist in order for the privilege to arise?

If a lawyer-client relationship does not exist, then legal advice privilege will not arise. Thus, for example, if C asks L, his friend, for his confidential advice in respect of a legal matter, the advice given by L will not be privileged, even though L is a lawyer, if L does not give it in the course of performing his professional duties (*Smith v Daniel* (1875)). It seems, however, that if the client does not know that the lawyer is no longer practising, communications with the lawyer may still be privileged (*Dadourian Group International Inc v Simms* (2008)).

Does legal advice privilege arise in relation to communications with professionals other than lawyers?

At common law, legal advice privilege does not arise in relation to communications with professionals other than lawyers. Thus, for example, communications between an accountant and the accountant's client are not subject to legal professional privilege (*Prudential v HMRC* (2010)). As is seen below, litigation privilege may attach to communications with non legal professionals which take place for the purposes of litigation. Moreover, statute may extend the ambit of legal professional privilege. Thus, for example, under s.190 of the **Legal Services Act 2007**, clients of Alternative Business Structures will be able to claim legal advice privilege in communications with individuals who are not lawyers provided that the client is the client of a lawyer and the individual acted under the direction or supervision of the lawyer.

Are all lawyer-client communications confidential?

Not all lawyer-client communications are confidential, and thus not all lawyer-client communications will be privileged. For example, if a client retains a solicitor and informs the solicitor of his address for correspondence purposes, it appears that, in the normal course of events, the solicitor's knowledge of the client's address does not amount to a professional confidence (*Ex p. Campbell* (1870)). Equally, it seems that where a solicitor is under a duty to disclose communications between solicitor and client to a third party, such as the client's accountants, the communications will not be confidential communications between legal adviser and client and, thus, legal advice privilege will not arise (*Nederlandse Reassurantie Groep Holding NV v Bacon and Woodrow (A Firm) and Others* (1995)).

[*Note:* where a communication with such a third party takes the form of a confidential communication between the solicitor or client and the third party for the dominant purpose of preparing for litigation which has commenced or is contemplated, then the communication may be protected by legal professional privilege in its litigation privilege form.]

Are communications with the client's in-house lawyers privileged?

Whilst communications with in-house lawyers are privileged in English Law, the European Court of Justice has held that communications between a client and their in-house lawyers are not privileged in the context of investigations by the European Commission (*Akzo Nobel Chemicals Limited and Akcros Chemicals Limited v Commission of the European Communities* (2010)).

Are communications between opposing parties confidential?

Communications between opposing parties to legal proceedings are not confidential and are thus not subject to legal professional privilege (*Parry v News Group Newspapers* (1990)) though, as was seen above, they may be still be privileged if they amount to "without prejudice communications".

In order for the privilege to arise, is it necessary that litigation has commenced or is contemplated?

So far as confidential communications between lawyer and client are concerned, all that is necessary is that the purpose of the communications was that of obtaining or giving legal advice. Therefore, in order for the form of legal professional privilege referred to as "legal advice privilege" to arise, it is not necessary that litigation had commenced or was contemplated at the time when the communication was made. Thus, for example, legal advice privilege may arise in the context of communications between solicitor and client concerning the drafting of a lease by the solicitor for the client even though litigation had not arisen and was not contemplated at the relevant time (*Balabel v Air India*). In order for legal advice privilege to arise, however, it appears that the advice which is sought or given must take place in a "relevant legal context" (and, thus, some forms of business advice which a solicitor gives to his client may not be privileged) (*Three Rivers DC v Governor and Company of the Bank of England (No.4)*).

As regards communications with third parties (i.e. expert witnesses or witnesses of fact), such communications are only privileged by legal professional privilege in the form of "litigation privilege" if the dominant purpose of the communications was that of preparing for litigation which has commenced or is contemplated.

KEY CASE

WAUGH V BRITISH RAILWAYS BOARD (1980)
In *Waugh v British Railways Board* the relevant communication was a report concerning the details of a railway accident which had been prepared equally for the purpose of accident prevention and for the purpose of providing the Board's legal adviser with information which he required in the context of contemplated litigation. Since informing the Board's legal adviser was not the dominant purpose of the two, the House of Lords held that the report was not privileged.

It appears that litigation privilege will not arise merely because litigation is possible but will only arise if litigation is at least reasonably in prospect (*USA v Philip Morris Inc* (2004)).

Finally, it should be noted that litigation privilege will not arise where a communication was made for the purposes of non-adversarial proceedings, such as an inquiry set up to enquire into the supervision of a bank by the Bank of England (*Three Rivers DC v Governor and Company of the Bank of England (No.5)* (2003)) or care proceedings (*L (a minor) (police investigation: privilege), Re*).

Can the privilege attach to pre-existing documents which the client subsequently sends to the lawyer or to the third party?

Where a document was not privileged at the time it was created, the fact that it is subsequently sent by the client to a lawyer or to an expert witness does not entitle the client to subsequently claim that it is privileged. Thus, if a client sends an invoice containing a sample of his handwriting to his solicitor and the solicitor sends the invoice to a handwriting expert, the client is not entitled to claim privilege in respect of the invoice (*R. v King* (1983)).

Where, for the purposes of litigation which has commenced or is contemplated, a lawyer makes a copy of an unprivileged document which has never been in the client's hands, the copy may be privileged (*Watson v Cammell Laird* (1959); *Dubai Bank v Galadari* (1989)). Equally, copies of unprivileged documents in the lawyer's hand may be privileged if the lawyer used his skill to compile the collection of documents, inspecting the documents might reveal the nature of his advice to his client and the documents are not the client's own document's (*Lyell v Kennedy* (1884); *Sumitomo Corp v Credit Lyonnais* (2002)).

Does the operation of the privilege prevent a witness of fact from giving evidence of facts which he has personally perceived?

Where a third party (i.e. an expert witness or a witness of fact) has perceived relevant facts, the fact that he has engaged in privileged communications with the lawyer or the client does not prevent him from being called as a witness by another party to the relevant legal proceedings. If the client asserts his privilege, the witness cannot give evidence as to the content of the privileged communications, but the existence of the privilege does not prevent the third party from giving evidence of the facts which he has perceived (*Harmony Shipping Co v Saudi Europe*).

Similarly, a solicitor may be compelled to give evidence of facts personally perceived by the solicitor, such as the fact that the solicitor was present in court when his client was disqualified from driving (*R. (on the application of Howe) v South Durham Magistrates' Court* (2005)).

Where two clients jointly retain a common legal adviser, can one successfully claim privilege against the other in respect of communications between the clients and the legal adviser?

Where two clients jointly retain a legal adviser, either may claim that communications made to the lawyer in the capacity of their joint legal adviser are privileged as against third parties but neither may claim that such communications are privileged as against each other (*Konigsberg, Re* (1989)).

Can the client successfully claim privilege against another party who shares a joint interest with him in the subject-matter of the privileged communication or with whom he has a common interest in the outcome of litigation?

A client cannot successfully claim privilege against a person with whom the client shares a joint interest in the subject-matter of the privileged communication. Thus, for example, trustees cannot maintain privilege against a beneficiary in respect of communications concerning a disposition of trust property (*In Re Postlethwaite* (1887)). They could, however, maintain privilege in such communications against third parties. The same may be true where parties with a common interest in litigation retain a common legal adviser and exchange information (*Buttes Gas and Oil Co v Hammer (No.3)* (1981)). A trustee who was potentially facing legal action from his beneficiaries would, however, be entitled to claim legal professional privilege in communications with his own solicitor which had taken place for the purpose of advising the trustee as to his personal liability (*Thomas v Secretary of State for India in Council* (1870)).

Can the right to claim legal professional privilege be waived?

Legal professional privilege can only be claimed or waived by the client or on behalf of the client (*Proctor v Smiles* (1886)). If the client chooses to claim privilege it cannot be waived on their behalf by the legal adviser or the third party. Equally, where the client chooses to waive privilege, it cannot be claimed on their behalf by the legal adviser or the third party. It should be noted, however, that the legal adviser, whilst acting in the capacity of the client's agent, may possess the authority to waive privilege on the client's behalf. Thus, if a solicitor, whilst acting on his client's behalf, mistakenly permits another party to inspect a privileged document, this may amount to a waiver of privilege (*Guinness Peat Properties Ltd v Fitzroy Robinson Partnership* (1987)). Equally, if a client's barrister mistakenly reads out part of a privileged document in court, this, too, may amount to a waiver of privilege in the entire document (*Great Atlantic Insurance v Home Insurance* (1981)). Moreover, where, in the course of legal proceedings, privilege is waived by one party in a communication which concerns a particular transaction (e.g. concerning what was said during a particular conversation), this may result in the other party being entitled to disclosure of other communications concerning the same transaction (*General Accident Fire and Life Assurance Corp Ltd v Tanter* (1984)). Similarly, where a former client sues his former solicitor in negligence, this may give rise to an implied waiver of privilege by the client in relation to communications between the former client and the former solicitor concerning the transaction which forms the subject matter of the negligence proceedings (*Lillicrap v Nalder* (1993)).

Where a party has obtained possession of copies of privileged documents can he use these as secondary evidence to prove the contents of the originals?

Essentially, where a party to legal proceedings obtains possession of copies of privileged documents, the party may use the copies as secondary evidence to prove the contents of the originals regardless of how the party obtained them (*Calcraft v Guest* (1898)). It may be, however, that, before the secondary evidence is adduced, a court will be prepared to grant the party entitled to claim privilege an injunction preventing the party in possession of the copies from making use of them in subsequent legal proceedings (*Lord Ashburton v Pape* (1913)).

Basically, it appears that a court will be prepared to grant an injunction preventing the use of secondary evidence to prove the contents of a privileged document if the party entitled to claim the privilege applies for the injunction before the copies have been adduced in evidence and provided that there is no reason why the court, in the exercise of its discretion, should refuse to grant an equitable remedy (*Goddard v Nationwide Building Society*

(1987)). In general, such an injunction will be granted even though the conduct of the party wishing to adduce the secondary evidence has been entirely proper. Where, however, the party entitled to claim privilege permitted the party wishing to adduce the secondary evidence to inspect the relevant document in the course of disclosure under **CPR** Pt 31, then the latter party is normally entitled to assume that there has been a waiver of privilege (*Guinness Peat Properties Ltd v Fitzroy Robinson Partnership*). Exceptionally, however, even in these circumstances an injunction may be granted where inspection was obtained by fraud, where the party obtaining inspection or his solicitors realised that they were only permitted to inspect the relevant document in consequence of a mistake or where the mistake would have been obvious to the reasonable solicitor (*Guinness Peat Properties Ltd v Fitzroy Robinson Partnership*; *Pizzey v Ford Motor Company* (1994)). Moreover, it should be noted that **CPR** 31.20 provides that where a party was permitted to inspect a privileged document in consequence of the inadvertence of another party, the inspecting party may only use the privileged document or its contents with the court's permission (though normal practice appears to remain to apply promptly for an injunction) (*Breeze v John Stacey* (1999)).

KEY CASE

GUINNESS PEAT PROPERTIES V FITZROY ROBINSON PARTNERSHIP (1987)
In the context of an action for breach of contract and / or negligence the defendant's solicitors accidently permitted the opposing solicitors to inspect and copy a letter sent to the defendant's insurer in which they identified defects for which they may have been liable. The defendants had intended to claim privilege in the document and as a result applied for an injunction to prevent the plaintiffs from using the copy and requiring all copies to be delivered to the defendants.

The Court of Appeal held that the judge had properly granted an injunction because the defendants' mistake had been an obvious one of which the plaintiffs had been aware and the defendants had applied promptly for the injunction as soon as they had become aware of the error.

It appears that an injunction will not be granted to prevent the prosecution from making use of secondary evidence in criminal proceedings (*Butler v Board of Trade* (1971)). In such circumstances the court might, however, be prepared to exclude the secondary evidence in the exercise of its exclusionary discretion under s.78 of **PACE**.

Can the court order the production of privileged documents where the interests of the client who claims the privilege are outweighed by those of a defendant to criminal proceedings?

It was formerly believed that a claim of legal professional privilege would not be upheld where a defendant to criminal proceedings established on the balance of probabilities that the person claiming privilege no longer had an interest to protect and that the defendant did have a legitimate interest in adducing the privileged information in evidence. The House of Lords has now made clear, however, that once the privilege arises there is no exception to its absolute nature (*R. v Derby Magistrates' Court Ex p. B* (1995)). Thus, a court cannot order the disclosure of privileged information in such circumstances, it being for the party entitled to claim the privilege to decide whether he wishes to waive it.

Will the privilege arise where confidential communications took place for the purpose of facilitating the commission of a crime of a fraud?

It appears that where the purpose of confidential communications was to facilitate the commission of criminal or fraudulent activity, the client cannot maintain the privilege even though neither the legal adviser nor the client were aware of the criminal or fraudulent purpose (*R. v Central Criminal Court Ex p. Francis and Francis* (1989)).

Can the privilege be removed by statute?

Statute may override legal professional privilege but will only do so where the intention to override the privilege is either expressly stated in the statute or where there is a necessary implication to that effect (*R. (on the application of Morgan Grenfell & Co Ltd) v Special Commissioners of Income Tax*). This does not mean, however, that rules of court made under a statutory provision that does not expressly or impliedly override the privilege may not provide for a sanction (e.g. the inadmissibility of evidence) if a party declines to disclose privileged information (e.g. the identity of its witnesses) pre-trial, but a court order made under rules of court which were made under such a statutory provision will be unlawful if it requires a party to disclose privileged information (*R. (on the application of Kelly) v Warley Magistrates' Court*).

PUBLIC INTEREST IMMUNITY

What is the effect of claiming public interest immunity?

DEFINITION CHECKPOINT
Essentially, successfully claiming public interest immunity may entitle a party to civil or criminal proceedings to withhold disclosure or inspection of documents or to refuse to answer questions.

How can public interest immunity be claimed?

In civil proceedings, under **CPR** Pt 31, a party may claim the right to withhold inspection of a document (such that the other party knows that the document exists but cannot obtain inspection of it) or may even apply for permission to withhold disclosure of the document (such that the other party will not even know that the document exists).

In criminal proceedings, under **CrimPR** Pt 22, a prosecution application for a public interest immunity ruling need only be served on the defendant to the extent to which its service would not disclose the material that the prosecution believe should not be disclosed and the court may direct that the public interest immunity hearing takes place wholly or partly in the defendant's absence.

Who can claim public interest immunity?

It is not merely central government that may claim public interest immunity, rather, other bodies, such as police forces, local authorities and even the National Society for the Prevention of Cruelty to Children, have also made successful claims (*D v National Society for the Prevention of Cruelty to Children* (1978)).

When will a public interest immunity claim succeed?

A public interest immunity claim may either take the form of a contents claim or a class claim.

DEFINITION CHECKPOINT
Contents claim
A claim that disclosing the particular document is against the public interest
Class claim
A claim that the document falls within a class of documents the production of which is against the public interest.

In practice, central government will no longer make class claims but will only claim public interest immunity if disclosing the particular document could cause real damage to the public interest. Other bodies may still make contents claims or class claims.

In determining whether a public interest immunity claim is successful, the court is required to balance the public interest against disclosure with the public interest in favour of disclosure (*Conway v Rimmer* (1968)). The public interest against disclosure might, for example, take the form of potential damage to national security, such as revealing plans of secret weapons during a war (*Duncan v Cammell Laird* (1942)) or that of revealing the identity of an informant (whether an informant to the police or to some other body, such as the National Society for the Prevention of Cruelty to Children (*D v National Society for the Prevention of Cruelty to Children*). Essentially, the public interest in favour of disclosure is that of doing justice in the proceedings before the court. Thus, for example, where withholding the identity of a police informant might prevent a person charged with a serious criminal offence from proving his innocence, it is likely that the court will order disclosure on the basis that the public interest against disclosure is outweighed by the public interest in favour of disclosure (*R. v Keane* (1994)).

KEY CASE

R. v H (2004)
Where public interest immunity is claimed in criminal proceedings, if the material might weaken the case for the prosecution or strengthen the case for the defence, the court will order disclosure if non-disclosure would make the accused's trial unfair even if this results in the prosecution discontinuing the proceedings against the accused.

The result of a public interest immunity claim will not necessarily be that the court either orders full disclosure of the relevant material or orders its non-disclosure. Rather, in appropriate circumstances, the court may be prepared to order an appropriate form of limited disclosure, such as providing anonymised versions of documents (*R. v H*).

Is the court entitled to inspect the documents before reaching its public interest immunity decision?

The court is entitled to inspect the documents to which a public interest immunity claim relates before deciding whether the claim is successful (*Conway v Rimmer*). It seems that the court will do so as a matter of practice in the context of criminal proceedings (*R. v Douglas* (1993)) and will normally do so in the context of civil proceedings (*Goodridge v Chief Constable for Hampshire* (1999)).

Is there a right to waive public interest immunity?

Unlike privilege there is no right to waive public interest immunity because, where it arises, the evidence to which it relates is rendered inadmissible. In practice, however, where the party who is entitled to claim public interest immunity (e.g. a government minister) does not believe that it is in the public interest to do so, this will be a matter which the court will take into account when balancing the public interest against disclosure with the public interest in favour of disclosure, and which may well persuade the court that the relevant material should be disclosed (*R. v Chief Constable of West Midlands Police Ex p. Wiley* (1995)).

Human rights

Where the prosecution withhold disclosure of material evidence for or against the accused, this may give rise to a violation of art.6 of the **European Convention on Human Rights** (*Rowe and Davis v UK* (2000)). This, it appears, will be the case either if withholding disclosure is not strictly necessary or if the procedures adopted by the court fail to satisfy the requirements of a fair trial. Where a public interest immunity claim follows the procedure which is now laid down under **CrimPR** Pt 22, however, and withholding disclosure on public interest grounds is strictly necessary, it appears that withholding disclosure is unlikely to give rise to a violation of art.6 (see *Jasper v UK* (2000); *Fitt v UK* (2000)).

In exceptional circumstances, in order to ensure that the accused is given a fair trial, it may be necessary for the court to order that "special counsel" be appointed to represent the interests of the accused in the context of a public interest immunity claim (*R. v H*). It should be noted, however, that special counsel is not responsible to the accused. Moreover, special counsel must not disclose to the accused the material which the public interest immunity claims concerns.

Revision checklist

You should now know and understand:

- **the effect of a communication being privileged and the rationale behind why a communication may be privileged, with reference to the various types of privilege referred to below;**

- **the nature and operation of the privilege against self incrimination;**

- **the nature and operation of the without prejudice privilege;**

- the nature and operation of the two forms of legal professional privilege, namely legal advice privilege and litigation privilege;

- the nature and operation of public interest immunity.

QUESTION AND ANSWER

The Question

Jack is suing BiggCo Ltd for an accident in which his hand was injured using an industrial press. In the course of disclosure between Eric, Jack's solicitor and Amanda, the solicitor acting on behalf of BiggCo Ltd, Amanda obtained possession of a copy of a letter concerning the accident, written by Jack to his solicitor, Eric, in which Jack stated:

> "I had been operating the machine for a number of hours when the accident took place. If I hadn't been half asleep and had been concentrating I'm sure that I could have moved my hand in time."

The copy of the letter was improperly made from a file in Eric's office by a friend of Amanda's who worked for Eric as a secretary.

Furthermore BiggCo wish to rely upon an admission made by Jack that he was "at least partly responsible" for the accident. Jack made the admission during negotiations with BiggCo in which both parties sought to settle the dispute outside of court.

Consider whether the letter from Jack to his solicitor and/or the admission made by Jack are privileged communications and whether either the letter or the admission is likely to be admissible in the proceedings.

Advice and the Answer

General guidance

This chapter has considered four types of privilege, namely; without prejudice privilege, the privilege against self incrimination and the two types of legal professional privilege, legal advice privilege and litigation privilege as well as considering the concept of public interest immunity. In order to be able to successfully answer a question relating to privilege it is vitally important that you are able to identify the correct type of privilege to apply or alternatively when a public interest immunity application may need to be made.

It is relatively straightforward to apply the correct kind of privilege once you know how to spot the situations in which the various forms of privilege arise. The without prejudice privilege applies specifically to communications made during a genuine attempt to settle a dispute and therefore arises in situations such as negotiations to settle a dispute. Legal advice privilege can only apply to communications between legal advisor and client, you can rule out legal advice privilege where the communication is with a third party or a professional other than a legal advisor. Litigation privilege only applies to communications made in the context of adversarial litigation; again you can rule out litigation privilege where the dominant purpose of the communication is for something other than litigation or the proceedings to which it relates are non-adversarial in nature. The privilege against self incrimination only exists where producing a document or answering a question would tend to expose the person doing so to a criminal charge or penalty (or, in the context of criminal proceedings only, to a forfeiture). An application for public interest immunity will arise where it may be in the public interest to withhold a piece of information, for example where a piece of evidence comes from a police informant who the police wish to remain anonymous. Public interest immunity claims are decided by balancing the competing public interests for and against the disclosure of the information.

Model Answer

A communication in confidence between a client and his legal adviser for the purpose of obtaining or giving legal advice is subject to legal professional privilege in the form of "legal advice privilege" (*Balabel v Air India*). In order for legal advice privilege to arise, however, the advice must take place in a "relevant legal context" (e.g. some forms of business advice given by solicitors may not be privileged) (*Three Rivers DC v Governors and Company of the Bank of England (No.4)*). Here, the correspondence between Jack and his solicitor presumably took place for the purposes of giving Jack legal advice and, thus, appears to be subject to legal advice privilege. Consequently, had the letter not fallen into Amanda's possession, Jack could have refused to produce it or to answer questions concerning its contents and could have required his solicitor to do the same. Since the letter has fallen into Amanda's hands, however, she will be able to adduce it in evidence (*Calcraft v Guest*) unless Jack obtains an injunction, thus preventing the use of the copy as secondary evidence (*Goddard v Nationwide Building Society*). In this instance the court would likely be entitled to grant an injunction as it appears that the document was obtained by fraud (*Guinness Peat Properties Ltd v Fitzroy Robinson Partnership*). If the copy has already been adduced in evidence, however, then Jack will be too late to obtain an injunction (*Goddard v Nationwide Building Society*). Moreover, the court may refuse to grant him an injunction in the exercise of its equitable discretion (e.g. if there has been undue delay in applying for it) (*Goddard v Nationwide Building Society*).

Negotiations between Jack and BiggCo in an attempt to settle the dispute between them will (unless the negotiations took place on an "open basis") be subject to the without prejudice privilege (*Rush and Tompkins v GLC*). Thus, unless both parties to the proceedings waive the privilege, Jack's statement made during the negotiations will not be admissible in the proceedings as evidence of Jack's contributory negligence even though it contains admissions of his contributory negligence.

Estoppel by Record and the Use of Previous Convictions and Judicial Findings as Evidence of the Facts upon which they were Based

Introduction

In this chapter we will consider both the operation of the doctrine of res judicata (estoppel by record) in civil and criminal proceedings and the extent to which previous convictions and judicial findings in civil cases may be adduced as evidence of the facts upon which they were based in proceedings between parties other than the parties to the proceedings in which the accused was convicted or the findings were made.

THE DOCTRINE OF RES JUDICATA IN CIVIL PROCEEDINGS

Is the judgment of a civil court conclusive evidence against all persons of the facts upon which it was based?

The judgment of a civil court is conclusive evidence against all persons of "the state of things which it actually effects" but not of the findings on which it is based (*Hollington v Hewthorn* (1943)). Thus, for example, if a court awards C £10,000 damages against D in consequence of D's breach of contract, the judgment conclusively proves that C was awarded £10,000 damages against D but does not conclusively prove that D breached his contract with C.

Where the judgment of a civil court does not merely determine the interests of the parties to it (i.e. whether one is liable in damages for breach of contract or in negligence to the other) but, rather, determines the "status" of a person or thing, however, then such status is determined conclusively as against all persons. For example, a decree of nullity is conclusive evidence against all persons of the invalidity of the relevant marriage (*Salvesen v The Administrator of Austrian Property* (1927)). A judgment of the former type (e.g. one which merely determines liability in tort or contract) is termed a judgment in personam. A judgment of the latter type (i.e. one which determines status) is termed a judgment in rem.

Are parties to civil proceedings ever estopped from re-litigating findings made by a court in the course of civil proceedings between them?

DEFINITION CHECKPOINT

"Estoppel by record"

A party to civil proceedings or his privies may be estopped from re-litigating findings made by a court in the course of civil proceedings between himself or his privies and another party or his privies. This form of estoppel is known as estoppel by record or estopped per rem judicatam and, as is the case with estoppels generally, will only take effect if pleaded (i.e. if set out in the party's statement of case) (*Vooght v Winch* (1819)). Such an estoppel may either take the form of a cause of action estoppel (preventing the re-litigation of a previously litigated cause of action) or that of an issue estoppel (preventing the re-litigation of an issue which formed an essential element of a previously litigated cause of action).

Thus, where P successfully sued D, a builder, for damages in respect of D's breach of a contract to complete a building in a "good and workmanlike manner", P could not, by bringing subsequent proceedings in respect of the same cause of action against D, recover further damages arising from consequences of D's defective workmanship which P had not particularised for the purposes of the original action (*Conquer v Boot* (1928)). P was prevented from re-litigating this cause of action by virtue of the operation of a cause of action estoppel.

KEY CASE

WALL v RADFORD (1991)

In legal proceedings brought by P's passenger T, P and D were found equally liable in negligence in respect of the car crash in which T was injured. In the course of subsequent proceedings brought by P against D, P was estopped (an issue estoppel) from asserting other than that he was 50 per cent contributorily negligent, the issue having been determined in the course of the earlier proceedings brought by T.

What conditions must be satisfied in order for a cause of action estoppel or an issue estoppel to arise?

A cause of action estoppel or an issue estoppel may arise only if the following requirements are satisfied:

(1) The parties to the latter proceedings must be (or be the privies of) the parties to the original proceedings. Thus, P was not estopped from denying contributory negligence in an action which he brought against D concerning injuries which P had suffered in a vehicle collision even though D had previously proved contributory negligence in an action brought against D by P's father, who owned the car which P had been driving, in respect of the damage to his car (*Townsend v Bishop* (1939)). It should be noted that at the time when *Townsend* was decided, contributory negligence provided a complete defence to liability and consequently had P been estopped from denying contributory negligence his action must have failed.

(2) The parties to the latter proceedings must be litigating in the same capacities in which they litigated the original proceedings. Thus, where, in legal proceedings brought by T, P and D had been found equally to blame for a collision between vehicles in which T's property had been damaged, P, litigating in the capacity of personal representative of his wife (who had been killed in the collision), was not estopped, in the course of subsequent proceedings against D, from denying contributory negligence (*Marginson v Blackburn BC* (1939)). P was, however, estopped from denying contributory negligence when litigating on his own behalf. It should be noted that at the time when *Marginson* was decided, contributory negligence provided a complete defence to liability and consequently the effect of the estoppel was that P could not bring his personal action against D though he could bring the action on behalf of his wife's estate.

(3) The cause of action or issue which is being litigated in the latter proceedings must have been determined in the original proceedings. In *Wall v Radford* (considered above), Popplewell J. held that, for the purpose of determining whether P was estopped from denying that he was 50 per cent contributorily negligent, the factual issues raised in the subsequent proceedings were the same as those which had been determined in the original proceedings. His Lordship declined to follow earlier authority to the effect that where the subsequent proceedings involve consideration of legal duties of care different from those which the original proceedings concerned, the issues raised in the subsequent proceedings are not the same as those determined in the earlier proceedings (*Bell v Holmes* (1956)). In *Conquer v Boot* (considered above), the plaintiff was debarred from bringing a second

action in respect of the same cause of action. In contrast, in *Brunsden v Humphrey* (1884), a cab driver was not debarred from bringing an action to recover damages for personal injuries which he had sustained in an accident by virtue of the fact that he had already recovered damages from the same defendant in earlier proceedings concerning damage to his cab resulting from the same accident. This was so as the two actions concerned two distinct causes of action (the former concerning damage to property, the latter concerning personal injuries).

(4) Fourthly, the court which determined the relevant issue in the original proceedings must have been a court of competent jurisdiction and must have given a final judgment upon the merits. The decision of a court or tribunal which does not determine a dispute between contending parties cannot become conclusive evidence of the facts upon which it was based against the parties to subsequent civil proceedings, the court or tribunal not being a "court of competent jurisdiction" (*The European Gateway* (1987)). Moreover, even where the decision of a court or tribunal does determine a dispute between contending parties, its decision will not become conclusive evidence of the facts upon which it was based against the parties to subsequent civil proceedings if the court or tribunal did not possess jurisdiction to finally determine the relevant issue (*R. v Hutchings* (1881)). It should be noted that the fact that it is possible to appeal from the decision of a court or tribunal does not prevent its decision from being final for this purpose.

Are there "special circumstances" in which exceptions to estoppel by record exist?

In "special circumstances" a party may not be prevented, by issue estoppel, from re-opening a previously litigated issue. Such circumstances include those in which new evidence has become admissible which could not, by exercising reasonable diligence, have been adduced in the original proceedings and those in which, following the original proceedings, there has been a change in the law (*Arnold v National Westminster Bank* (1991)).

Special circumstances do not entitle a party to re-litigate a cause of action where a cause of action estoppel arises.

Should a party to legal proceedings pursue every cause of action available to him?

Where a party to legal proceedings seeks to bring a claim or to raise a defence which he could have brought in the context of earlier proceedings, the court may (under what is commonly referred to as "the rule in *Henderson v Henderson*") be prepared to strike out the claim or the defence as an abuse of process. The court may be prepared to do this if the other party to the proceedings persuades the court that the claim or defence should have been brought or raised in the earlier proceedings (*Johnson v Gore Wood* (2001)). Whether the court is prepared to strike out a claim or defence on this basis will depend upon the circumstances of the case as a whole, relevant considerations including, for example, whether the claimant was aware of the facts underlying the second claim at the time of the original litigation (*Joseph v Joseph* (2003)) and whether the claimant could have discovered the relevant facts had reasonable diligence been exercised (*Stuart v Goldberg Linde (a Firm)* (2008)).

Examples of factual situation in which the court might, in appropriate circumstances, be prepared to strike out a claim as an abuse of process under the rule in *Henderson v Henderson* (1843) are (as the Court of Appeal recognised in *Talbot v Berkshire CC* (1994)) provided by the facts of *Brunsden v Humphrey* and *Wall v Radford* (both seen above).

Collateral attacks

It may be an abuse of process (and thus result in a claim being struck out) for a claimant (or in some circumstances a defendant) to challenge a judicial decision by a parallel judicial process (i.e. via a collateral attack). Thus, for example, where an accused whose criminal appeal is unsuccessful brings a civil claim for damages against a police force as a means of challenging his criminal conviction "by the back door", the claim may be struck out on this basis (*Hunter v Chief Constable of the West Midlands Police* (1982)).

KEY CASE

HUNTER V CHIEF CONSTABLE OF WEST MIDLANDS POLICE (1982)
In *Hunter*, where D had claimed that the police had assaulted him prior to D's confessing but the judge had found that D had not been assaulted and had admitted D's confession in evidence, the House of Lords held that D's subsequent action for damages relating to the alleged assault was an abuse of process because its dominant purpose was to show that D's confession had been obtained by police violence.

THE ADMISSIBILITY OF PREVIOUS CONVICTIONS AND JUDICIAL FINDINGS AS EVIDENCE OF THE FACTS UPON WHICH THEY WERE BASED IN CIVIL PROCEEDINGS BETWEEN PARTIES OTHER THAN THE PARTIES TO THE PROCEEDINGS IN WHICH THE ACCUSED WAS CONVICTED OR THE FINDINGS WERE MADE

The effect of the decision of the Court of Appeal in *Hollington v Hewthorn* was that previous convictions and judicial findings were not admissible as evidence of the facts upon which they were based in civil proceedings between parties other than the parties to the proceedings in which the accused was convicted or the findings were made.

KEY CASE

HOLLINGTON V HEWTHORN (1943)

In *Hollington v Hewthorn*, a case in which P's car was damaged in a collision with a car driven by D and D was convicted for careless driving, P was not entitled to adduce evidence of D's conviction for careless driving as evidence of D's negligence. [Note that if the facts of this case were to arise today, the conviction would now be admissible under s.11 of the **Civil Evidence Act 1968**, which is considered below.]

HOWEVER, the ambit of the rule in *Hollington v Hewthorn* in civil proceedings has been substantially reduced by ss.11, 12 and 13 of the **Civil Evidence Act (CEA) 1968**. Other than in relation to adultery and paternity (which are considered below), however, the rule still applies so as to render a civil judgment inadmissible in subsequent civil proceedings as evidence of the findings made by the civil court (*R. v D* (1996); *Secretary of State for Trade and Industry v Bairstow* (2004)). As is seen below, the current status of the rule in criminal proceedings is unclear.

The admissibility of previous convictions in civil proceedings

LEGISLATION HIGHLIGHTER

Section 11 **Civil Evidence Act 1968**

Essentially, s.11(1) of the **CEA 1968** provides that a person's subsisting conviction (i.e. a conviction which has not been quashed) is admissible in civil proceedings to prove that the person committed the offence of which he was convicted provided that proving that the person committed the offence is relevant to an issue before the court.

> The section also provides that where a person's conviction is admitted under s.11, the person shall be taken to have committed the offence of which he was convicted unless the contrary is proved.

Thus, s.11 gives rise to a rebuttable presumption of law (see Chapter 1, above). It appears that this presumption imposes a legal burden of proof upon the party who wishes to prove that the person convicted did not commit the offence, the requisite standard of proof being proof on the balance of probabilities (*McCauley v Hope* (1999)).

Thus, were the facts of *Hollington v Hewthorn* to arise today, D's conviction would not merely be admissible as evidence of his negligence but, moreover, D would be presumed to have driven carelessly unless he proved that he had not done so. Thus, D would bear the legal burden of proving on the balance of probabilities that he did not commit the offence of which he was convicted. What is unclear, however, is whether the effect of s.11 is merely to place the burden of proving that he did not commit the offence on D or whether, additionally, a conviction which is admitted under s.11 acts as evidence proving that D did, in fact, commit the relevant offence (*Stupple v Royal Insurance Co Ltd* (1971)). Whichever view is correct, it does appear that the task of rebutting the presumption that the person convicted of an offence in fact committed it is, in general, not an easy one to accomplish (*Hunter v Chief Constable of the West Midlands Police*).

Where a party intends to adduce evidence of a previous conviction under s.11, the **CPR** provide that he must include a statement of such intent in the particulars of claim.

LEGISLATION HIGHLIGHTER

Section 13 of the **Civil Evidence Act 1968**

Where the commission of a criminal offence by the claimant is relevant to an issue in proceedings for libel or slander, the claimant's subsisting conviction for the relevant offence is, under s.13 of the **CEA 1968**, admissible as conclusive evidence that he committed it. Thus, the effect of s.13 is to give rise to a conclusive or irrebuttable presumption of law (see Chapter 1, above).

The admissibility of previous findings of adultery and paternity in civil proceedings

LEGISLATION HIGHLIGHTER

Section 12 of the **Civil Evidence Act 1968**

Essentially, s.12 of the **CEA 1968** provides that subsisting findings of adultery made in matrimonial proceedings in the High Court or in a County Court, subsisting findings of paternity and subsisting adjudications of paternity in affiliation proceedings are admissible in civil proceedings as evidence of adultery or paternity provided that proving that the relevant person committed the relevant adultery or fathered the relevant child is relevant to an issue before the court. The section also provides that where a finding or adjudication is admitted under the section then the person who was found guilty of the relevant adultery or was found to be the father of the relevant child shall be taken to have committed the relevant adultery or to have fathered the relevant child unless the contrary is proved.

THE DOCTRINE OF RES JUDICATA IN CRIMINAL PROCEEDINGS

Can a person who has been convicted or acquitted of a criminal offence be subsequently tried for that offence?

DEFINITION CHECKPOINT

"autrefois convict" and "autrefois acquit"

A person who has been convicted of a criminal offence may plead autrefois convict in order to bar subsequent proceedings for the same offence against him. Similarly, a person who has been acquitted of a criminal offence may plead autrefois acquit in order to bar subsequent proceedings for the same offence against him. Further, the pleas of autrefois convict and autrefois acquit also bar proceedings against a person in respect of lesser offences of which he could have been convicted in earlier proceedings when charged with a more serious offence. Authority for the above propositions is provided by *DPP v Connelly* (1964). Moreover, it may be an abuse of process to bring proceedings against a person for an offence of which he could not have been convicted in earlier proceedings if the later proceedings concern substantially the same facts as the earlier proceedings (*DPP v Connelly*; *R. v Beedie* (1997)).

Upon an application by the prosecution made with consent of the Director of Public Prosecutions, there may now be circumstances in which, in the context of new and compelling evidence, the Court of Appeal will, under Pt 10 of the **Criminal Justice Act (CJA) 2003**, be required, in the interests of justice, to quash a conviction for an offence such as murder, kidnapping or rape and order a retrial.

Can the prosecution dispute a previous acquittal in subsequent criminal proceedings?

As was seen above, where proceedings concern an offence of which the accused has already been acquitted, the accused may plead autrefois acquit. Where, however, proceedings concern an offence of which the accused could not have been convicted in earlier proceedings and do not concern substantially the same facts as the earlier proceedings, the doctrine of autrefois does not apply and, moreover, there is no abuse of process. In such circumstances, and subject both to the operation of the rules of evidence which regulate the admissibility of evidence of bad character (see Chapter 13, below) and to the exercise of the court's exclusionary discretion under s.78 of **PACE** (see Chapter 11, below), the prosecution can, if this is relevant to an issue in the proceedings, dispute a previous acquittal of the accused (*R. v Z* (2000)). Thus, for example, where the accused is charged with rape, evidence concerning the facts of his previous acquittals for rape may be admissible for the prosecution even though the evidence contradicts the correctness of the previous acquittals (*R. v Z*) (though he may not be re-tried for an alleged rape for which he has previously been acquitted unless his conviction has been quashed under Pt 10 of the 2003 Act).

Can an issue estoppel lie in criminal proceedings?

KEY CASE

R. v HUMPHREYS (1977)

In *R. v Humphreys* the House of Lords held that an issue estoppel cannot lie in criminal proceedings. Thus, during Humphrey's trial for perjury, a police officer was properly permitted to testify that he had seen Humphreys driving a motor vehicle in 1972 even though the police officer had previously testified to the same effect during a trial at the end of which Humphreys had been acquitted of driving a motor vehicle whilst disqualified.

THE ADMISSIBILITY OF PREVIOUS CONVICTIONS AS EVIDENCE OF THE FACTS UPON WHICH THEY WERE BASED IN CRIMINAL PROCEEDINGS BETWEEN PARTIES OTHER THAN THE PARTIES TO THE PROCEEDINGS IN WHICH THE ACCUSED WAS CONVICTED

The ambit of the rule in *Hollington v Hewthorn* (see above) in criminal proceedings has been reduced by s.74 of **PACE**.

LEGISLATION HIGHLIGHTER

Section 74 of the **Police and Criminal Evidence Act 1984**

Essentially, s.74(1) of **PACE** (as amended by the **CJA 2003**) provides that a person's previous conviction is admissible in criminal proceedings in which he is not the accused to prove that the person committed the offence of which he was convicted if evidence that the person committed the offence is admissible. The conviction must, however, be a subsisting conviction (i.e. one which has not been quashed) (s.75(4)). Section 74(2) provides that where a conviction is admitted under s.74, then the person convicted shall be taken to have committed the offence of which he was convicted unless the contrary is proved. Thus, s.74(2) creates a rebuttable presumption of law (see Chapter 1, above).

In order for a conviction to be admissible under s.74(1) it appears that evidence that the relevant person committed the relevant offence must be admissible under the bad character provisions of the **CJA 2003** (see Chapter 13, below). Even where such evidence is admissible, however, it seems that the trial judge may find it necessary to exclude evidence of the conviction in the exercise of his discretion under s.78 of the 1984 Act upon the basis that its admission would have such an adverse effect on the fairness of the proceedings that it ought not to be admitted (*R. v O'Connor* (1987)). This may be necessary (e.g. in the context of a conspiracy trial) in circumstances in which the jury might infer if the conviction was admitted that because the relevant person (e.g. a conspirator who pleaded guilty) committed the offence of which he was convicted, the logical conclusion was automatically that the accused (e.g. a conspirator who pleaded not guilty) was guilty of the offence with which he was charged. Moreover, where a conviction is admitted under s.74, the judge should explain to the jury why it has been admitted (*R. v Kempster* (1990)).

Finally, s.74(3) essentially provides that where evidence that the accused has committed an offence is admissible (i.e. under the bad character provisions of the **CJA 2003**), if the accused is proved to have been convicted of the relevant offence, he shall be taken to have committed the offence unless the contrary is proved. Thus, s.74(3) creates a rebuttable presumption of law (see Chapter 1, above).

Human rights

It appears that the admission for the prosecution of a conviction of a person other than the accused under s.74(1) in the context of a proper exercise by the judge of his exclusionary discretion and the giving of an appropriate direction by the judge to the jury in circumstances in which the accused could have called the person whose conviction was admitted under s.74(1) to give defence evidence will not give rise to a violation of art.6(1) of the European Convention on Human Rights (*MH v UK* (1997)).

Does the rule in *Hollington v Hewthorn* still prevent the admissibility in criminal proceedings of evidence of civil judgments?

The Court of Appeal in *R. v Kordasinski* (2006) (which concerned evidence of foreign convictions, which do not fall within s.74 of **PACE**), held that s.99 of the **CJA 2003** (see Chapter 13, below) has abolished the rule in *Hollington v Hewthorn* in criminal proceedings. It is submitted, however, that two other decisions of the Court of Appeal, *R. v Levey* (2007) and *R. v Hogart* (2007), provide authority for the proposition that the rule in *Hollington v Hewthorn* still exists in the criminal context and still applies where a party to criminal proceedings wishes to rely upon evidence of a civil judgment, though following *Hogart* it seems that evidence of a civil judgment may be admissible under the bad character provisions of the 2003 Act, which are considered in Chapter 13. It should be noted, however, that *Levey* was decided prior to *Kordasinski* and that *Kordasinski* was not cited in *Hogart*.

Revision checklist

You should now know and understand:

- the doctrine of res judicata in civil proceedings and the operation of estoppel by record;

- when a party will be able to plead a cause of action estoppel;

- when a party will be able to plead an issue estoppel;

- the special circumstances in which an issue estoppel may be re-opened;

- when a claim or defence may be struck out as an abuse of process either under the rule in *Henderson v Henderson* or in consequence of a collateral attack;

- the admissibility of criminal convictions in civil proceedings under **s.11 and s.13 of the CEA 1968** and the effect of admitting criminal convictions into civil proceedings;

- **the effect of admitting criminal convictions into criminal proceedings under PACE s.74;**

- the operation of and restrictions on the doctrine of res judicata in criminal proceedings and the human rights implications.

QUESTION AND ANSWER

The Question

Shane is bringing an action in negligence arising from an incident in which he was hit and injured by Lizzy's car whilst crossing the road. Lizzy denies that she was negligent. Lizzy was convicted of careless driving in relation to the incident in which Shane was injured, she appealed the conviction but the conviction was upheld.

If Shane's claim is unsuccessful he may decide to bring a second action against Lizzy to once again recover damages for the injuries he sustained, alternatively he may decide to bring an action against the manufacturer of the car in respect of the faulty brakes.

If Shane's claim is successful he has decided that he will bring a second claim against Lizzy in order to recover damages for a valuable watch that was broken when he was hit by Lizzy's car.

Consider the evidential issues raised by the above scenario.

Advice and the Answer

General guidance

As with a number of evidential issues it is first important to distinguish whether the proceedings are civil or criminal in nature as different rules will apply depending on the type of proceedings. It is more likely that you will face a question relating to estoppel in the context of a question on civil proceedings. In civil proceedings there are a number of issues that you may need to consider. Firstly you should consider whether the parties have previously litigated the course of action or whether any issue in the proceedings has previously been decided in earlier proceedings. If so then you need to consider whether there is an estoppel by record (i.e a cause of action or issue estoppel).

Where there is no estoppel consider whether the issue could have been raised in earlier proceedings, if so the court possess a power to strike out a later attempt to raise the issue as an abuse of process (*Henderson v Henderson*).

You should also consider the possibility of admitting previous court findings, for example criminal convictions, into civil proceedings. Although the rule in *Hollington v Hewthorn* is that a previous finding by a court is not admissible as evidence of the findings upon which the decision was based the effect of this rule has been reduced by ss.11–13 of the **Civil Evidence Act 1968**. The effect of ss.11–13 of the 1968 Act is that previous findings may be admissible in certain situations. For example s.11 of the 1968 act allows a criminal conviction to be admitted into civil proceedings where the conviction is relevant and subsisting. The effect of admitting a conviction under s.11 is that the conviction gives rise to a rebuttable presumption that the person convicted did what they were convicted of.

In criminal proceedings you need to be aware of when a defendant will be able to plead autrefois convict or autrefois convict in relation to an earlier decision made by a criminal court. You should also be familiar with the exceptions to the general rules of autrefois convict and acquit created by the **Criminal Justice Act 2003**, the human rights implications and also with the operation of s.74 of the **Police and Criminal Evidence Act 1984**.

Answer plan

1 Although the rule in *Hollington v Hewthorn* is that a previous finding by a court is not admissible as evidence of the findings upon which the decision was based in proceedings between parties other than those to the original proceedings, the effect of this rule has been restricted by s.11 of the **Civil Evidence Act 1968**.

2 Under s.11 of the **Civil Evidence Act 1968** Lizzy's careless driving conviction will be admissible if proving that Lizzy committed the offence is relevant and the conviction is a subsisting conviction. It would appear that the conviction is relevant to an issue in the proceedings as it arises from the same set of facts as Shane's negligence claim and is thus relevant to prove that Lizzy did drive carelessly on the occasion to which Shane's negligence claim relates. The conviction is subsisting as it was not quashed on appeal.

3 The effect of admitting the conviction under s.11 is that it creates a

rebuttable presumption that Lizzy did what she was convicted of i.e. that she drove carelessly at the time that she ran over Shane. Lizzy would bear the burden of rebutting the presumption of the criminal conviction, on the balance of probabilities, if she is to successfully defend the claim (*McCauley v Hope*).

4 If Shane's claim is unsuccessful it would appear he would be unable to bring a second claim against Lizzy to recover damages in respect of the incident in which he was injured. To do so would be to attempt to relitigate the cause of action for the second time. Lizzy would therefore be able to plead a cause of action estoppel (a type of estoppel by record) stopping Shane from bringing the claim (*Conquer v Boot*).

5 It would appear that no cause of action estoppel arises if Shane wishes to bring a claim against the manufacturer as the second claim would involve different parties and would therefore be a new cause of action.

6 If Shane's first claim is successful he will not be estopped from bringing a second claim in relation to the damage to his watch (although the parties are the same the cause of action issue will be different and therefore a cause of action estoppel will not arise) (*Brunsden v Humphrey*). However Shane's second claim may be struck out as an abuse of process because it appears that he should have raised the issue relating to the watch in the first set of proceedings (*Henderson v Henderson*). The court may be prepared to do this if Lizzy persuades the court that Shane should have brought the claim in the earlier proceedings (*Johnson v Gore Wood* (2001)).

The Hearsay Rule and its Common Law Exceptions in Criminal Proceedings

Introduction

This chapter considers the operation of the hearsay rule in criminal proceedings. In this chapter we will consider what types of statements fall within the hearsay rule and which do not. We will also consider some examples of common law exceptions to the hearsay rule, preserved by s.118 of the **Criminal Justice Act 2003 (CJA),** under which hearsay may be admissible in criminal proceedings. Statutory exceptions to the hearsay rule under which hearsay evidence may be admissible in criminal proceedings are considered in Chapters 11 and 12 below, some having already been encountered in Chapter 5, above.

In the context of criminal proceedings, ss.114 and 118 of the **CJA 2003** have abolished the common law hearsay rule and its exceptions (other than the common law exceptions which s.118 preserves) and have created a new statutory hearsay rule (*R. v Singh* (2006)).

The position regarding the admissibility of hearsay evidence is found in s.114(1) of the **CJA 2003,** the general position being that hearsay evidence is not admissible save for four specified situations in which hearsay evidence may be used; this rule is often referred to as the "rule against hearsay" and the situations in which hearsay evidence may be admitted as "hearsay exceptions".

Basically, the effect of s.114(1) of the **CJA 2003** is that a statement which was not made in oral evidence in the proceedings and which is tendered as evidence of the matters stated (i.e. a hearsay statement) is only admissible in criminal proceedings:

- where statute makes the hearsay evidence admissible;
- where a common law exception to the hearsay rule which has been preserved by s.118 of the **CJA 2003** makes it admissible;
- where the parties agree to its admission; or
- where the court admits it in the exercise of the inclusionary discretion conferred upon it by s.114(1)(d) of the 2003 Act.

The effect of s.114(3) of the 2003 Act is, however, that the hearsay provisions of the 2003 Act do not affect the exclusion of a hearsay statement other than on the ground that the statement was not made in oral evidence in the proceedings. Thus, for example, hearsay evidence is not admissible if it is not relevant (*R. v T* (2006)). It should be noted that it is a general principle of the law of evidence that evidence that is not relevant to an issue in the proceedings is not admissible. Evidence is not relevant to a fact in issue if it is neither capable of increasing or reducing the probability that a fact in issue exists (*R. v Randall* (2004)).

The admissibility of hearsay statements as confessions under s.76 or s.76A of **PACE** is considered in Chapter 11, below. The admission of hearsay evidence in criminal proceedings under other statutory exceptions to the hearsay rule or in the exercise of the court's inclusionary discretion and the various safeguards which the 2003 Act imposes are considered in Chapter 12, below. Hearsay exceptions that relate to the examination of witnesses and to the evidence of expert witnesses have already been considered in, respectively, Chapters 5 and 6, above. The present chapter is concerned both with the nature of those circumstances in which a statement is an hearsay statement (and thus will be inadmissible in criminal proceedings unless a hearsay exception applies) and with the nature of some of the common law exceptions to the hearsay rule which s.118 of the **CJA 2003** preserves.

To what types of statement does the hearsay rule apply in criminal proceedings?

The hearsay rule, as it applies in the context of criminal proceedings, applies to statements as defined by s.115(2) of the **CJA 2003**. Section 115(2) defines a statement as "... any representation of fact or opinion made by a person by whatever means; and it includes a representation made in a sketch, photofit or other pictorial form". Thus, the hearsay rule applies to statements made by a person whether they take the form of written statements, oral statements or statements made by conduct. The effect of s.114(1), however, is that a statement is only a hearsay statement if the statement was not made in oral evidence in the proceedings and is relied on in those proceedings as evidence of a matter stated. Moreover, as is seen below, the effect of s.115(3) is that whether a statement falls within the ambit of the hearsay rule may also depend upon the purpose for which the statement was made.

To what types of statement does the hearsay rule not apply in criminal proceedings?

The purpose for which a statement was made may determine its hearsay status

Section 115(3) of the **CJA 2003** essentially provides that the hearsay provisions of the **CJA 2003** only apply to a matter stated if the purpose (or at least one of the purposes) of the person making the statement appears to the court to have been either to cause another person to believe the matter or to cause another person to act or a machine to operate upon the basis that the matter is as stated.

> **DEFINITION CHECKPOINT**
>
> In the context of criminal proceedings a hearsay statement is a statement not made in oral evidence in the proceedings relied upon as evidence of the matter stated, provided that the purpose (or at least one of the purposes) of the person making the statement appears to the court to have been either to cause another person to believe the matter or to cause another person to act or a machine to operate upon the basis that the matter is as stated.

The major effect of the provision which now exists as s.115(3) was intended by the Law Commission (Evidence in Criminal Proceedings: Hearsay and Related Topics (Law Com No. 245)) to be that (unlike the former position at common law) implied statements do not amount to hearsay statements if it appears that their maker did not make them for either or both of the above-mentioned purposes. Thus, the Law Commission intended that this provision would reverse the decision of the House of Lords in *R. v Kearley* (1992), in which statements made by persons during telephone calls to the accused's house asking for the accused and asking for drugs which were tendered by the prosecution in order to prove that the accused deals in drugs were held to fall within the ambit of the hearsay rule at common law.

It is submitted that in *R. v Leonard* (2009), the Court of Appeal did not apply s.115(3) in the way in which the Law Commission would have intended. In *Leonard,* their Lordships held that evidence of text messages on the accused's mobile phones, one apparently thanking him for supplying drugs and one apparently criticising him for drugs that he had supplied, fell within the ambit of the hearsay rule when relied upon to prove that the accused was a drug dealer. Their Lordships held that s.115(3) was satisfied because the persons who sent the text messages to the accused must have done so for the purposes of making the accused aware that they were, respectively, happy and unhappy with the drugs that the accused had provided. It is suggested, however, that upon a proper construction of s.115(3), the statements that *Leonard* concerned should not have been regarded as falling within the ambit of the hearsay rule if relied upon by the prosecution to prove that the accused was a drug dealer because the persons who sent the text messages had, presumably, not done so for the purpose of making anyone believe that this was so.

Subsequent to *Leonard*, it appears that the Court of Appeal in *R. v*

Chrysostomou (2010) (in which *Leonard* was referred to but was not expressly criticised) applied s.115(3) in the way in which the Law Commission would have intended.

KEY CASE

R. v CHRYSOSTOMOU (2010)

In *Chrysostomou*, the Court of Appeal was concerned with the admissibility of text messages on the accused's mobile phone, asking the accused to supply drugs. Their Lordships, recognising that the purpose for which the prosecution had relied on the text messages was not that of proving matters stated therein but, rather, was as evidence of implied assertions to the effect that the accused was a drug dealer, held that the text messages did not fall within the ambit of the hearsay regime that the CJA 2003 had created.

It is suggested that another example of the application of s.115(3) in the way in which the Law Commission would have intended is provided by the decision of the Court of Appeal in *R. v Knight* (2007). In *Knight*, the Court of Appeal held that where the alleged victim of sexual offences had made a statement concerning her relationship with the accused in a diary that she had not intended anyone else to read, the statement was not a hearsay statement when relied on at the accused's trial as evidence of the matters stated.

Where a statement does not fall within the hearsay regime created by the CJA 2003 due to the operation of s.115(3), it seems that the statement is admissible, provided that it is relevant and is not excluded by virtue of the operation of other rules of evidence, such as s.78 of the **Police and Criminal Evidence Act 1984** (*R. v Knight*), or the bad character provisions of the 2003 Act which are considered in Chapter 13 below (R. v *Chrysostomou*).

Representations which were not made by persons are not hearsay statements in criminal proceedings

---

DEFINITION CHECKPOINT

The definition of "statement" in s.115(2) of the CJA 2003 only applies to representations made by persons. Thus, under the CJA 2003, the hearsay rule does not apply to representations which were not made by persons (i.e. it does not apply to representations which were made by machines).

Where a machine makes a representation but the representation depends for its accuracy on information which was supplied by a person, the effect of s.129(1) of the **CJA 2003** is, however, that the representation is not admissible as evidence of the fact represented unless it is proved that the information was accurate. In contrast, where a machine makes a representation without relying upon information supplied by a human, the s.129(1) requirement will not apply.

Thus it is submitted, where A types an email to B into his computer, A makes his statement using a machine and the statement, if relied on as evidence of the matter stated, falls within the hearsay rule and will only be admissible if an exception to the hearsay rule is applicable. If C types data into a database, it is submitted that a printout of certain fields from the database, being a representation made by a machine, does not fall within the **CJA 2003** hearsay rule, but will be subject to the s.129(1) accuracy requirement. Finally, if D puts an item onto a pair of scales and the scales give a reading of the object's weight, it is submitted that the reading, being a representation made by a machine, does not fall within the **CJA 2003** hearsay rule and that the s.129(1) accuracy requirement does not apply because the representation did not depend for its accuracy upon information provided by a person.

The purpose for which the statement is tendered

The hearsay rule does not apply where a statement is relied upon other than as evidence of a matter stated (see s.114(1) of the **CJA 2003**). Thus, for example, the rule did not apply at common law (and presumably would not apply under the **CJA 2003**) where the accused, whose defence was duress, wished to repeat in court threats made to him by terrorists (*Subramaniam v Public Prosecutor* (1956)). The rule did not apply because, in the context of the defence of duress, the statements were relevant regardless of whether they were true (in the sense that the terrorists actually intended to carry out the threats which they made) or false (in the sense that the terrorists had lied to the accused and did not intend to carry out the threats). Rather, what was important in that context was whether the threats had been made (which depended upon the truth of the accused's testimony in court and not upon that of the terrorists' statements). This was so because if the threats had been made and believed by the accused, they were potentially capable of amounting to duress whether or not there was, in reality, any intention to carry them out.

Photographs, video recordings and films

At common law it was clear that the hearsay rule did not apply to photographs or video recordings of persons, places or events, such evidence being classified as "real evidence" (see, for example, *Taylor v Chief Constable of Cheshire* (1987)). "Real evidence" basically means evidence in the form of objects that the court can examine for itself, such as the weapon that was allegedly used by the accused in committing a murder.

It is submitted that such evidence will continue to be admissible as real evidence, and will not be governed by the hearsay provisions of the **CJA 2003**, because the content of such photographs, recordings or films will not amount to "statements" under s.115(2) of the **CJA 2003**, they not amounting to "representations of fact or opinion made by a person". In contrast, however, it is submitted that a photograph, film or video recording of a document written by a person, of a statement made by a person by conduct, or of an audio recording of words spoken by a person will amount to a hearsay statement if relied upon as evidence of a matter stated.

Identifying hearsay

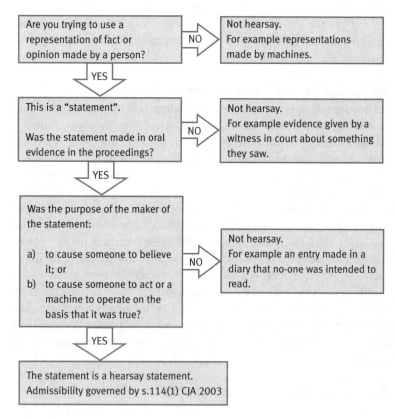

Note: If the statement does not fall within the ambit of the hearsay rule then its admissibility will depend upon a common law test of relevance or, if it is a representation made by a machine upon the operation of s.129 **CJA 2003**.

MAJOR COMMON LAW EXCEPTIONS TO THE HEARSAY RULE

Where a hearsay statement falls within an exception to the hearsay rule the statement is admissible in evidence even though it is a hearsay statement. The **CJA 2003** abolished certain common law exceptions to the hearsay rule, such as the dying declaration, but preserved a number of others. Examination of all of the preserved common law hearsay exceptions falls outside the scope of the present book. Rather, the examples of preserved common law hearsay exceptions which we will consider are the four categories of hearsay statement, preserved by s.118(1)(4), which are commonly said to be admissible in criminal proceedings because they "form part of the *res gestae*" (i.e. because they are closely associated with an act or state of affairs the performance or existence of which is of relevance in legal proceedings).

LEGISLATION HIGHLIGHTER

Section 118(1)(4) of the **Criminal Justice Act 2003**;

Under this section a hearsay statement can be admitted in any of the following three situations;

(a) the statement was made by a person so emotionally overpowered by an event that the possibility of concoction or distortion can be disregarded,

(b) the statement accompanied an act which can be properly evaluated as evidence only if considered in conjunction with the statement, or

(c) the statement relates to a physical sensation or a mental state (such as intention or emotion).

Essentially, a statement may be admissible under s.118(1)(4) (i.e. because it "forms part of the *res gestae*") if it concerns its maker's contemporaneous actions, physical sensations or mental state or if it is closely associated with a dramatic event.

It should be noted that the common law hearsay exceptions which s.118(1)(4) preserves apply only in criminal proceedings as they have not been preserved by s.7 of the **CEA 1995** (see Chapter 10, below). Indeed, given the width of the statutory hearsay exceptions which are examined in Chapter

12, these common law exceptions are now of limited practical significance in criminal proceedings.

Statements concerning the contemporaneous actions, physical sensations or mental state of their maker

A statement explaining its maker's contemporaneous actions may be admissible to prove why they were performed. Thus, if a person, whilst away from home, writes a letter explaining why he is staying away from home, the letter may be admissible to prove why he stayed away from home, should this be of relevance to an issue before the court (*Rouch v Great Western Railway Co* (1841)). Moreover, it has been held that where a witness cannot remember whom he identified via an identification procedure, a police officer who attended the parade can repeat in court the statement which the witness made at the time identifying the accused, the statement accompanying and explaining the activities of seeing and recognising (*R. v McKay* (1990)).

A statement concerning its maker's contemporaneous physical sensations is admissible to prove that he experienced the relevant sensations but is not admissible as evidence of their cause. Thus, if a patient, whilst being examined by a doctor, tells the doctor that he has a pain in his leg and also tells the doctor that the pain was caused by an insect sting, the doctor may repeat the statement in court for the purpose of proving that the patient was in pain but may not do so for the purpose of proving that the patient had been stung by an insect (*Amys v Barton* (1911)). Moreover, where a patient is ill for several days, a statement made several days into the period of illness may be admissible to prove that the illness had been on-going from the date of its commencement (*Aveson v Lord Kinnaird* (1805)).

Finally, a statement concerning its maker's contemporaneous mental state is admissible to prove what its maker intended to do or believed to be the case at that time but is not admissible as evidence of the truth of its maker's beliefs. Thus, where a man states that he is insolvent, his statement may be repeated in court to prove that he was aware of his insolvency but the fact of his insolvency must be proved by other admissible evidence (*Thomas v Connell* (1838)). A statement of intent may be admissible whether it was made at the time when the intended act was carried out or whether it was made prior to performance of that act, in which case the court may be entitled to infer that the intent was still possessed by the maker at the relevant time (*R. v Moghal* (1977)). The longer the time gap between the making of the statement and the performance of the act, however, the lower the probative value of the statement, if it is admitted in evidence, will be. Moreover, if the statement was made after the performance of the relevant act, a court will be unlikely to admit it if the time gap was substantial (*R. v Moghal*).

It should be noted that the requirement that the statement be contemporaneous to the act, physical sensation or mental state does not necessarily mean that in order to be admissible the statement must have been made exactly at the same time as the performance of the act or the existence of the physical sensation or mental state. Rather, whether the statement is a contemporaneous statement is a question of fact and degree for the court (*R. v Moghal*).

Statements closely associated with a dramatic event

Statements closely associated with a dramatic event are admissible as evidence of matters stated if the possibility that they have been concocted or distorted can be disregarded. In other words, to adopt the wording of s.118(1)4(a) of the **CJA 2003,** a statement is admissible as evidence of matters stated if its maker was "... so emotionally overpowered by an event that the possibility of concoction or distortion can be disregarded". As the House of Lords made clear in *R. v Andrews* (1987), the judge must determine whether this is so by considering whether the maker's mind was so dominated by the event at the time when the statement was made that the possibility of concoction or distortion can be ruled out. The judge must take into account any factors which might increase the risk of concoction or distortion, such as whether the maker had a motive to concoct or distort. Moreover, the judge should consider any factors which give rise to a particular risk of error. For example, where the statement relates to an identification which the maker made, it may be that the identification was made in circumstances in which the reliability of identification evidence would be doubtful (e.g. a fleeting glimpse of a person a long way away in the dark). Finally, if the judge decides that the statement is admissible, he should still draw the jury's attention to factors which might increase the risk of concoction or distortion or which might give rise to a particular risk of error and direct them that they must be satisfied that there was no concoction or distortion.

In *Andrews*, the question before the House of Lords was whether a statement made by a murder victim identifying the accused as the murderer had properly been admitted in evidence. The statement had been made by Andrews a few minutes after he was fatally stabbed. The statement had been admitted by the trial judge even though there was evidence to suggest that Andrews had a motive to concoct evidence against the accused and even though the possibility of error was increased because Andrews had been drinking heavily. The House of Lords held that, upon the facts of the case, the trial judge had been entitled to decide that there was no possibility of concoction or distortion and, consequently, that the evidence had properly been admitted.

In order for a statement to be admitted under this exception to the hearsay rule, it is necessary both that the existence of the dramatic event and that the fact that the statement was made in its context are both proved by evidence other than the content of the statement itself (*R. v Ratten* (1972)).

| KEY CASE |

R. V RATTAN (1972)
In the above case the relevant statement was a request for the police made to a telephone operator by an hysterical woman, the Privy Council held that evidence that the statement was closely associated with a dramatic event was provided by the fact that the accused's wife had been shot and killed in the house from which the call was made a few minutes after it was made, by the fact that she made the statement in a call requesting the police and by her tone of voice when she made the call.

It should be noted that a statement may be admitted under this exception to the hearsay rule even though the maker of the statement is available to be called though, where the hearsay evidence is tendered by the prosecution, the court may, in such circumstances, find it necessary to exclude the hearsay in the exercise of its exclusionary discretion (i.e. under s.78 of **PACE**) so as to give the accused the possibility of cross-examining the relevant witness (*Attorney General's Reference (No.1 of 2003)*). It should also be noted that a statement may be admitted under this exception to the hearsay rule whether it was made by the victim of a crime, by a third party or even by the accused (see, for example, *R. v Glover* (1991)).

HUMAN RIGHTS

In relation to the human rights consequences of the admission of hearsay evidence for the prosecution, see Chapter 12, below.

| Revision checklist |

You should now know and understand:

- **the operation of the rule against hearsay in criminal proceedings as a rule of exclusion which is subject to exceptions;**
- **the nature of a hearsay statement in criminal proceedings;**
- **the major preserved common law exceptions to the rule against hearsay.**

QUESTION AND ANSWER

Raoul is charged with robbery relating to an incident in which a masked man stole diamond rings from a jewellery store at gunpoint. Amongst other evidence the prosecution intend to rely on the following;

- A diary entry written by Sue the cashier who was working in the jewellery store at the time of the robbery. The entry was made in Sue's personal diary on the night of the robbery in which she noted that "the man with the gun had a strange symbol tattooed on his thumb...". Sue was run over and killed on her way to make a statement at the police station the following day. Raoul has a distinctive symbol tattooed on his thumb.
- A text message found on Raoul's phone from Roger, a pawnbroker, reading "I don't know of anyone who'd be interested in diamonds mate, not really my area of business. Are they legit?".
- The recording of a 999 call from Fred, a witness who was outside of the store at the time of the robbery. Fred, who was clearly shocked by events, reported seeing a man with a gun come out of the jewellery store and get into a blue car which the witness went on to describe.
- A printout from the DVLA database showing that Raoul owns a blue car of the make and model described by the witness.

Consider whether any of the above pieces of evidence fall within the ambit of the hearsay rule and, if so, whether they may be admissible under any of the preserved common law hearsay exceptions.

General guidance

This chapter has been concerned with identifying statements that will or will not fall within the ambit of the hearsay rule and the application of the preserved common law exceptions to the rule. You should note that the admissibility of hearsay statements under the statutory exceptions to the hearsay rule created by the **Criminal Justice Act 2003** is discussed in Chapter 12 and this chapter (including the question and answer) should be read in conjunction with that chapter. Generally you should examine the issue of hearsay in two parts, firstly deciding whether a statement falls within the ambit of hearsay rule (i.e. whether the statement is "hearsay") and secondly, if the statement is hearsay, deciding whether or not it is admissible.

Model Answer

A statement will fall within the ambit of the hearsay rule if it is a statement, not made in oral evidence in the proceedings, used as evidence of the matter stated. According to s.115(2) of the **Criminal Justice Act (CJA) 2003** a statement is any representation of fact or opinion made by a person by whatever means and includes representations made in sketch, photofit or other pictorial form. Not made in oral evidence in the proceedings means statements not made by witnesses giving evidence in court about things that they have personally perceived. Whether the statement is being used as evidence of the matter stated depends, according to s.115(3) **CJA 2003**, on whether the purpose (or one of the purposes) of the person making the statement appears to the court to have been either; to cause a person to believe the matter, or to cause a person to act or a machine to operate on the basis that the matter is as stated.

The diary entry appears to fall outside of the hearsay rule. Although it is a statement as it is a representation of fact made by Sue and the statement was made outside of court it does not appear that it was Sue's purpose to cause anyone to believe the matter stated as the entry was made in her personal journal which she presumably did not intend anyone to read.

The text message also appears to fall outside of the hearsay rule. Again it appears to be a statement; in this case a representation of opinion by Roger that he will not be able to find anyone interested in buying diamonds. Again the statement was made outside of court but again it does not appear that the statement is being relied upon as evidence of the matter stated (i.e. whether Roger's purpose was to cause Raoul to believe the truth of his statement). Instead it appears that the text message is being used as an "implied assertion" that Raoul was trying to sell diamonds. Despite the decision in *R. v Leonard* (2009) where the court held that text messages did fall within the ambit of the hearsay rule if would seem that the correct position in this case would be to follow the decision of the court in *R. v Chrysostomou* (2010). In *Chrysostomou* the Court of Appeal held that text messages implying that the defendant had offered drugs for sale were not being relied upon as evidence of the matter stated but were instead being relied upon as an implied assertion that the defendant was known to offer drugs for sale. The text messages were therefore not hearsay.

Fred's 999 call will fall within the ambit of the hearsay rule. Fred has made an out of court statement relating to the incident at the jewellery store. Presumably Fred's purpose was to cause the 999 operator to believe the matter stated and also to cause the police to act on the basis of the statement. Because of this the rule against hearsay (s.114(1) **CJA 2003**) means that the statement will not be admissible unless an exception to the rule can be found. In this case it would appear that the common law exception preserved by s.118 (1)(4) may apply and that the statement may be admissible as a statement forming part of the *res gestae*. Section 118(1)(4) allows the admission of a hearsay statement where the statement was made by a person "so emotionally overpowered by an event that the possibility of concoction or distortion can be disregarded". There is evidence that the dramatic event (i.e. the robbery) has affected Fred given that he was "clearly shocked", this may be sufficient to allow the admission of the statement under s.118(1)(4) (*R. v Rattan* (1972)). It is for the trial judge to decide whether Fred was "so emotionally overpowered" that concoction or distortion can be disregarded (*R. v Andrews* (1987). It should be noted there may also be a statutory hearsay exception that could apply to this statement, these exceptions are dealt with in Chapter 12. The possibilities might include s.116 or s.117 of the **CJA 2003** (if Fred was unavailable to testify) or s.114(1)(d) of **CJA 2003**.

The computer printout is not hearsay as it is a representation made by a machine and so is not a statement for the purposes of s.115(2) **CJA 2003**. It must be noted that if the statement relies upon information supplied by a person for its accuracy (which presumably must be the case) then, before it is admissible, the accuracy of the information must first be proved (s.129(1) **CJA 2003**).

Civil Evidence Act 1995   **10**

Introduction

The **Civil Evidence Act (CEA) 1995** provides a statutory regime which makes hearsay evidence admissible in civil proceedings. This chapter will consider the procedural requirements and safeguards which the 1995 imposes in relation to the admission of hearsay evidence in civil proceedings, for example the importance of giving notice, and the mechanisms by which hearsay evidence can be tested.

It should be noted, however, that the effect of the definition of "civil proceedings" in s.11 of the **CEA 1995** is that the provisions of the Act do not apply to civil proceedings to which the strict rules of evidence are inapplicable (e.g. to claims which have been allocated to the small claims track).

ADMISSIBILITY

> **LEGISLATION HIGHLIGHTER**
>
> Section 1 of the **Civil Evidence Act 1995**
>
> Section 1 of the **CEA 1995** makes hearsay evidence admissible in civil proceedings. Hearsay is defined by s.1 of the **CEA 1995** as "... a statement made otherwise than by a person while giving oral evidence in the proceedings which is tendered as evidence of the matters stated..." and a statement is "... any representation of fact or opinion, however made" (s.13).

Section 14 provides, however, that s.1 does not make hearsay evidence admissible if the hearsay evidence is inadmissible for some reason other than its hearsay nature (e.g. if it is inadmissible due to the operation of some other rule of evidence, of some other statutory provision or of rules of court). Thus, for example (as was seen to be the case in Chapter 9, above, in relation to criminal proceedings), hearsay evidence will not be admissible in civil proceedings if it is not relevant to an issue in the proceedings.

Section 1(4) provides that ss.2 to 6 (considered below) do not apply where hearsay evidence is admissible under some exception to the hearsay rule other than the general exception provided by s.1. Thus, for example, ss.2 to 6 will not apply where hearsay evidence is admitted in civil proceedings under a common law exception to the hearsay rule preserved by s.7 (considered below), or under an exception to the hearsay rule provided by some other statutory provision, such as the **Children (Admissibility of Hearsay Evidence) Order 1993)**.

Hearsay notices

Section 2(1) of the **CEA 1995** requires a party intending to adduce hearsay evidence in civil proceedings to give such notice of this fact to the other parties to the proceedings (and, if requested, to provide the other parties with such particulars concerning the hearsay evidence) as is reasonable and practicable to enable the other parties to deal with matters arising from the hearsay nature of the evidence. The parties may, however, agree to dispense with the requirements of s.2(1) and a party entitled to receive a hearsay notice, etc., may waive his entitlement (s.2(3)). It should be noted that the requirements of s.2(1) do not apply in relation to evidence at hearings other than trials or to affidavits or witness statements not containing hearsay evidence or to statements allegedly made by persons whose estates form the subject matter of probate actions (**CPR 33.3**).

The **Civil Procedure Rules 1998 (CPR)** make provision, for the purposes of s.2(1) of the **CEA 1995**, for the giving of notice of the fact that a party proposes to adduce hearsay evidence (**CPR 33.2**). If the party intends to call a witness to prove the hearsay statement, notice takes the form of the service of the witness' witness statement on the other parties within the time limits for serving witness statements. If the party intends to prove the hearsay statement by means of the witness statement of a witness whom he does not intend to call, then notice takes the form of the service of the witness's witness statement on the other parties within the time limits for serving witness statements but, in addition, when the witness statement is served, the serving party must also inform the other parties that the witness is not being called and give the reason why the witness will not be called. If the hearsay statement is not to be proved in either of the above-mentioned ways, then the party who wishes to rely upon it must serve a notice on the other parties within the time limits for serving witness statements, identifying the hearsay evidence, stating that he intends to rely on it and giving the reason why the witness will not be called.

Where a party fails to comply with the requirements of s.2 this does not affect the admissibility of the hearsay evidence (s.2(4)). Section 2(4) provides, however, that such failure may be taken into account by the court when determining the weight of the hearsay evidence, may result in an adjournment and may be of relevance when the court is exercising its powers in relation to costs.

Calling the maker of a hearsay statement for cross-examination upon it

---

LEGISLATION HIGHLIGHTER

Section 3 of the **Civil Evidence Act 1995**

The effect of s.3 of the **CEA 1995** in conjunction with **CPR 33.4** is that where a party to civil proceedings intends to adduce a hearsay statement in evidence instead of calling its maker as a witness, another party may, within 14 days of the service of notice of intention to rely upon the hearsay evidence upon him, seek the permission of the court to call the maker and cross-examine him on the contents of the hearsay statement as though he had been called by the party who adduced it in evidence.

Where the court does give a party permission to call the maker of a hearsay statement tendered by another party for cross-examination and the maker of the hearsay statement fails to attend the proceedings, the court may exclude the hearsay evidence in the exercise of its exclusionary discretion under **CPR 32.1**, though it seems that the court should only do so in exceptional circumstances, as the court can take account of the failure when assessing the weight of the hearsay evidence under s.4 of the 1995 Act (see below) (*Polanski v Condé Nast Publications Ltd* (2004)). Where a party is given permission to call the maker of a hearsay statement for cross-examination and the party who served notice of intention to rely on the hearsay does not adduce the hearsay statement in evidence, the maker of the hearsay statement may not be called for cross-examination under CPR 32.1 (*The Green Opal* (2003)).

The evidential weight of a hearsay statement

LEGISLATION HIGHLIGHTER

Section 4 of the **Civil Evidence Act 1995**

Essentially, s.4 of the **CEA 1995** provides that the court, when estimating what, if any, weight (i.e. probative value) hearsay evidence possesses, may take into account any circumstances from which it is reasonable to draw an inference as to the reliability of the hearsay evidence.

The hearsay evidence of a witness may well possess considerably less weight than the evidence of a witness who has appeared in court for cross-examination on his or her witness statement and, in some circumstances, may possess no weight at all (*R. (on the application of Cleary) v Highbury Magistrates' Court* (2007)). It seems that if a judge exercises his "discretion" under s.4 properly, admitting hearsay evidence in civil proceedings would not be likely to result in a violation of art.6(3)(d) of the European Convention on Human Rights (*Solon South West Housing Association Ltd v James* (2004)). It should be noted that the nature of art.6(3)(d) and the extent to which admitting hearsay evidence in criminal proceedings has the potential to result in a violation of art.6(3)(d) are considered in Chapter 12, below.

Section 4 provides that in estimating the weight of hearsay evidence the court may have particular regard to the following matters:

(1) Would it have been reasonable and practicable to have called the maker of the hearsay statement to give evidence?
(2) Was the hearsay statement made contemporaneously with the occurrence of the matters stated?
(3) Does the hearsay evidence take the form of multiple hearsay?
(4) Did any person involved have a motive to conceal or misrepresent matters?
(5) Was the hearsay statement edited, made in collaboration with another person or made for a particular purpose?
(6) Do the circumstances in which the hearsay evidence is adduced suggest an attempt to prevent its weight being properly evaluated?

Competence and compellability

LEGISLATION HIGHLIGHTER

Section 5(1) of the **CEA 1995**

Section 5(1) provides that a hearsay statement is inadmissible in civil proceedings if its maker would not have been a competent witness at the time of its making.

Section 5(1) also provides that a hearsay statement is inadmissible in civil proceedings if proved by a statement made by a person who was not a competent witness at the time when he made his statement.

The burden of proving that the relevant person was not competent at the relevant time is borne by the party who asserts that this was so (*C v C* (2001)). The competence of witnesses in civil proceedings was considered in Chapter 2, above.

Credibility

> **LEGISLATION HIGHLIGHTER**
>
> Section 5(2) of the **CEA 1995**
>
> Section 5(2) provides that, where the maker of a hearsay statement is not called as a witness, evidence is admissible to attack or support his credibility to the extent to which it would have been admissible had he been called.

Moreover, again under s.5(2), evidence of other inconsistent statements which he has made is admissible to contradict his hearsay evidence. The section makes identical provision concerning the credibility and inconsistent statements of the maker of a statement used to prove a hearsay statement. In either case, however, subject to the exceptions identified in Chapter 5 above, the section effectively upholds the principle that evidence cannot be called in rebuttal of answers to collateral questions by providing that evidence relating to a matter cannot be adduced if it could not have been adduced if the maker of the relevant statement had been called as a witness and had denied the matter when cross-examined.

Where a party to civil proceedings intends to attack the credibility of the maker of a hearsay statement which is to be adduced in evidence by another party without calling the maker, **CPR** 33.5 requires the former party to notify the latter party of his intention within 14 days of service of a hearsay notice upon him.

Common law exceptions to the hearsay rule preserved in civil proceedings

Section 7(1) of the **CEA 1995** abolishes what was formally the most important remaining common law exception to the hearsay rule in civil proceedings, namely, the rule that informal admissions (namely, statements adverse to their maker's interests) made by a party were admissible in evidence against him. Informal admissions are now admissible under s.1 of the **CEA 1995** and are thus subject to the provisions of ss.2 to 6 of the **CEA 1995**.

Section 7(2) preserves a number of minor common law exceptions to the hearsay rule (e.g. the rule that published works (such as dictionaries) concerning public matters are admissible in evidence). Where evidence is admissible under a preserved common law exception to the hearsay rule, the provisions of ss.2 to 6 do not apply to it (see above).

Finally, s.7(3) partially preserves a number of common law rules concerning the admissibility of evidence of reputation, though such evidence must now satisfy the requirements of ss.2 to 6.

Proving statements contained in documents

Section 8 of the **CEA 1995** provides that, provided that they are admissible in evidence, statements contained in documents may be proved in civil proceedings either by producing the original documents or by producing copies of the documents or of the relevant parts thereof, authenticated in a manner approved by the court. The section also provides that, for this purpose, a copy need not be directly copied from the original document but may be a copy of a copy, it being irrelevant how many levels of copying there are between the original document and the copy. Section 13 provides that a document is "anything in which information of any description is recorded".

KEY CASE

MASQUERADE MUSIC LTD V SPRINGSTEEN (2001)
In the context of proceedings for infringement of copyright the claimant was unable to produce a written copy of the assignment of the copyright in question. The judge permitted secondary evidence to be called to prove the contents of the document assigning copyright and the defendant's appealed, arguing that the judge should not have permitted the admission of the secondary evidence unless the claimants had carried out an exhaustive search for the original document.

The court held that where an original document is not readily available to a party, the court may permit the party to prove its contents at common law by relying upon the oral evidence of a witness who read the document. Whether the court will be prepared to admit such evidence appears to depend upon the weight of the evidence.

Production of a document essentially appears to entail calling a witness to produce a document, though it appears that a document may, alternatively, be proved by other admissible evidence (i.e. by admissible hearsay evidence) (*Ventouris v Mountain* (1992)). Where a witness is called solely for the purpose of producing a document, the witness need not take the oath (*Perry v Gibson* (1834)).

Essentially, s.9 of the **CEA 1995** provides that it is unnecessary to call witnesses or to adduce other evidence to prove documents which are certified to form part of business or public authority records by officers of the relevant businesses or public authorities. The court may, however, in appropriate circumstances, direct that the provisions of s.9 do not apply to particular documents or types of document.

WITNESS STATEMENTS IN CIVIL PROCEEDINGS

Under **CPR** Pt 32 the court will order parties to civil proceedings who intend to call witnesses of fact (i.e. non-expert witnesses) to serve witness statements on the other parties. These are written statements of the admissible evidence to be given by such witnesses. Unless the court orders otherwise, witness statements will stand as the evidence in chief of the relevant witnesses, though cross-examination and re-examination will still take place, and the court, under **CPR** 32.5, may permit a witness to give evidence in chief amplifying his witness statement or concerning matters that have arisen since it was served.

Where a party is unable to obtain a witness statement the court may, under **CPR** 32.9, permit the party to serve a witness summary instead.

> **DEFINITION CHECKPOINT**
>
> A witness summary is a summary of the evidence which would be in the witness statement or, if this is not known, of the matters about which the party intends to question the witness.

Where a party fails to serve a witness statement or a witness summary as required by rules of court, the oral evidence of the relevant witness is only admissible with the permission of the court (**CPR** 32.10). If permission to call the witness is not given in such circumstances, this would not prevent the party who failed to serve the witness statement from relying on the witness statement as hearsay evidence even though the failure to serve the witness statement amounted to a failure to comply with the hearsay notice requirements laid down by **CPR** Pt 33.

If a party who serves a witness statement neither calls the witness nor adduces the witness statement as hearsay evidence, any other party may adduce the witness statement as hearsay evidence.

EXCLUSIONARY DISCRETION

Under **CPR** 32.1 the civil courts now possess discretion to exclude evidence which would otherwise be admissible in civil proceedings. Rule 32.1 entitles the court to:

- give directions as to the issues in relation to which it requires evidence;
- give directions as to the nature of the evidence which it requires;
- give directions as to the way in which evidence is to be placed before it;
- exclude admissible evidence; and
- limit cross-examination.

The **CPR** 32.1 discretion is an important case management power that the court may exercise in line with the overriding objective of the **CPR** so as to prevent it from being required to consider evidence of marginal relevance that would add significant length and expense to the trial. A good example of a context in which the **CPR** 32.1 discretion is exercised is provided by "similar fact evidence", which is considered in Chapter 13, below.

It should be noted that the civil courts should exercise their powers under the **CPR** in line with the "overriding objective", which can be found in **CPR** 1.1. This requires the court to deal with cases justly, which includes saving expense and dealing with the case expeditiously, but also requires the court to ensure that the parties are on an equal footing, to deal with the case fairly, to allocate an appropriate share of the court's resources to the case and to deal with the case in a way which is proportionate to the money involved, its importance, its complexity and the financial positions of the parties.

Revision checklist

You should now know and understand:

- that, due to the operation of s.1 of the **Civil Evidence Act 1995**, the rule against hearsay does not apply in civil proceedings;

- the requirement to give notice when relying upon hearsay evidence and the consequences of failing to give notice;

- the procedure for giving notice of the intention to rely upon hearsay evidence;

- the mechanisms by which the weight of hearsay evidence can be challenged in civil proceedings;

- the way in which the credibility of the maker of a hearsay statement can be challenged;

- the exercise of the court's exclusionary discretion in civil proceedings.

QUESTION AND ANSWER

The Question

Dan is bringing a civil claim against JimCo Ltd in relation to an accident he had at the factory, owned by JimCo Ltd, where Dan was employed. Dan is suing JimCo for damages for a broken leg and resulting damaged nerves after he slipped on a wet floor that had just been mopped but where no warning signs were displayed.

Dan has obtained a witness statement from Gina another employee of JimCo who was present at the time of the accident. Gina's statement indicates that "the floor was wet and there were no warning signs, Dan was just walking between workshops and fell really awkwardly". Dan does not intend to call Gina but instead intends to rely upon her witness statement as forming her evidence in chief.

JimCo also have a statement from Gina taken a few days after the accident in which she asserts "Dan must have been late because he was running towards the workshop. It was probably his own fault".

Dan also wishes to rely upon an entry in the companies' accident book indicating that at the time of the accident the floor was wet but that the signs warning of the wet floor were locked in the cleaner's cupboard whilst the cleaner was on his lunch break. The accident book relating to Dan's injury can no longer be located but George, the foreman in charge on the day of the accident, read the entry in the book and is willing to testify as to the contents. Dan has so far been unable to obtain a witness statement from George but George is able to come to court to give evidence if required.

JimCo have obtained a statement from Madeline a receptionist at the factory who claims to have seen Dan running shortly before the accident, JimCo do not intend to call Madeline but instead intend to rely upon her witness statement as hearsay evidence. Dan does not remember seeing Madeline that day as she works in a different part of the building, he remembers hurrying past her the previous day and wishes to have her called for cross examination about whether she could have been mistaken about when she saw him.

Advise Dan about the admissibility of the evidence he wishes to adduce (including any steps JimCo might take to challenge the weight of the evidence) and whether he can have Madeline called for cross examination?

General guidance

In civil proceedings hearsay evidence is admissible by virtue of s.1 of the **Civil Evidence Act 1995** therefore the majority of the discussion is usually centred around the procedural requirements for the admission of hearsay evidence and the steps that can be taken to challenge it. Some things that you will almost always need to consider are;

- The party adducing the evidence is required to give notice that they will be relying upon hearsay evidence (s.2). [It is important to remember that the failure to give such notice does not render the evidence inadmissible but may have consequences re adjournment and costs and/or the assessment of the weight of the hearsay evidence under s.4.]
- Steps can be taken by the opposing party to challenge the hearsay evidence, either by applying to the court within 14 days of receipt of notice to have the witness called for cross examination (s.3) or by challenging the weight of the statement (s.4) or the credibility of its maker (s.5(2)).
- In order for hearsay evidence to be admissible the maker of the statement must have the required capacity (i.e. must be a competent witness) (s.5(1))
- Statements contained in documents can be proved by producing copies (s.8) or by calling witnesses to testify as to the contents of the document (*Masquerade Music v Springsteen*).

Answer plan

1 The evidence of Gina; Dan intends to rely upon Gina's witness statement as hearsay evidence. The witness statement will be admissible by virtue of the provision in s.1 of the **Civil Evidence Act 1995** that abolishes the rule against hearsay in civil proceedings.

2 In relation to this hearsay evidence, Dan should comply with the notice requirements imposed by s.2(1) of the **CEA 1995** and **CPR 33.2**. Since the hearsay evidence is contained in a witness statement of a person who is not being called, it appears that the witness statement should be exchanged at the normal time for exchanging witness statements and that Dan should indicate both that he is not calling Gina and why he is not doing so.

3 If Jack fails to comply with these notice requirements this will not affect the admissibility of the hearsay evidence but may reduce its weight (under s.4) and may have costs and/or adjournment implications.

4 Within 14 days of receiving notice that Dan will be relying upon Gina's hearsay evidence as her evidence in chief JimCo can apply to the court for permission to have Gina called for cross-examination on her witness statement (s.3 of the 1995 Act in conjunction with **CPR** 33.4). *Note: Gina is likely to be a competent and compellable witness in the proceedings—see Chapter 2 above.* [Note: if Gina is called for cross-examination then, as was seen in Chapter 5, above, her previous inconsistent statement may potentially be proved under **CPA 1865** s.5 (the inconsistent statement being admissible under s.1 and s.6 of the **CEA 1995**.]

5 Alternatively, rather than calling Gina for cross-examination, JimCo might seek to adduce Gina's earlier (inconsistent) statement in her absence under s.5 of the 1995 Act in an attempt to reduce the weight that the judge might give to her evidence.

6 George's evidence is admissible by virtue of s.1 of the 1995 Act and is subject to the notice requirement contained in s.2. If Dan is unable to obtain a witness statement from George the court may grant him permission, under CPR 32.9, to serve a witness summary instead. If he fails to serve either a witness statement or a witness summary George will not be able to testify except with the court's permission (**CPR** 32.10).

7 Dan is unable to prove the content of the accident book by producing a copy under CEA 1995 s.8 but, at common law, the court may be prepared to permit him to call George to give evidence of the content of the statement (*Masquerade Music v Springsteen*).

8 Madeline's hearsay evidence will be admissible under **CEA 1995** s.1, again subject to the s.2 notice procedure. Within 14 days of receiving notice of JimCo's intention to rely upon the hearsay evidence of Madeline, Dan can apply to the court for permission to have Madeline called for cross examination (s.3 of the 1995 Act in conjunction with **CPR** 33.4). *Note: Madeline is also likely to be a competent and compellable witness in the proceedings—see Chapter 2 above.*

9 In general, it is worth noting in respect of those witness who are not called and whose hearsay evidence is adduced before the court that the likelihood is that the judge, under s.4, will give significantly less weight to hearsay evidence than he would to the evidence of a witness who has given evidence in the proceedings.

Confessions and Improperly Obtained Evidence

Introduction

In this chapter, we will consider:

- what constitutes a confession;
- how the courts determine whether confessions are admissible in evidence;
- the exercise of the court's discretion to exclude prosecution evidence on the grounds of fairness;
- the position regarding the admissibility of illegally, unfairly or improperly obtained evidence.

. . . .

CONFESSIONS

> **DEFINITION CHECKPOINT**
>
> The meaning of "confession"
> Section 82(1) of the **Police and Criminal Evidence Act 1984 (PACE)** defines a confession as including;
>
> > ". . . any statement wholly or partly adverse to the person who made it, whether made to a person in authority or not and whether made in words or otherwise . . ."

Thus, a statement, whether made orally, in writing or by conduct (e.g. by video re-enactment), is a confession either if it takes the form of a "wholly inculpatory statement" (i.e. a full confession of guilt) or if it takes the form of a "mixed statement" (i.e. a statement that is only partly adverse to its maker). For example, where D admitted to the police that he had been in the vicinity of a burglary but gave an innocent explanation for his presence, D's mixed statement was admissible as a confession (*R. v Sharp* (1988)).

A statement which is totally in the accused's favour (i.e. a "wholly exculpatory statement") is not a confession, but may be admissible in evidence in the accused's favour as a previous consistent statement under principles that were considered in Chapter 5, above. A statement which was a wholly exculpatory statement at the time when the accused made it is not a confession even though it subsequently becomes adverse to its maker (e.g.

by being inconsistent with the accused's testimony in court) (*R. v Hasan* (2005)).

Where a mixed statement is admitted in evidence as a confession the jury are entitled to consider not just the inculpatory parts of the statement but also the exculpatory parts (*R. v Sharp*). This common law rule is preserved by s.118 of the **Criminal Justice Act 2003** (*R. v Papworth* (2008)).

Whilst confessions are often made to the police, s.82(1) makes clear that a confession need not be made to "a person in authority". Thus, for example, in *R. v B* (2009) a confession was made by the accused to the mother of a sexual offence complainant.

Determining the admissibility of a confession: the voir dire

DEFINITION CHECKPOINT
The "voir dire"
The voir dire is often referred to as a "trial within a trial". It is a hearing in the absence of the jury in which witnesses will be examined and evidence heard in order to determine collateral matters such as the admissibility of a confession.

The statutory provision which regulates the admissibility of confessions is s.76 of **PACE** (see below). Challenges to the admissibility of confessions are determined "on the voir dire" during which the jury is not present and the judge is not concerned with the truthfulness of the confession. If the confession is not admitted, then the jury is not told of its existence. If the confession is admitted, it is put before the jury but the defence may still try to persuade the jury that it should not be believed (as the jury is concerned with its truthfulness). If the defence do not challenge the admissibility of a confession before it is put before the jury, it appears that its admissibility cannot subsequently be challenged under s.76 (*R. v Sat-Bhambra* (1988)), though the defence may still try to persuade the jury that the confession should not be believed. Moreover, if the defence do not assert that the accused's confession is inadmissible but simply assert that no confession was ever made there is no need for a voir dire as it is for the jury, not the judge, to decide whether this is so (*Ajodha v The State* (1982)).

Where a voir dire is held, the Privy Council stated, in *R. v Wong Kam Ming* (1980), that:

- the accused cannot be questioned about the truthfulness of his confession during the voir dire;
- statements which he makes during the voir dire cannot be made known to the jury; and
- inconsistencies between the accused's evidence and statements which

he made during the voir dire cannot be made known to the jury unless his confession is admitted and the accused gives evidence concerning its reliability.

Finally, if the admissibility of a confession is challenged under s.76 during summary trial, the magistrates must, similarly, hold a trial within a trial (*R. v Liverpool Juvenile Court* (1988)). During the voir dire the magistrates, like the judge in a jury trial, are not concerned with the truthfulness of the confession.

Determining the admissibility of a confession: the statutory conditions of admissibility

A confession is hearsay evidence. However, a confession made by the accused may be admissible under the hearsay exception provided by s.76(1) of **PACE**. The effect of s.128(2) of the **CJA 2003** is that where a confession is inadmissible under s.76(1), it cannot be admissible under any other exception to the hearsay rule except s.76A (which is considered below).

LEGISLATION HIGHLIGHTER

Section 76 of the **Police and Criminal Evidence Act 1984**

Section 76(1) provides for the admissibility of relevant confessions at the criminal trials of their makers, as evidence against their makers, subject to conditions of admissibility laid down by s.76(2). Section 76(1) and (2) provide as follows:

"(1) In any [criminal] proceedings a confession made by an accused person may be given in evidence against him in so far as it is relevant to any matter in issue in the proceedings and is not excluded by the court in pursuance of this section.

(2) If, in any proceedings where the prosecution proposes to give in evidence a confession made by an accused person, it is represented to the court that the confession was or may have been obtained

    (a) by oppression of the person who made it; or

    (b) in consequence of anything said or done which was likely, in the circumstances existing at the time, to render unreliable any confession which might be made by him in consequence thereof,

the court shall not allow the confession to be given in evidence against him except in so far as the prosecution proves to the court beyond reasonable doubt that the confession (notwithstanding that it may be true) was not obtained as aforesaid."

Thus, if the defence suggest (or the court of its own motion raises the issue in accordance with s.76(3)) that the means by which, or circumstances in which, a confession was obtained fall within para.(a) or (b) of s.76(2), the confession will only be admissible if the prosecution can prove beyond reasonable doubt that the confession was not obtained in either of the ways set out in those paragraphs. Further, s.76(2) makes clear (and the court has confirmed this in *R. v Crampton* (1991)) that whether the confession is true or not is not a relevant consideration in assessing its admissibility.

Oppression (s.76(2)(a))

In order to establish that a confession was not "obtained by oppression", the prosecution must prove, to the criminal standard of proof, either that the accused did not confess in consequence of the oppression to which he was subjected or that he was not subjected to oppression.

When is a confession "obtained" by oppression?

It appears from the wording of s.76(2)(a) that if the prosecution can prove that the accused did not confess because he was oppressed but, rather, confessed for some other reason, then the confession is not rendered inadmissible by para.(a). In determining whether the oppression to which the accused was subjected may have "produced" the accused's confession, it seems that the court will take relevant aspects of his personality into account in deciding whether these render it more or less likely that he may have "cracked" under pressure. Thus, the courts have recognised that conduct which might "persuade" a person of very low intelligence to confess (*R. v Seelig* (1992)) might not have this effect when directed at someone who is intelligent and sophisticated (*R. v Miller, R. v Paris, R. v Abdullahi* (1992)).

The nature of oppression

A confession is not rendered inadmissible by s.76(2) if the prosecution can prove that the conduct to which the accused was subjected did not amount to oppression. Section 76(8) provides that oppression includes:

> "... torture, inhuman or degrading treatment, and the use or threat of violence (whether or not amounting to torture)."

KEY CASE

R. v FULLING (1987)

A more comprehensive definition was adopted in *R. v Fulling* by Lord Lane C.J. who stated that oppression should be given its dictionary meaning which, according to the *Oxford English Dictionary*, is:

> "Exercise of authority or power in a burdensome, harsh or wrongful manner; unjust or cruel treatment of subjects, inferiors etc; the imposition of unreasonable or unjust burdens."
>
> His Lordship was of the view that oppression in this sense would almost certainly involve improper conduct by persons interviewing the accused.

Examples of conduct on the part of police officers which appears potentially capable of giving rise to oppression include breaches of the requirements of **PACE** or of the Codes of Practice made under **PACE** and "heavy handed" questioning or distortion of evidence on the part of interviewing officers. For example, it appears that failure to provide access to a solicitor as required by s.58 of **PACE** may, potentially, amount to oppression (*R. v Samuel* (1988)), though it is, perhaps, more likely that (as in *R. v Samuel*) such failure will result in the exclusion of a confession under **PACE** s.78 (which is considered below). Similarly, where interviewing officers persistently shouted allegations at the accused even though he had consistently denied his guilt several hundred times over a number of days, their conduct was held to amount to oppression (*R. v Miller, R. v Parris, R. v Abdullahi*). Again, where interviewing officers deliberately set out to persuade the accused that the case against him is stronger than, in fact, it is, it appears that their conduct may amount to oppression (*R. v Beales* (1991)).

Conversely, the mere fact that conduct is improper does not, in itself, mean that the conduct is oppressive if the degree of impropriety is trivial (*R. v Emmerson* (1990) and *R. v Parker* (1995)).

Unreliability (s.76(2)(b))

In order to establish that a confession was not "obtained in consequence of anything said or done which was likely, in the circumstances existing at the time, to render unreliable any confession which [the accused] might [have made] in consequence [of the thing said or done]", the prosecution must prove, to the criminal standard of proof, either that the accused did not confess in consequence of the thing said or done, or that the thing said or done was not likely to have rendered unreliable any confession made by him in consequence of the thing said or done, in the circumstances in which he did confess (*R. v Barry* (1992); *R. v Proulx* (2001)).

When is a confession "obtained" in consequence of the thing said or done?

The wording of s.76(2)(b) makes clear that if the prosecution can prove that the accused did not confess because the thing was said or done but for some other reason, then the confession is not rendered inadmissible by para.(b) (*R. v Barry*; *R. v Proulx*). In determining whether the thing said or done may have "produced" the accused's confession, it seems that the court will take relevant aspects of his personality into account. Such factors may sometimes make it more likely that the accused confessed in response to the thing said or done but sometimes may have the opposite effect. For example, failure to provide access to a solicitor as required by s.58 of **PACE** might be a factor which could lead a person of low intelligence who knows little about the criminal process to confess, but may well be less likely to have this effect upon a person who has the ability to cope with an "interview situation" and is aware of his legal rights (see, respectively, *R. v Harvey* (1988) and *R. v Alladice* (1988)).

What types of "things" and "circumstances" are capable of producing unreliability?

A confession is not rendered inadmissible by s.76(2)(b) if the prosecution can prove that the thing said or done was not likely to have rendered unreliable any confession made by the accused in consequence of the thing said or done in the circumstances in which he did confess (*R. v Barry*; *R. v Proulx*).

In contrast with oppression, improper conduct does not form an essential pre-requisite of unreliability (*R. v Fulling*). Further, whether or not the accused's confession is or is not likely to be unreliable is not the issue before the court, the court being concerned with the likely reliability of any confession which he might have made in the circumstances, in consequence of the thing said or done (*R. v Crampton* (1991)). Thus, the issue for the court is not whether the confession that the accused made is untruthful but is whether, in the circumstances, such a confession as the accused made is likely to have been rendered unreliable by the thing that was said or done (*R. v Proulx*).

The court, when deciding whether to exclude a confession under s.76(2)(b), must consider four issues (see *R. v Barry* and *R. v Proulx*):

(1) Whether anything relevant was said or done.
(2) The nature of the circumstances existing at the time when the thing was said or done.
(3) Whether, in those circumstances, the thing said or done was likely to render any confession which the accused might have made in consequence of the thing said or done unreliable.
(4) Whether the confession was made in consequence of the thing said or done.

Examples of things said or done which might, in appropriate circumstances, be relevant to the operation of para.(b) are:

- breaches of requirements laid down by **PACE** or by the Codes of Practice made under **PACE** (*R. v Trussler* (1988));
- inducements to confess in the form of offers of favourable treatment (*R. v Mathias* (1989)); or
- statements to the effect that close friends or relatives of the accused are implicated in the commission of the crime under investigation (*R. v Harvey*).

The thing said or done must be said or done by someone other than the accused himself (*R. v Goldenberg* (1988) and *R. v Wahab* (2003)). Thus, if the accused confesses in the hope that he will be released on bail and, consequently, will be able to obtain alcohol or drugs in order to satisfy his craving, this will not be sufficient to render his confession inadmissible under para.(b) unless this hope has been created or fostered by the words or conduct of others.

KEY CASE

R. v WAHAB (2003)

The defendant was arrested, along with a number of members of his family on suspicion of conspiracy to supply Class A drugs. After a number of interviews the defendant's solicitor, acting on instructions from the defendant, approached the police to ask whether, if the defendant made a confession, the other members of his family would be released. The police indicated that no guarantees could be made and the defendant's solicitor advised him that the police would consider the case as a whole and that if the evidence against his family members was "borderline" they would be released. On the basis of his solicitor's advice the defendant subsequently confessed to being a "middle man" in the supply chain.

At trial the defendant argued that he had been improperly advised by his solicitor and sought to have his confession excluded. The trial judge admitted the confession and the defendant was convicted. He then appealed on the basis that his confession was unreliable and therefore should have been excluded under s.76(2)(b) **PACE**.

The court dismissed the appeal and held that reliance on legal advice properly given to the defendant did not normally give rise to grounds for exclusion on the basis of unreliability. Unless directly relevant to the reliability of the confession the 'concerns' or 'motives' of the person making the statement are not relevant to s.76(2)(b).

The circumstances existing at the time when the "thing" was said or done may make it more or less likely that a consequent confession would be unreliable. For example, the absence of a legal adviser may result in the accused attaching more weight to an inducement to confess than he would have done had he received proper legal advice before confessing (*R. v Mathias*). Similarly, the mental illness and low intelligence of the accused may increase the likelihood that, upon hearing that her lover has confessed to a crime, she would confess in order to protect her (*R. v Harvey*).

Finally, the fact that circumstances which make it more likely that a confession made by the accused will be unreliable are unknown to the interviewing officers at the time when they say or do the relevant thing does not prevent the court from taking account of those circumstances when determining the admissibility of the accused's confession under para.(b). Thus, for example, the fact that the officers are not aware of the accused's low mental age would not prevent the court from considering this factor when considering whether things said or done by the officers were likely to have rendered unreliable a consequent confession by him (*R. v Everett* (1988)).

Oppression, unreliability and the role of the jury

Where the accused asserts that a confession was obtained by oppression or in consequence of something said or done, etc. but the judge admits the confession, the accused may adduce evidence of oppression or of the thing said or done before the jury. In such circumstances the judge must direct the jury that they should ignore the confession if they consider that it was or may have been so obtained (*R. v Mushtaq* (2005)). The position is the same if the accused does not challenge the admissibility of his confession before the judge but adduces evidence of oppression or of the thing said or done before the jury (*R. v Pham* (2008)).

Determining the admissibility of confessions

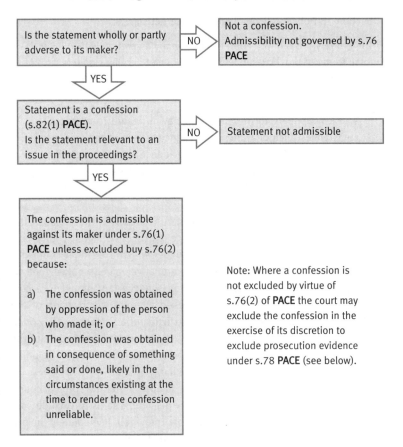

Is the statement wholly or partly adverse to its maker? — **NO** → Not a confession. Admissibility not governed by s.76 **PACE**

↓ YES

Statement is a confession (s.82(1) **PACE**). Is the statement relevant to an issue in the proceedings? — **NO** → Statement not admissible

↓ YES

The confession is admissible against its maker under s.76(1) **PACE** unless excluded buy s.76(2) because:

a) The confession was obtained by oppression of the person who made it; or

b) The confession was obtained in consequence of something said or done, likely in the circumstances existing at the time to render the confession unreliable.

Note: Where a confession is not excluded by virtue of s.76(2) of **PACE** the court may exclude the confession in the exercise of its discretion to exclude prosecution evidence under s.78 **PACE** (see below).

Judicial discretion to refuse to permit the prosecution to adduce a confession in evidence

Where the operation of s.76(2) of **PACE** does not render a confession inadmissible as prosecution evidence, the court (trial judge or magistrates) may permit the prosecution to adduce the confession in evidence, but is not obliged to do so. Rather, the court possesses discretion to refuse to permit the prosecution to adduce a confession (or any other evidence tendered by the prosecution) in evidence.

Section 78 **Police and Criminal Evidence Act 1984**

The primary basis of the court's exclusionary discretion (which extends to all forms of prosecution evidence, not just to confessions) is s.78 of **PACE**, which provides that the court may refuse to allow the prosecution to adduce evidence:

"... if it appears to the court that having regard to all the circumstances, including the circumstances in which the evidence was obtained, the admission of the evidence would have such an adverse effect on the fairness of the proceedings that the court ought not to admit it."

In addition to the s.78 discretion, **PACE** s.82(3) preserves the common law discretion to exclude prosecution evidence which the criminal courts possessed prior to the enactment of **PACE**, under which a criminal court may exclude prosecution evidence either if its probative value is outweighed by its prejudicial effect or if takes the form of evidence tantamount to a confession that was obtained from the accused after the commission of the offence by means that would justify the exclusion of a confession (*R. v Sang* (1980)). In practice, however, the criminal courts normally make use of the s.78 discretion, rather than the common law discretion, when excluding confessions in the exercise of their discretion.

Examples of circumstances in which it appears that the criminal courts are prepared to exercise their exclusionary discretion so as to exclude confessions tendered by the prosecution are provided immediately below, though it is not suggested that this list is exhaustive.

Where there has been a breach of requirement laid down either by PACE or by one of the Codes of Practice made under PACE

It appears that the exercise of exclusionary discretion is justified where the breach is "significant and substantial", though the fact that a breach is significant and substantial does not automatically require the exclusion of a confession in every case (*R. v Walsh* (1989)).

Thus, it may not be appropriate to exclude a confession in respect of a breach which is trivial (such as not showing the accused the record of his interview (*R. v Matthews* (1989)) or which has insignificant practical consequences. For example, the court may decline to exercise its discretion where, although there has been a failure to provide the accused with a solicitor as requested, the court is satisfied that this has not adversely affected the accused's interests because he has the ability to cope with an "interview situation" and is aware of his legal rights (*R. v Alladice*).

In contrast, if a breach has significant practical consequences, the exercise of exclusionary discretion may well be appropriate. Thus, if the court is of the opinion that the accused would probably not have confessed had he received legal advice as requested, the court is likely to exercise its exclusionary discretion (*R. v Samuel*).

Further, even where a breach does not have significant practical consequences, bad faith on the part of the interviewer may make the breach significant and substantial and may thus persuade the court to exercise its discretion, though good faith will not make a significant and substantial breach less significant and substantial (*R. v Walsh*). Thus, where the court is satisfied that failure to provide the accused with a solicitor did not adversely affect his interests, the court may still be prepared to exercise its exclusionary discretion if the failure to comply with the accused's request amounted to a deliberate decision not to comply with the requirements of **PACE**.

Where a confession has been obtained by unfair means

KEY CASE

R. v Mason (1987)
In *R. v Mason* police officers told the accused and his solicitor that the accused's fingerprints had been found at the scene of the crime (arson) on a bottle containing inflammable liquid. This was a deliberate lie but it persuaded the accused's solicitor to advise him to answer police questions and explain his involvement in the offence with the result that he confessed. The Court of Appeal held that the trial judge should have excluded the confession in the exercise of his exclusionary discretion.

Where the probative value of the confession is outweighed by its prejudicial effect

If the judge feels that the evidential value of a confession is small (perhaps, for example, because of the mental illness of the accused at the time when he made it), he may be prepared to exercise his exclusionary discretion so as to prevent the jury being prejudiced by knowledge of the confession upon the basis that the probative value of the confession is outweighed by its prejudicial effect (*R. v Miller* (1986), a case concerning the preserved common law discretion).

What if a first confession is excluded but the accused also confessed at a later interview which was properly conducted?

Sometimes, following the making of a confession which the court either cannot admit, due to the operation of s.76(2), or will not admit in the exercise of its exclusionary discretion, it may be that the accused was interviewed again, and made a further confession. Where this is the case, even if nothing happened in the course of the second interview which would require or justify exclusion of the confession, the courts have held that the conduct which required or justified exclusion of the first confession may remain an operative factor which either requires the exclusion of the second on grounds of oppression or unreliability or justifies its exclusion in the exercise of judicial discretion (see, respectively, *R. v Ismail* (1991); *R. v McGovern* (1991); and *R. v Gillard and Barrett* (1991)).

Is an accused's confession admissible evidence for the prosecution against his co-accused?

Usually, a confession is only admissible in evidence for the prosecution against the person who made it. It cannot be used against a co-accused whom it implicates as this would infringe the hearsay rule, the hearsay exception contained in s.76 of **PACE** only permitting the admission of a confession as evidence against its maker. Thus, *in R. v Natheeswaran* (2009), the accused's appeal was successful because the judge had directed the jury that they could rely on confessions made by a co-accused as evidence against the accused. However, if an accused, whilst being interviewed, accepts that a confession, implicating him, which was made by a co-accused is true, the confession also becomes his confession and may be used against him (*R. v Christie* (1914)).

Where, upon the basis of a confession made by the accused, a jury finds that the accused is guilty, whilst the accused's confession is not admissible against a co-accused, the jury is entitled to take its finding that the accused is guilty into account when deciding whether the co-accused is guilty if, in the circumstances, the accused's guilt is relevant to that of the co-accused (*R. v Hayter* (2005)). Thus, in *Hayter*, where D had allegedly found, for B, a person, R, who was prepared to kill B's husband, the House of Lords held that the jury had been entitled to take R's guilt into account when deciding whether D was guilty of murder even though the main evidence against R had been a confession that R had made to his girlfriend. The principle from *Hayter* does not apply, however, if the statement made by the accused is an exculpatory statement, rather than a confession (*Persad v The State of Trinidad and Tobago* (2007)). In *Persad*, in which three men had allegedly committed a robbery, one had also allegedly committed a rape and one (but not the rapist) had also allegedly committed buggery, the Privy Council held that the jury should have been directed that an out of court statement made by one of the men in which he admitted robbery but denied rape and buggery was not evidence against the second man because it was an exculpatory statement in relation to the sexual offences (the third man had made an out of court statement admitting robbery and rape but denying buggery).

Is an accused's confession admissible in evidence for a co-accused?

Section 76A of **PACE** provides that an accused's confession is admissible in evidence for a co-accused in so far as it is relevant to a matter in issue and is not excluded under s.76A. Where oppression or unreliability are alleged, the judge will, essentially, be required to exclude the confession as evidence for a co-accused (under s.76A(2)(a) and (b)) in the same circumstances in which the judge would be required to exclude a confession tendered by the prosecution (i.e. the accused's confession will be inadmissible for a co-accused if it was, or may have been, obtained by oppression or in consequence of anything said or done which was likely, in the circumstances existing at the time, to render unreliable any confession which might be made by him in consequence thereof). However, there is a difference between s.76 and s.76A in that the standard of proof required where the co-accused seeks to prove that the accused's confession was not obtained in either of these ways is only proof on the balance of probabilities (whereas, as was seen above, the standard of proof for the prosecution under **PACE** s.76 is proof beyond reasonable doubt).

Is a confession made by a person other than the accused admissible?

Where a confession is made by someone other than the accused (e.g. a confession made by a third party or a confession made by a former co-accused who has pleaded guilty), the confession will not be admissible under **PACE** s.76 or s.76A but may be admissible under some other statutory hearsay exception, such as s.114(1)(d) of the **CJA 2003**, which is considered in Chapter 12, below (*R. v Finch* (2007)). Section 128(2) of the 2003 Act (which was considered above) will not apply in such circumstances as the confession (made by a third party or a former co-accused) is not made by a "defendant".

Where a confession is excluded, is evidence of facts discovered as a result of the confession admissible?

Sometimes when an accused makes a confession, he also provides information as to the whereabouts of items connected with the offence (e.g. that the murder weapon is in his car) which the prosecution may later wish to adduce in evidence against him. If the confession is admissible the prosecution will be entitled to reveal how the items were discovered, but if the confession is excluded the position is more complicated.

If the confession is excluded under s.76 of **PACE**, the effect of s.76(4) is that the facts discovered in consequence of the confession are still admissible. The effect of ss.76(5) and 76(6) is, however, that the prosecution cannot reveal to the jury how the facts were discovered. Thus, to continue the above example, if the confession was excluded under s.76 the jury could be told that the murder weapon was found in the accused's car but could not be told that the accused had told the police that it was there.

Section 76(4) only applies where a confession is "excluded in pursuance of" s.76 and, thus, s.76(4) does not apply where a confession is excluded in the exercise of the court's exclusionary discretion (i.e. under **PACE** s.78). It appears, however, that in such circumstances, common law principles, the effect of which are similar to that of s.76(4), will probably apply (*R. v Warickshall* (1783)).

Like s.76(4), s.76(5) and s.76(6) only apply where a confession is "excluded in pursuance of" s.76. The common law position concerning the extent to which the prosecution may reveal to the jury how the items were discovered where the court excludes a confession in the exercise of its exclusionary discretion is unclear.

Excluded confessions as evidence of their makers' manner of communication

Section 76(4) also provides that where a confession excluded under s.76 is relevant to show that the accused "speaks, writes or expresses himself in a particular way", this does not affect the admissibility "of so much of the confession as is necessary to show that he does so".

Confessions made by unaccompanied mentally handicapped persons

Where a confession made by a mentally handicapped person in the absence of an independent person is admitted in evidence against him during trial on indictment and the prosecution case is based wholly or substantially upon the confession, s.77 of **PACE** applies. The effect of s.77 is, essentially, that the trial judge must explain to the jury that, in the circumstances, they must exercise especial caution prior to convicting the accused. The s.77 requirement does not apply if an independent person (i.e. a person independent of the police force) was present when the accused confessed.

In many cases in which a mentally handicapped person confesses in the absence of an independent person, s.77 will be irrelevant in practice as the confession will be excluded either under s.76 or in the exercise of the court's exclusionary discretion. The provision of a warning under s.77 does not render admissible a confession which otherwise would be excluded (*R. v Moss* (1990)).

JUDICIAL DISCRETION TO EXCLUDE ILLEGALLY, UNFAIRLY OR IMPROPERLY OBTAINED PROSECUTION EVIDENCE OTHER THAN CONFESSIONS

As has already been seen in the course of this chapter, the admissibility of confessions for the prosecution in criminal proceedings is now governed by s.76 of **PACE**. The fact that prosecution evidence other than a confession was obtained illegally, unfairly or improperly does not render the evidence inadmissible at common law (*Kuruma v R.* (1955); *R. v Sang*) and there is no statutory provision equivalent to s.76 of **PACE** which might render such evidence inadmissible. Rather, where evidence other than a confession which was illegally, unfairly or improperly obtained is relevant to an issue in criminal proceedings it will be admissible for the prosecution unless the court excludes it in the exercise of its exclusionary discretion, either under s.78 or (much less likely in practice) in the exercise of its common law exclusionary discretion.

> **DEFINITION CHECKPOINT**
>
> Where the prosecution intend to rely upon illegally, unfairly or improperly obtained evidence (other than confessions) the general position is that there is no rule of law which renders the evidence inadmissible, however the court **may** decide to exercise its exclusionary discretion so as to exclude the evidence if the admission of the evidence would have such an adverse effect on the fairness of the proceedings that it ought not to be admitted. It must be noted that the power to exclude under s.78 **PACE** only applies to prosecution evidence.

Thus, for example, where the defence alleges that evidence was obtained in consequence of breaches of requirements imposed by Code D (concerning the conduct of identification procedures) the evidence will only be excluded if the judge, in the exercise of his exclusionary discretion, decides that the admission of the evidence would, in the circumstances, have such an adverse effect on the fairness of the proceedings that it ought not to be admitted (*R. v Quinn* (1990)). In relation to breaches of requirements of **PACE** or of the **PACE** Codes of Practice, exclusion under s.78 is likely where the breach is significant or substantial or in bad faith (*R. v Walsh*). Where the breach is not significant, substantial or deliberate and the evidence is admitted, an appropriate direction to the jury may be required (*R. v Quinn*).

Where entrapment (e.g. by an undercover police officer acting as an agent provocateur) is alleged, the grant of a stay of proceedings will normally be the appropriate remedy (*R. v Loosely* (2001)). If the issue of entrapment arises in the context of the exercise of the s.78 discretion, however, the evidence should be excluded either if there has been procedural unfairness or if condoning the police conduct would bring the administration of justice into disrepute (*R. v Loosely*). In this context, relevant factors will include whether the accused was enticed to commit the offence, the nature of the entrapment, the nature of the evidence against the accused, how active or passive the undercover officer had been, whether there was an unassailable or strongly corroborated record of what had occurred (e.g. tape recordings) and whether the officer had abused his role by conducting an interview in breach of requirements of **PACE** Code C (*R. v Smurthwaite* (1994)).

The admission for the prosecution in criminal proceedings of illegally, improperly or unfairly obtained evidence (e.g. evidence obtained by entrapment) may give rise to a violation of art.6 of the **European Convention on Human Rights** (*Teixeira de Castro v Portugal* (1999)). It is submitted, however, that where a criminal court, having properly considered the exercise of the s.78 exclusionary discretion (and, where appropriate, having properly considered whether the proceedings should be stayed as an abuse of process) and having properly taken into account any relevant human rights arguments, determines that evidence, such as evidence obtained by entrapment (*Nottingham City Council v Amin* (2000)) or evidence obtained in consequence of violation of art.8 of the Convention (*Khan v UK* (1997)), should be admitted, the admission of such evidence will be unlikely to give rise to a violation of art.6.

Revision checklist

You should now know and understand:

- what makes a statement a confession in the context of criminal proceedings;
- when a confession will be admissible in criminal proceedings;
- when a confession should be excluded in criminal proceedings by virtue of s.76(2) **PACE 1984**;
- when the court may exercise its exclusionary discretion to exclude a confession;
- the position regarding the admissibility of evidence obtained as a result of an inadmissible confession;

- the position regarding the admissibility of illegally, unfairly or improperly obtained evidence;

- when the court may exercise its exclusionary discretion to exclude illegally, unfairly or improperly obtained evidence.

QUESTION AND ANSWER

The Question

Sylvia has been charged with criminal damage to her boyfriend's car. The prosecution allege that, upon finding out that Dave, her boyfriend, was also seeing his secretary behind her back, Sylvia went to Dave's office car park and poured paint stripper all over his brand new Mercedes, causing extensive damage. Sylvia denies damaging the car. Amongst other things the prosecution wish to rely upon a confession made by Sylvia when questioned by the police that she had damaged the car.

Sylvia says that she only confessed to damaging the car because she is a diabetic and had been held at the police station for 24 hours without access to her insulin. She felt unwell and was anxious to get home for an injection of insulin but did not inform the police about her diabetes as she has always been acutely embarrassed about her illness and refuses to tell anyone about it. She had asked to see a solicitor but he was delayed and the police continued to question her in his absence. She confessed to the offence before her solicitor arrived.

Advise the prosecution as to the admissibility of Sylvia's confession

Advice and the Answer

General guidance

There may be a number of issues that you need to consider if you face a question concerning the admissibility of confession evidence. The first thing you need to consider is whether the statement is in fact a confession i.e. whether it falls within the definition of a confession under s.82(1) of **PACE 1984**. Next you need to consider whether the confession is admissible under s.76(1) of **PACE** and finally whether the confession should be excluded under either s.76(2)(a) or (b) of **PACE** or, alternatively, might be excluded under **PACE** s.78.

The s.78 discretion applies only to prosecution evidence and can be used where it appears that admitting the evidence would, in the circumstances, have such an adverse effect on the fairness of the proceedings that it ought not to be admitted.

It is also worth noting that where a confession is found to be inadmissible, although the jury cannot be told about the confession itself (ss.75 and 76 **PACE 1984**), any evidence discovered as a result of the inadmissible confession will usually still be admissible (s.74 **PACE 1984**).

Model answer

A confession is admissible against its maker under s.76(1) of **PACE** if it is relevant to an issue in the proceedings unless the judge is required to exclude it under s.76(2). In order to determine the admissibility of Sylvia's confession the judge will hold a voir dire. The effect of s.76(2) is that the confession will not be admissible unless the prosecution can prove beyond reasonable doubt that it was not obtained as a result of oppression (s.76(2)(a)) or in consequence of anything said or done which, in the circumstances existing at the time, was likely to render unreliable any confession which Sylvia might make in consequence thereof (s.76(2)(b)). Thus, it is the manner in which the confession was obtained which determines its admissibility, not whether the confession may be true (*R. v Crampton*).

Oppression has a partial definition in s.76(8) as including "... torture, inhuman or degrading treatment, and the use or threat of violence (whether or not amounting to torture)". Clearly, Sylvia was not subjected to such treatment at the police station. However, as the statutory definition is not an all-encompassing definition, the courts have provided their own definition. In *R. v Fulling*, the court gave the word its *Oxford English Dictionary* meaning which is, "Exercise of authority in a burdensome, harsh or wrongful manner; unjust or cruel treatment of subjects, inferiors, etc.; the imposition of unreasonable or unjust burdens." Lord Lane C.J. took the view that improper conduct on the part of the interviewer was an essential ingredient of oppression as defined above. Sylvia did not have access to her insulin and was questioned in the absence of her solicitor. The failure to provide insulin would not constitute oppression as the police officers were not aware she was a diabetic and so there was no impropriety on their part in this regard. As for the questioning in the absence of her solicitor, the court stated, obiter, in *R. v Samuel*, that refusal to allow access to a solicitor, if accompanied by bad faith, might constitute oppression. Although a solicitor was in fact called in this case, Sylvia was questioned before he arrived which, unless properly authorised (of which there is no suggestion in the question), is contrary to s.58 of **PACE**. The court may treat this in the same way as if the police had refused to let Sylvia call a solicitor and, if the police acted in bad faith, this may amount to oppression. If it does, the confession will be excluded under s.76(2)(a) unless the prosecution can prove beyond a reasonable doubt that the confession was not obtained by the oppression (i.e. that there was no causal link between the two).

Should the judge determine that there was no oppression, or that if there was oppression that there was no causal link between the oppression and the confession, the prosecution will still be required to prove that the confession was not obtained in consequence of anything said or done which (in the circumstances existing at the time) was likely to render any confession so obtained unreliable (s.76(2)(b)). There is no statutory definition of unreliability but it is clear that impropriety is not required (*Fulling*). In approaching s.76(2)(b), the judge must consider four issues (*R. v Barry*; *R. v Proulx*), namely:

- whether anything relevant was said or done;
- the nature of the circumstances existing at the time when the thing was said or done;
- whether, in those circumstances, the thing said or done was likely to render any confession which the accused might have made in consequence of the thing said or done unreliable; and
- whether the confession was made in consequence of the thing said or done.

On the facts, the something said or done could be the questioning in the absence of a solicitor (*Samuel*). The failure to provide insulin could not constitute something said or done as the interviewing officers were unaware of Sylvia's diabetes (*R. v Goldenberg*). Her diabetes could, however, constitute a circumstance, despite the officers' ignorance of Sylvia's condition (*R. v Everett*), as could her lack of legal advice. Should the judge determine that something was said or done, the prosecution must prove beyond reasonable doubt either that the accused did not confess in consequence of it or that in the circumstances existing at the time it was not likely to render any confession that the accused might have made in consequence of the thing said or done unreliable. If they fail to do so, the confession must be excluded under s.76(2)(b).

If the confession is not excluded under s.76(2), it may still be excluded by the judge in the exercise of his discretion, either at common law or under s.78 of **PACE**. Section 82(3) preserves the discretion which existed at common law but since the enactment of **PACE**, the courts have tended to rely on their exclusionary discretion under s.78. Section 78 permits the judge to exclude evidence tendered by the prosecution if he considers that, having regard to all the circumstances, including the circumstances in which it was made, its admission would have such an adverse effect on the fairness of the proceedings that the judge ought not to admit it. In deciding whether to exercise his discretion, the judge may take into account the fact that there was a breach of **PACE** or the Codes of Practice. The police in this question appear to have breached s.58 of **PACE**. It seems that the judge is likely to exclude Sylvia's confession under **PACE** s.78 on the basis that there has been a significant and substantial breach of a requirement of **PACE**, though the existence of such a breach will not automatically result in exclusion under s.78 (*R. v Walsh*). Thus, the judge may decline to exercise his s.78 discretion if he is satisfied that the breach of s.58 did not adversely affect Sylvia's interests because she had the ability to cope with the interview and was aware of her legal rights (*R. v Alladice*). In contrast, if the judge decides that the breach of s.58 had significant practical consequences, the exercise of the s.78 exclusionary discretion would appear to be appropriate. Thus, if the court is of the opinion that Sylvia might not have confessed had she received legal advice as requested, the court is likely to exercise its s.78 exclusionary discretion so as to exclude her confession (*R. v Samuel*). Moreover, if the judge decides that the breach of s.58 was deliberate, this will be an additional factor which will be likely to persuade the court to exercise its s.78 discretion so as to exclude the confession (*R. v Walsh*).

If the judge admits the confession, the judge should direct the jury that they should ignore the confession if they consider that it was or may have been obtained by oppression or in consequence of something said or done which (in the circumstances existing at the time) was likely to render any confession so obtained unreliable (*R. v Mushtaq*).

Statutory Exceptions to the Hearsay Rule in Criminal Proceedings (other than Confessions)

Introduction

In Chapter 9 we considered when a statement will fall within the ambit of the hearsay rule. This chapter deals with some of the major statutory exceptions to the hearsay rule, created by the **Criminal Justice Act (CJA) 2003,** which permit the admission of hearsay evidence in criminal proceedings.

Further examples of statutory exceptions to the hearsay rule in criminal proceedings have already been considered in earlier chapters (i.e. those relating to the examination of witnesses, created by s.119 and s.120 of the 2003 Act were considered in Chapter 5, s.127 of the 2003 Act and section 30 of the **Criminal Justice Act 1988,** relating to expert evidence, were considered in Chapter 6, above, and those relating to confessions, created by s.76 and s.76A of **PACE,** were considered in Chapter 11, above). There are a variety of other minor statutory exceptions to the hearsay rule, consideration of which falls outside the scope of this book.

Moreover, s.118 of the 2003 Act preserved a number of common law exceptions to the hearsay rule, some of which were considered in Chapter 9, above, and one of which was considered in Chapter 6, above.

The statutory hearsay exceptions that the 2003 Act created are exceptions to the hearsay rule only. Consequently, as was seen in Chapter 9, above, they do not render admissible statements which are inadmissible because they fall within another exclusionary rule of evidence in addition to the hearsay rule (e.g. they do not render admissible hearsay statements which are irrelevant).

SITUATIONS WHERE A WITNESS IS UNAVAILABLE— SECTION 116

LEGISLATION HIGHLIGHTER

Section 116 of the **Criminal Justice Act 2003**

Section 116 permits the admission of a hearsay statement provided that the following three conditions are **all** satisfied:

(1) The oral evidence of the maker of the statement would be admissible as evidence of the matter stated. Thus, for example, if the maker could not have given direct oral testimony of the matter stated because his oral evidence would not have been relevant to an issue in the proceedings, the statement will be inadmissible under s.116 (*R. v T* (2006)).

(2) The maker of the statement is identified to the court's satisfaction. In *R. v Mayers* (2008), the Court of Appeal held that the evidence of an anonymous witness is not admissible under s.116.

(3) **One** of the conditions contained in s.116(2) for not calling the maker of the statement is satisfied. The conditions are (a) that the maker is dead **OR** (b) is unfit to be a witness by reason of his bodily or mental condition **OR** (c) is outside the United Kingdom and it is not reasonably practicable to secure his attendance **OR** (d) cannot be found, all reasonable steps having been taken to find him, **OR** (e) does not give oral evidence (or does not continue to give evidence) either at all or in connection with the relevant matter through fear and the court grants leave for the statement to be admitted in evidence.

When is a s.116(2) condition satisfied?

It appears that the party who wishes to adduce hearsay evidence under s.116 will bear the burden of proving that the evidence is admissible under s.116, the prosecution being required to do so beyond reasonable doubt (*R. v Acton JJ., Ex p. McMullen* (1990)), the defence on the balance of probabilities (*R. v Mattey and Queeley* (1995)). It seems that in order to discharge this burden, the party who wishes to adduce the hearsay evidence will be required to adduce admissible evidence to prove that the s.116 condition on which the party relies has been satisfied (*Neill v North Antrim Magistrates' Court* (1992)).

For example, in *R. (on the application of Meredith) v Harwich Justices* (2006), the Divisional Court held that a statement by a doctor that it would be in the best interests of a witness not to attend court in consequence of her depressive illness and panic attacks had not been sufficiently positive to prove that she was unfit to be a witness.

In *R. v C and K* (2006), where a foreign witness suddenly informed the police that he was no longer prepared to travel to England to give evidence, the Court of Appeal held that the judge should not have ruled at a preparatory hearing that the witness's evidence was admissible under s.116 and that further enquiries were required to determine why the witness had changed his mind. The Court of Appeal also indicated that the **PACE** s.78 exclusionary discretion was relevant in this context, the fairness of admitting the hearsay evidence depending in part on the efforts that should reasonably be taken either to secure the witness's attendance or to arrange a procedure via which the contents of the witness's statements could be clarified and challenged.

Fear

With regard to condition (e) (i.e. that the witness is unavailable through fear), s.116(3) provides that the term "fear" is to be widely construed and includes fear of the death or injury of another person and fear of financial loss. Where a party wishes to rely on this condition, s.116(2) provides that the leave of the court must be obtained. Section 116(4) provides that leave may be given only if the court considers that the statement ought to be admitted in the interests of justice.

In applying the interests of justice test, the court is directed by s.116(4) to consider any relevant circumstances but is specifically directed to consider the following specific matters:

(1) The contents of the statement.
(2) The risk that admitting or excluding the statement will result in unfairness to any party to the proceedings (and, in particular, how difficult it will be to challenge the statement if its maker does not give oral evidence).
(3) If appropriate, the fact that a special measures direction under **YJ&CEA** 1999 s.19 (see Chapter 5) could be made in relation to the maker of the statement.

In *R. v Davies* (2006), the Court of Appeal held that a judge had been entitled to find that a witness was in fear where, in one statement, the witness had indicated that she did not want to be face to face with the accused because she was frightened of the accused (who had held a knife to the witness' throat), and in a later statement had indicated that she wanted no further involvement in the case because she felt that there could be repercussions if the accused was sent to prison, and she did not want to cause her family problems.

In *R. v Doherty* (2006), the Court of Appeal held that a judge had been entitled to find that a witness was in fear where the witness had informed a police officer, via emails and a fax, that he was not prepared to give evidence for the prosecution because, in consequence of telephone calls to the witness and his wife by an unknown man who knew where the witness lived, the witness felt that his wife and child were at risk.

What happens if a s.116(2) condition was caused by the party who wishes to adduce the hearsay evidence?

Section 116(5) provides that where any of the five s.116(2) conditions is satisfied, the condition will be treated as not being satisfied if it is shown that the relevant circumstances were caused, either by the party who wishes to rely on the hearsay statement or by someone acting on his behalf, with the aim of preventing the maker of the hearsay statement from testifying. Thus, for example, where the reason why a defence witness who is overseas and will not return is that the accused or his associates have "persuaded" the witness not to return, the effect of s.116(5) is that the defence will not be entitled to adduce the witness's hearsay evidence under s.116 (though the prosecution would potentially be entitled to do so).

Exclusionary discretion

Where hearsay evidence is admissible for the prosecution under s.116 (or under any other statutory or common law hearsay exception) its admissibility will be subject to the possibility of exclusion in the court's discretion under **PACE** s.78 (which was considered in Chapter 11, above), the operation of which in the context of the hearsay provisions of the **CJA 2003** was preserved by s.126 of the **CJA 2003** (*Gian v CPS* (2009)) though a defence application under s.78 will only be successful if admitting the hearsay evidence would have such an adverse effect on the fairness of the proceedings that the court ought not to admit it (*R. v Musone* (2007)).

. . . .
BUSINESS AND OTHER DOCUMENTS—SECTION 117

LEGISLATION HIGHLIGHTER

Section 117 of the **Criminal Justice Act 2003**

Section 117 permits the admission of a hearsay statement provided the following requirements are satisfied:

(1) The statement must be contained in a document. A document may (under s.134) be "anything in which information of any description is recorded".

(2) Oral evidence would be admissible as evidence of the matter stated. Thus, for example, as was seen to be the case under s.116, s.117 will not make irrelevant hearsay evidence admissible.

(3) The document (or the part of the document that contains the statement) was created or received by a person in the course of a trade, business, profession or other occupation, or as the holder of a paid or unpaid office.

(4) The person who supplied the information that the statement contains had (or may reasonably be supposed to have had) personal knowledge of the matters dealt with. Section 117(3) provides that this may be the same person as the person who created or received the document or may be a different person.

(5) If the information was supplied to the person who created or received the document from the person who supplied the information via an intermediary or intermediaries, the intermediaries must have received the information in the course of a trade, business, profession or other occupation, or as the holder of a paid or unpaid office.

In *Maher v DPP* (2005), a witness saw an accident in a car park in which a parked car was damaged and left a note of the registration number of the car that had collided with the parked car under the windscreen wiper of the damaged car. The owner of the parked car telephoned the police, and a clerk recorded the registration number. The Divisional Court held that the record made by the clerk should not have been admitted in subsequent criminal proceedings under s.117 because the owner of the parked car (the intermediary) had not transmitted the information to the clerk in the course of a trade, business, profession, occupation or office.

The additional requirement

An additional requirement is imposed by s.117(4) and (5), but this additional requirement only applies if the statement was prepared for the purposes of pending or contemplated criminal proceedings or for the purposes of a criminal investigation. Such a statement will not be admissible under s.117 unless **EITHER** one of the s.116(2) conditions for not calling the person who supplied the information is satisfied **OR** the person who supplied the information cannot reasonably be expected (having regard to the time since the person supplied the information and to all other circumstances) to have any recollection of the matters dealt with in his statement.

Section 117 and statements of doubtful reliability

The court, under s.117(6) and (7), may direct that a statement is not admissible under s.117 if the court is satisfied that the reliability of the statement as evidence for the purpose for which the statement is tendered is doubtful because of the contents of the statement, the source of the information, the way or circumstances in which the information was supplied or received or the way or circumstances in which the document was created or received.

MULTIPLE HEARSAY—SECTION 121

DEFINITION CHECKPOINT
Section 121 imposes an additional requirement for the admissibility of multiple hearsay. Multiple hearsay is where a statement which is itself hearsay is used to prove that another hearsay statement was made. For example, W makes a statement to X who repeats it to Y. Z overhears X repeating the statement to Y. The repetition of the statement in court by Y or Z would be multiple hearsay.

Section 121 provides that a hearsay statement is only admissible to prove that an earlier hearsay statement was made (i.e. s.121 provides that multiple hearsay is only admissible) if one of the following three **alternative** conditions is satisfied:

(1) A hearsay statement is admissible to prove that an earlier hearsay statement was made if either of the hearsay statements is admissible under s.117 (see above), s.119 (which concerns inconsistent statements made by witnesses see Chapter 5, above) or s.120 (which concerns previous consistent statements made by witnesses see Chapter 5, above).

(2) A hearsay statement is admissible to prove that an earlier hearsay statement was made if all the parties to the proceedings so agree.

(3) A hearsay statement is admissible to prove that an earlier hearsay statement was made if the value of the hearsay evidence, taking into account how reliable the hearsay statements appear to be, is so high that the interests of justice require the later hearsay statement to be admissible for the purpose of proving the earlier hearsay statement.

The Court of Appeal in *R. v Walker* (2007) recognised that a judge should not apply s.121 without first considering whether the statements that constitute the multiple hearsay are admissible under hearsay exceptions. In *Walker*, the hearsay exception in question was s.114(1)(d) (which is considered immediately below) and the Court of Appeal indicated that s.121(3) "imposes a higher threshold" than s.114(1)(d).

In *Maher v DPP*, the facts of which were considered above, the Divisional Court held that the hearsay evidence that the case concerned was admissible under s.114(1)(d) (which is considered below) and s.121(1)(c), the admission of the multiple hearsay being in the interests of justice.

In *R. v Musone*, two prisoners were charged with murdering a third prisoner in a cell. The victim, before he died, named the person who had stabbed him to a fourth prisoner. The fourth prisoner refused to give evidence at the murder trial but the Court of Appeal held that the judge had properly admitted evidence, under s.114(1)(d) and s.121(1)(c), of a statement that the fourth prisoner had made to a prison officer in which the fourth prisoner had repeated the statement that the victim had made to him.

INCLUSIONARY DISCRETION—SECTION 114(d)

LEGISLATION HIGHLIGHTER

Section 114(1)(d) of the Criminal Justice Act 2003

Under s.114(1)(d) the court possesses discretion to admit hearsay evidence in the interests of justice. Thus, even where no other statutory or common law hearsay exception is applicable, the court may grant leave to admit an otherwise inadmissible hearsay statement where satisfied that it is in the interests of justice to do so.

In determining whether to admit a hearsay statement under s.114(1)(d), s.114(2) requires the court to consider a number of specific factors (as well as any others it considers relevant). Essentially, the specific factors comprise:

(a) the probative value of the hearsay statement (assuming it to be true) in relation to the matter in issue;
(b) what other evidence can be given in relation to the matter in issue;
(c) the importance of the matter in issue;
(d) the circumstances in which the hearsay statement was made;
(e) the reliability of the maker of the hearsay statement;
(f) the reliability of the evidence of the making of the hearsay statement;
(g) whether (and if not, why not) oral evidence of the matter stated can be given;
(h) how much difficulty would be involved in challenging the hearsay statement; and

(i)   the extent to which the difficulty in challenging the hearsay statement would be likely to prejudice the party facing that difficulty.

Whilst s.114(2) requires the court to consider these specific factors, the court is not required to reach a specific conclusion in relation to each individual factor but, rather, must take them (plus any other relevant factors) into consideration and must give each appropriate weight in reaching a conclusion concerning the admissibility of the evidence (*R. v Taylor* (2006)). In *R. v Z* (2009) the Court of Appeal recognised that applying s.114(1)(d) too generously will negate the s.116 admissibility conditions (which were considered above) but that if s.114(1)(d) is applied too cautiously it will be ineffective. Thus, for example, the Court of Appeal has indicated that it would rarely be appropriate to admit the hearsay evidence of a witness who is alive, well, able to testify and not in fear just because the witness is reluctant to testify (*R. v Z* (2009). Moreover, the Court of Appeal has indicated that the court will need to exercise considerable care in circumstances in which hearsay evidence that the prosecution wishes to adduce under s.114(1)(d) forms the prosecution case against the accused and would be difficult for the defence to challenge (*R. v Y* (2008)).

For example, in *R. v CW and T* (2010), the Court of Appeal held that the hearsay evidence of a child sexual offence complainant should not have been admitted under s.114(1)(d) in circumstances in which the complainant was available to testify. In *R. v Finch* (2007), the Court of Appeal held that the trial judge had correctly ruled that evidence of a confession made by a co-accused who had pleaded guilty was not admissible for the accused under **PACE** s.76A (see Chapter 11, above) and the Court of Appeal also upheld the judge's decision that it was not in the interests of justice to admit the evidence under s.114(1)(d) because the co-accused was available to give evidence.

DEFINITION CHECKPOINT

It would appear that the authorities suggest that the s.114(1)(d) inclusionary discretion should only be used as a last resort where no other exception to the hearsay rule applies. It is therefore important to note that before attempting to use the s.114(1)(d) inclusionary discretion you should seek to exhaust all other options (both statutory and common law) first. In particular, it seems that it will rarely be appropriate to use s.114(1)(d) to admit the hearsay evidence of a witness who is available to testify but is reluctant to do so.

DISCRETION TO EXCLUDE HEARSAY EVIDENCE—SECTION 126

The court has a discretion under s.126(1) to exclude hearsay evidence where satisfied that the case for excluding the hearsay evidence, taking into account the danger that its admission would result in undue waste of time, substantially outweighs the case for admitting the hearsay evidence, taking into account the value of the hearsay evidence. The purpose of the s.126(1) discretion appears to be to permit the court to exclude hearsay evidence (whether tendered by prosecution or defence) which is otherwise admissible under a statutory or common law hearsay exception if the evidence is of limited probative value and admitting it would waste the court's time. Thus, for example, it seems that the court should use the s.126(1) discretion to exclude hearsay evidence if its admission would waste the court's time by diverting attention of the jury towards "satellite disputes" (*R. v Horncastle*).

Apart from the s.126 discretion, s.126(2) makes clear that the court retains its discretion (considered in Chapter 11, above), both under **PACE** s.78 and at common law, to exclude prosecution evidence, which includes evidence which would otherwise be admissible under a hearsay exception. Thus, the court could exclude hearsay evidence tendered by the prosecution either if it would have such an adverse affect on the fairness of the proceedings that it should not be admitted or if its probative value is outweighed by its prejudicial effect.

REQUIRED CAPABILITY OF THE MAKER/SUPPLIER, ETC. OF A HEARSAY STATEMENT—SECTION 123

Section 123 provides that a hearsay statement will not be admissible under s.116 (see above), s.119 (see Chapter 5, above) or s.120 (see Chapter 5, above) if it was made by a person who lacked the required capability at the time the statement was made. Similarly, a hearsay statement will not be admissible under s.117 (see above) if the person who supplied or received the information, the person who created or received the document or any intermediaries via whom the information contained in the statement passed, lacked the required capability (or, if the person cannot be identified, cannot reasonably be assumed to have the required capability) at the time the information was supplied/received or the document was created/received.

Under s.123(3), a person has the required capability if the person is capable both of understanding questions put to the person about the matters stated and of giving answers to those questions which can be understood.

Section 123(4) provides that where the issue of required capability is raised, the party seeking to adduce the hearsay evidence bears the burden of proving that person's capability on the balance of probabilities. Proceedings to determine the issue will take place in the absence of the jury and expert evidence and evidence from a person to whom the statement was made may be received for the purpose of determining the issue.

Section 123 does not apply where hearsay evidence is tendered under s.114(1)(d). In *R. v SJ* (2009), the hearsay evidence of a witness who was two and a half years old was properly admitted under s.114(1)(d) (the Court of Appeal did not refer to s.123).

CREDIBILITY—SECTION 124

Under s.124, where the maker of a hearsay statement does not give oral evidence in connection to the subject matter of the hearsay statement, the following evidence is admissible to attack his credibility:

(1) Evidence which would have been admissible as relevant to his credibility had he given oral evidence.

(2) Evidence of matters (i.e. of collateral matters see Chapter 5, above) which could have been put to him during cross-examination had he given oral evidence but of which the cross-examining party could not have adduced evidence. Evidence of such matters may only be given under s.124, however, with the leave of the court.

(3) Evidence which tends to prove that he made a statement inconsistent with the hearsay statement is admissible in order to show that he has contradicted himself.

Where a statement is admitted under s.117, the effect of s.124(4) is that s.124 applies to the person who supplied or received the information, to the person who created or received the document and to any intermediaries via whom the information contained in the statement passed.

If the admission of evidence under s.124 results in the making of an allegation against the maker of the hearsay statement, the court, under s.124(3), may allow a party to adduce evidence to deny or answer the allegation.

PROOF OF STATEMENTS IN DOCUMENTS—SECTION 133

Section 133 provides that a statement contained in a document which is admissible in evidence in criminal proceedings may be proved either by producing the document itself or by producing a copy thereof, the document or copy being authenticated in a manner approved by the court. Under s.134, a copy is "anything onto which information recorded in the document has been copied, by whatever means and whether directly or indirectly" and a document is "anything in which information of any description is recorded".

Where an original document is not readily available to a party, the court may permit the party to prove its contents at common law by relying upon the oral evidence of a witness who read the document (*Masquerade Music Ltd v Springsteen* (2001)). Whether the court will be prepared to admit such evidence appears to depend upon the weight of the evidence (*Masquerade Music Ltd v Springsteen*).

STOPPING THE CASE WHERE EVIDENCE IS UNCONVINCING—SECTION 125

Section 125 applies to jury trials only. Its effect is that the trial judge must either direct an acquittal or order a retrial where, at any time following the conclusion of the case for the prosecution, he is satisfied that the case against the accused is based wholly or partly on a hearsay statement which is so unconvincing that, considering its importance to the case against the accused, the conviction would be unsafe.

KEY CASE

R. v JOYCE (2005)
Three eyewitnesses had made statements to the police, incriminating the accused, prior to a trial, but retracted their statements before the trial, indicating that they had made mistakes. At the trial, the witnesses gave evidence which was inconsistent with their police statements, one witness admitting the making of the inconsistent statement and the other two (being treated as hostile witnesses) having their previous inconsistent statements proved under s.3 of the **CPA 1865** (see Chapter 5, above). The judge admitted the inconsistent statements under the hearsay exception created by s.119 of the **CJA 2003** (see Chapter 5, above). The defence asserted that the judge should direct an acquittal under s.125, but the judge left the case to the jury. The Court of Appeal upheld the judge's rulings.

RULES OF COURT

Part 34 of the **CrimPR** contains rules of court which apply when a party to criminal proceedings wishes to adduce hearsay evidence under certain provisions of the **CJA 2003**, namely, under s.114(1)(d), s.116, s.117 or s.121. Parties who wish to adduce hearsay evidence under any of these provisions must give notice to the court and the other parties as required by **CrimPR** Pt 34. Where a party receives such notice and wishes to oppose the introduction of the hearsay evidence, the party must serve notice on the court and the other parties as required by **CrimPR** Pt 34. In the absence of such an objection, **CrimPR** Pt 34 provides that the hearsay evidence is to be treated as if it were admissible by agreement.

The effect of s.132 of the 2003 Act is that if a party who wishes to tender hearsay evidence fails to comply with the **CrimPR** Pt 34 notice requirements, the hearsay evidence is only admissible with the leave of the court, if the court gives leave, the court or jury may still draw inferences from the failure (i.e. the court may infer that the party has been trying to prevent the other parties from investigating the hearsay evidence) and the failure may have costs implications. The court should not refuse leave merely for the purpose of disciplining a party for failing to comply with **CrimPR** Pt 34 but leave may properly be refused where admitting hearsay evidence in the context of a failure to comply with **CrimPR** Pt 34 would result in unfairness that could not be cured by adjourning the proceedings (*R. v Musone*). Moreover, it seems that where a prosecution failure to give notice was deliberate, the court will be likely to exclude the hearsay evidence (*Gian v CPS* (2009)).

CrimPR Pt 34 provides that the court may shorten or extend the time limits that it imposes and may dispense with the notice requirement. Moreover, a party may waive the right to receive notice to introduce hearsay evidence.

ARE THERE ANY HUMAN RIGHTS IMPLICATIONS OF ADMITTING HEARSAY EVIDENCE FOR THE PROSECUTION?

The admission of hearsay evidence for the prosecution may, in appropriate circumstances, be capable of giving rise to a violation of art.6 of the **European Convention on Human Rights**. This is so because art.6(3)(d) gives the accused the right to examine, or to have examined, the witness against him.

As was seen in Chapter 11 above, the court (under **PACE** s.78) possesses discretion to exclude evidence tendered by the prosecution the admission of which would have such an adverse affect on the fairness of the proceedings that it ought not to be admitted. Moreover, under s.3 of the **Human Rights Act 1998**, the court is under a duty to read and give effect to legislation, where possible, in a Convention-compatible way.

The court will not automatically be required to exercise its exclusionary discretion so as to exclude hearsay evidence tendered by the prosecution in circumstances in which the defence have not had the opportunity to cross-examine the maker of the hearsay statement, however, because admitting hearsay evidence for the prosecution will not automatically render the accused's trial unfair for the purposes of art.6. Rather, in determining whether art.6 requires the exclusion of hearsay evidence in such circumstances, the question for the court will be whether admitting the evidence is compatible with a fair trial (*R. v Cole; R. v Keet* (2007)).

KEY CASE

R. v HORNCASTLE (2009)
The Supreme Court held that the fact that the case against the accused is wholly or decisively based on the hearsay evidence of an unavailable witness does not necessarily mean that there has been a violation of art.6. In reaching its decision, the Supreme Court took into account the existence of the admissibility conditions imposed by the CJA 2003 (e.g. the s.116 admissibility conditions) and of the safeguards contained in the CJA 2003 Act (e.g. the safeguards created by ss.124, 125 and 126, including the preservation of **PACE** s.78 by s.126). Their Lordships also recognised that the prosecution bear the legal burden of proof and that the judge is under a duty to direct the jury concerning the dangers of hearsay evidence. To the extent to which the decision of the European Court of Human Rights in *Al-Khawaja v United Kingdom* (2009) was authority for the proposition that the fact that the case against the accused is wholly or decisively based on the hearsay evidence of an unavailable witness will inevitably result in a violation of art.6, the Supreme Court declined to follow the decision in *Al-Khawaja* on the basis that the European Court of Human Rights had not sufficiently appreciated the safeguards that exist in English Law.

Revision checklist

You should now know and understand:

- the operation of the s.116 of the **Criminal Justice Act 2003**;

- the operation of s.117 of the **Criminal Justice Act 2003**;

- the additional requirements for the admission of multiple hearsay imposed by s.121 of the **Criminal Justice Act 2003**;

- the operation of the s.114(1)(d) inclusionary discretion;

- the additional requirements necessary for the admission of hearsay evidence and the discretion to exclude hearsay evidence;

- the human rights implications of admitting hearsay evidence.

QUESTION AND ANSWER

The Question

Henry has been charged with the murder of Mandy and is pleading not guilty. The prosecution allege that Henry shot Mandy, his estranged wife, as she walked home from her night class. Henry denies that he saw Mandy on the evening when she was shot. The prosecution wish to call Jane, who also attended the night class, who will testify that as she left the night class she saw a man walk up to Mandy and Mandy said "Hello Henry, what do you want?". The prosecution also wish to call Tom who will testify that he found Mandy after she had been shot and, before she lapsed into unconsciousness, she said to Tom, "It was my husband Henry who shot me". Finally, the prosecution wish to adduce in evidence the notebook of PC King, a police officer. PC King attended Mandy in hospital, several days after the shooting, during a brief period when she was conscious and wrote down in his notebook Mandy's statement in which she named Henry as her assailant, Mandy reading the written statement through and signing it. Mandy died shortly after making this statement and PC King was killed later on the same day whilst trying to prevent a bank robbery.

Advise the prosecution as to the admissibility of the evidence of Jane, Tom and the notebook of PC King.

Advice and the Answer

The evidence of Jane

Essentially, a hearsay statement is a statement not made in oral evidence in the proceedings which is relied upon as evidence of a matter stated (see **CJA 2003** s.114). Subject to the exceptions recognised by s.114 of the **CJA 2003** (which are considered below), hearsay evidence is not admissible in criminal proceedings. Jane's evidence is not a hearsay statement, however, because under s.115(3) the hearsay provisions of the 2003 Act do not apply to a matter stated unless at least one of the purposes of the maker of the statement is either to cause a person to believe the matter stated or to cause a person to act or a machine to operate upon the basis that the matter is as stated. Here, it does not appear that when Mandy said "Hello Henry" she did so with the purpose of making anyone believe that the man to whom she was talking was called Henry (or making a person act or a machine operate upon that basis). Consequently, if the prosecution wish to rely upon Mandy's statement as evidence identifying the man she met as Henry, it is submitted that the statement is not hearsay evidence and will be admissible for this purpose provided (as is clearly the case on these facts) that it is relevant to an issue in the proceedings.

The evidence of Tom

Mandy's statement to Tom was not made whilst she was giving oral evidence in the proceedings and, presumably, will be relied upon by the prosecution as evidence of the matters stated (i.e. to prove that it was Henry who murdered her). Thus, since Mandy presumably made the statement for the purpose of making Tom believe the matter stated, it appears that the statement is a hearsay statement and will only be admissible under s.114 of the **CJA 2003** if the parties agree to its admission, if it is admissible under a statutory exception to the hearsay rule, if it is admissible under a preserved common law exception to the hearsay rule or if the court admits it in the exercise of its inclusionary discretion under s.114(1)(d). The statement might be admissible under a common law exception to the hearsay rule, preserved by s.118 of the 2003 Act, as forming part of the *res gestae*. Specifically, it might be admissible if the judge is satisfied that Mandy was so emotionally overpowered by the stabbing at the time when she made the statement (i.e. her mind was so dominated by the "exciting event") that the possibility of concoction or distortion can be disregarded (*R. v Andrews*). When considering the admissibility of the evidence, the trial judge should pay particular attention to any factors which might increase the risk of concoction (such as whether Mandy had a grudge against Henry) and to any special factors which might give rise to the possibility of error (e.g. whether Mandy was intoxicated at the time when she made the statement) (*R. v Andrews*).

The statement may also be admissible under s.116 of the **CJA 2003**. Essentially, this will be the case if Mandy could have given oral evidence of the matter stated, she is identified to the court's satisfaction and one of the s.116 reasons for not calling Mandy is satisfied. Here, there appears to be no reason why Mandy's oral evidence of the matters stated would not have been admissible, it appears that she can be identified to the court's satisfaction and one of the s.116 reasons for not calling her is satisfied (i.e. she is dead). Thus, the statement appears to be admissible under s.116.

Further, even if neither of the hearsay exceptions considered above were applicable, the hearsay statement would potentially be admissible, in the interests of justice, under the exclusionary discretion created by s.114(1)(d). In considering whether to admit the hearsay statement under s.114(1)(d), the court would be required (amongst other relevant matters) to consider the factors specified by s.114(2).

It should be noted that the trial judge possesses discretion to exclude evidence tendered by the prosecution in the exercise of his discretion under s.78 of the **PACE** if its admission would adversely effect the fairness of the trial such that it should be excluded. It is possible that admitting hearsay evidence for the prosecution may render the accused's trial unfair for the purposes of art.6 of the European Convention on Human Rights (which gives the accused the right to examine or have examined the witnesses for the prosecution). It should be noted, however, that the Supreme Court has held that if hearsay evidence is properly admitted under the provisions of the **CJA 2003** and subject to the various statutory and common law safeguards that relate to the admission of hearsay evidence, the fact that the case against the accused is wholly or mainly based on hearsay evidence does not mean that the accused's trial will inherently be unfair (*R. v Horncastle*).

PC King's notebook

Mandy's statement to PC King was not made whilst she was giving oral evidence in the proceedings and, presumably, will be relied upon by the prosecution as evidence of the matters stated (i.e. to prove that it was Henry who murdered her). Thus, it appears that the statement is a hearsay statement and will only be admissible, under s.114 of the **CJA 2003** if the parties agree to its admission, if it is admissible under a statutory exception to the hearsay rule, if it is admissible under a preserved common law exception to the hearsay rule or if the court admits it in the exercise of its inclusionary discretion under s.114(1)(d).

The preserved common law res gestae hearsay exception, considered above, does not appear to apply to the hearsay statement contained in the notebook because, after several days, it appears to be unlikely that Mandy would still have been so emotionally over-powered by the stabbing that the possibility of concoction or distor-tion can be disregarded.

The **CJA 2003** s.116 hearsay exception, also considered above, appears to apply because there appears to be no reason why Mandy's oral evidence of the matters stated would not have been admissible, it appears that she can be identified to the court's satisfaction and one of the s.116 reasons for not calling her is satisfied (i.e. she is dead).

The hearsay exception created by s.117 of the 2003 Act also appears to apply because the statement is contained in a document, oral evidence would be admissible to prove the matters stated, the supplier of information (Mandy) presumably had personal knowledge of the matters stated and the person who created the document (PC King) did so as the holder of the office of constable. Because the statement was presumably prepared for the purposes of a criminal investigation it appears that one of the statutory reasons for not calling Mandy must be satisfied, but since she is dead this is not a problem. It should be noted, however, that, under s.117(6) and (7), the court possesses discretion to determine that the hearsay statement will not be admissible under s.117 if satisfied that its reliability is doubtful.

Further, even if none of the three hearsay exceptions considered above were applicable, the hearsay statement would potentially be admissible, in the interests of justice, under the exclusionary discre-tion created by s.114(1)(d). In considering whether to admit the hearsay statement under s.114(1)(d), the court would be required (amongst other relevant matters) to consider the factors specified by s.114(2).

Moreover, prior to admitting the hearsay evidence contained in the notebook, the judge should (as was indicated in relation to Tom's hearsay evidence, above) consider the exercise of the **PACE** s.78 exclusionary discretion. Again, as was indicated above, the Supreme Court in Horncastle held that the fact that the case against the accused is wholly or mainly based on hearsay evidence does not mean that the accused's trial will inherently be unfair.

Finally, it should be noted that, under s.133 of the 2003 Act, a statement contained in a document may be proved either by produ-cing the original or by producing a copy, authenticated in a manner approved by the court. Here, the original notebook is available and, consequently, the statement may be proved by producing it.

Evidence of Character

Introduction

In this chapter, we will consider three topics.

First the extent to which the accused in a criminal trial can adduce evidence of his good character and the nature of judicial directions where such evidence is adduced.

Secondly, the nature of evidence of bad character under the **Criminal Justice Act (CJA) 2003** and the "gateways", created by the 2003 Act, through which evidence of the bad character either of the accused or of other witnesses may be admitted in criminal proceedings.

Finally, the nature of those circumstances in which evidence of character is admissible in civil proceedings as "similar fact evidence".

EVIDENCE OF THE ACCUSED'S GOOD CHARACTER

Admissibility of evidence of good character

At common law the general rule is that the accused is only entitled to adduce evidence of their general reputation as evidence of good character (i.e. as a general rule, evidence of specific examples of the accused's good character is not admissible).

KEY CASE

R. v ROWTON (1865)
A restrictive approach to the admissibility of evidence of the accused's good character was adopted in the leading case of *R. v Rowton* (1865). The court held that only evidence of the accused's general reputation in the community would be admissible. Thus, an accused could not call witnesses to testify or, through his counsel, cross-examine prosecution witnesses, regarding specific examples of his good deeds or their favourable opinion of him.

Rowton has never been overruled but has been applied flexibly by the courts. See, for example, *R. v Redgrave* (1981) in which the accused was charged with importuning for immoral purposes. Although the accused was not permitted to adduce photographs of himself with women and love letters in support of his contention that he was heterosexual, the Court of Appeal stated that he might, at the court's discretion, have been allowed to adduce evidence to show that he had a normal sexual relationship with his female partner.

How should the judge direct the jury where the accused adduces evidence of good character?
This depends on whether or not the accused chooses to testify.

KEY CASE

R. V VYE (1993)
R. v Vye considered the relevance of good character evidence where the accused chooses to testify. If the accused chooses to testify, evidence of the accused's good character is relevant in two ways;

(1) It is relevant to the accused's credibility (i.e. the jury should be directed to take the accused's good character into account in the accused's favour when deciding whether they believe the accused's testimony).

(2) It is relevant to the likelihood of the accused's guilt (i.e. the jury should be directed to take the accused's good character into account in the accused's favour when deciding whether the accused committed the offence with which the accused is charged).

An accused who is of good character is entitled to a direction by the judge on the relevance of his good character even if he is jointly charged with a co-accused who is of bad character, though it may be appropriate for the judge to direct the jury to the effect that they should not treat the absence of evidence of the co-accused's good character as evidence against the co-accused (*R. v Vye*).

What is the position if the accused chooses not to testify?
If the accused chooses not to testify, it will not be necessary to direct the jury concerning the relevance of the accused's good character to credibility unless the accused relies on the exculpatory parts of a mixed statement (see Chapter 11, above) which has been admitted in evidence (*R. v Vye*). Even if the credibility limb of the good character direction is not given, however, it will still be necessary for the judge to direct the jury concerning the relevance of the accused's good character to the likelihood of the accused's guilt.

> **DEFINITION CHECKPOINT**
>
> An accused who testifies in their defence is entitled to a direction about the relevance of their good character to BOTH their <u>credibility</u> and their <u>guilt</u>.
>
> Where the accused does not testify they are not entitled to the credibility limb of the direction (unless evidence of exculpatory statements that the accused made to the police in the course of making a confession is admitted) but are still entitled to a direction about the relevance of their good character to their guilt.

Does the judge possess discretion not to give, or to qualify, a good character direction?

The trial judge possesses discretion not to give a good character direction where the judge is satisfied that it would be an "insult to common sense" to do so (*R. v Aziz* (1995)). Equally, the judge possesses discretion to qualify a good character direction in order to give the jury a "fair and balanced picture" (*R. v Aziz*). A judge might, for example, find it necessary not to give, or to qualify, a good character direction in circumstances in which an accused who adduces evidence of good character has previous convictions or where, as in *Aziz*, the accused has admitted during the trial that he has engaged in serious criminal behaviour similar to the offence with which he is charged. The fact that the accused has previous convictions will, however, not necessarily require the judge not to give, or to qualify, the good character direction. It may be, for example, that in the context of the age and/or nature of the accused's convictions it is still appropriate to give the accused the benefit of a full good character direction even though he has previous convictions, though the jury should not be given a misleading direction (*R. v Gray* (2004)).

In *R. v Gray*, the accused, being charged with murder, made the jury aware of his previous convictions for road traffic offences, which were his only convictions, and of his involvement in non-fatal offences against the person, committed against the murder victim. The Court of Appeal held that the jury should have been directed concerning the relevance of the accused's good character to his credibility and should have been given a qualified version of the limb of the good character direction relating to the likelihood that a person of good character is guilty of the offence charged.

EVIDENCE OF BAD CHARACTER IN CRIMINAL PROCEEDINGS

The common law rules that previously governed the admissibility of evidence of bad character in criminal proceedings were abolished by s.99 of the **CJA 2003**. The only exception is that s.99 and s.118 preserve the common law rule

under which a person's bad character may be proved by evidence of reputation (though this preserved common law rule will only be relevant where
evidence of the person's bad character is admissible under provisions of the
CJA 2003).

The **CJA 2003** also repealed s.1(3) of the **Criminal Evidence Act 1898**,
which formerly concerned the admissibility of evidence of the accused's bad
character in criminal proceedings.

The admissibility of evidence of bad character in criminal proceedings
is now governed by the bad character provisions of the **CJA 2003** (contained
in Chapter 1 of Pt 11 of the 2003 Act) which are considered below.

What is evidence of bad character?

LEGISLATION HIGHLIGHTER

The definition of bad character is found in s.98 of the **Criminal Justice
Act 2003**

"98 "Bad character"
References in this Chapter to evidence of a person's "bad character"
are to evidence of, or of a disposition towards, misconduct on his part,
other than evidence which—
(a) has to do with the alleged facts of the offence with which the
    defendant is charged, or
(b) is evidence of misconduct in connection with the investigation or
    prosecution of that offence."

Under s.98 of the **CJA 2003**, evidence of a person's bad character means
either evidence of misconduct or evidence of a disposition towards misconduct, but s.98(a) provides that evidence of bad character does not include
evidence which has to do with the alleged facts of the offence with which the
accused is charged and s.98(b) provides that evidence of bad character does
not include evidence of misconduct in connection with the investigation or
prosecution of the offence with which the accused is charged. Misconduct is
defined in s.112 as "the commission of an offence or other reprehensible
behaviour".

Thus, evidence of a person's bad character does not merely include
evidence of the person's previous convictions but also includes, for example,
evidence of offences allegedly committed by the person in respect of which
the person has never been convicted and evidence of reprehensible behaviour on the part of the person which does not amount to an offence. For
example, in *R. v Moran* (2007), evidence of the accused's bad character took

the form of CCTV evidence showing that he had committed a previous offence with which he had never been charged and in *R. v Rossi* (2009)), evidence of the accused's bad character took the form of evidence of his "reprehensible behaviour" in following boys into public toilets.

Section 98(a) provides that evidence which has to do with the alleged facts of the offence with which the accused is charged does not amount to evidence of the accused's bad character. Thus, in *R. v Machado* (2006), the Court of Appeal held that evidence that the victim of an alleged robbery had offered to supply the accused with drugs immediately prior to the alleged commission of the alleged robbery was not evidence of the victim's bad character (and should have been admissible to support the accused's defence) because it had to do with the alleged facts of the offence with which the accused was charged. In order for evidence of misconduct to have to do with the alleged facts of the offence with which the accused is charged, however, it seems that there must be a nexus in time between the offence and the misconduct and, thus, for example, the mere fact that evidence of other misconduct helps to identify the accused as the person who committed the offence with which the accused is charged does not mean that the evidence "has to do" with the alleged facts of the offence with which the accused is charged for the purposes of s.98(a) (*R. v Tirnaveanu* (2007)). Where such a nexus does exist, even the accused's previous convictions may not amount to evidence of bad character on the basis that they have to do with the alleged facts of the offence with which the accused is charged. Thus, in *R. v Watson* (2006), the accused was charged with rape and his previous conviction for assault occasioning actual bodily harm related to an incident that had taken place on the same day as the alleged rape, the rape complainant having been the victim of the assault of which the accused had already been convicted. The Court of Appeal held that the previous conviction was not evidence of the accused's bad character and was admissible at common law, their Lordships rejecting the appellant's submission that the conviction should have been excluded under s.78 of the **Police and Criminal Evidence Act 1984**.

Section 98(b) provides that evidence of misconduct in connection with investigation or prosecution of the offence with which the accused is charged does not amount to evidence of bad character. Thus, it seems that evidence that the accused told lies to the police and evidence that the police fabricated evidence against the accused would not amount to evidence of the accused's bad character, provided that the lies or fabrication of evidence allegedly were told/took place in the course of the investigation of the offence with which the accused is charged.

The effect of s.112(2) of the **CJA 2003** is that where the accused is charged with two or more offences in the same proceedings, each offence is, for the purposes of the bad character provisions of the 2003 Act, treated as if it was charged in separate proceedings. Thus, in *R. v Chopra* (2007), where the accused was charged with indecently touching three different complainants on three different occasions, evidence that the accused indecently touched the first complainant was evidence of the accused's bad character in relation to the offences concerning the second and third complainants, evidence that the accused indecently touched the second complainant was evidence of the accused's bad character in relation to the offences concerning the first and third complainants and evidence that the accused indecently touched the third complainant was evidence of the accused's bad character in relation to the offences concerning the first and second complainants.

It should be noted that where the accused is charged with two or more offences in the same proceedings, s.101(3), which is considered below, does not apply as though each offence was charged in separate proceedings and, thus, the judge, when applying the s.101(3) fairness test (see below), is entitled to consider all of the offences with which the accused is charged.

If the accused is charged with several offences which arise out of the same facts, it seems that evidence relating to one count will not be evidence of the accused's bad character in relation to another, due to the operation of s.98(a), which was considered above. It is submitted that the position equates with that which was encountered, above, in relation to *R. v Watson*, which concerned the admissibility of the assault count in the context of the re-trial of the rape count, both counts having originally been tried together.

Is the admissibility of evidence of misconduct always governed by the bad character provisions of the CJA 2003?

Where evidence of misconduct amounts to evidence of bad character, its admissibility will be governed by the bad character provisions of the **CJA 2003**, which are considered below. Thus, for example, the admissibility of evidence of the accused's previous convictions and (as in *R. v Chopra*) the admissibility of evidence of other offences with which the accused is charged in the proceedings will be governed by the bad character provisions of the **CJA 2003**.

Where evidence of misconduct does not amount to evidence of bad character, its admissibility will be governed by the common law test of relevance (i.e. the evidence will be admissible if it is either capable of increasing or reducing the probability that a fact in issue exists see Chapter 12, above), though, if the evidence is tendered by the prosecution, its admissibility will be subject to the exercise of the **PACE** s.78 exclusionary discretion to exclude evidence the admission of which would make the trial so unfair that it ought to be excluded (in relation to which see Chapter 11, above). Thus, as was seen above, the assault conviction in *R. v Watson* did not amount to evidence of bad character due to the operation of s.98(a) and, consequently, the Court of Appeal held that it was admissible at common law and that its exclusion under **PACE** s.78 was not justified.

It is submitted that where the accused is charged with two or more offences which arise out of the same facts, the admissibility of evidence of one offence as evidence that the accused committed the other will not be governed by the bad character provisions of the 2003 Act, but will be governed by the common law test of relevance, because evidence relating to one count will have to do with the alleged facts of the other (see s.98(a), above).

What is the position where evidence of the accused's conduct does not amount to evidence of misconduct?

Where evidence of the accused's conduct does not amount to evidence of misconduct, its admissibility will be governed by the common law test of relevance and, if tendered by the prosecution, will be subject to the exercise of the PACE s.78 exclusionary discretion. Thus, in *R. v Manister* (2006), the Court of Appeal held that evidence that the accused, who was charged with indecently assaulting a 13 year old girl, had had a sexual relationship with a 16 year old girl, was not evidence of the accused's bad character and had properly been admitted for the prosecution, the evidence being relevant as evidence of the accused's interest in teenage girls and its admission not being unfair.

When is evidence of the bad character of the accused admissible?

Section 101(1) sets out the "gateways" (described as "gateways" by the Court of Appeal in *R. v Hanson* (2005)) through which evidence of the accused's bad character may be admissible. The effect of s.101(1) is that evidence of the accused's bad character will only be admissible if one or more of the seven s.101 gateways applies.

The Gateways

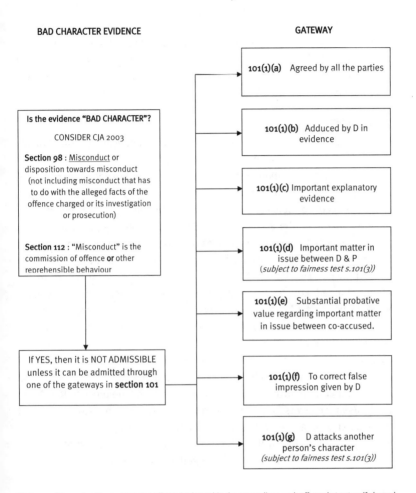

BAD CHARACTER EVIDENCE

GATEWAY

Is the evidence "BAD CHARACTER"?

CONSIDER CJA 2003

Section 98 : <u>Misconduct</u> or disposition towards misconduct (not including misconduct that has to do with the alleged facts of the offence charged or its investigation or prosecution)

Section 112 : "Misconduct" is the commission of offence **or** other reprehensible behaviour

If YES, then it is NOT ADMISSIBLE unless it can be admitted through one of the gateways in **section 101**

101(1)(a) Agreed by all the parties

101(1)(b) Adduced by D in evidence

101(1)(c) Important explanatory evidence

101(1)(d) Important matter in issue between D & P
(subject to fairness test s.101(3))

101(1)(e) Substantial probative value regarding important matter in issue between co-accused.

101(1)(f) To correct false impression given by D

101(1)(g) D attacks another person's character
(subject to fairness test s.101(3))

*Note s.112(2) requires if more than one offence is charged in the proceedings each offence is treat as if charged separately (apart from when considering the s.101(3) fairness test).

Each of the seven s.101 gateways will now be considered in turn.

Gateway "a"

Evidence of the accused's bad character may be admissible where all of the parties agree to its admission. It may be, for example, that the prosecution and the defence can come to an agreement concerning which of the accused's convictions will be revealed to the jury and which will not be revealed.

Gateway "b"

Evidence of the accused's bad character may be adduced (or intentionally elicited via cross-examination) by the accused.

There could be various reasons why the accused might wish to adduce evidence of the accused's own bad character under s.101(1)(b). For example, where the accused, being charged with a serious offence, gives evidence of his good character, the accused might decide to make the jury aware of his previous convictions for minor offences or for offences of a different nature to the offence charged in order that he may also make the jury aware of his lack of any previous convictions for serious offences of a similar nature to the offence charged. Equally, where the prosecution have not adduced evidence of the accused's bad character but the accused realises that the conduct of his defence (e.g. by attacking the character of a prosecution witness) is likely to result in the prosecution adducing such evidence (e.g. under gateway (g), which is considered below), the accused may decide that it is better to have evidence of his good character adduced sympathetically from him by his own counsel rather than having such evidence adduced by the prosecution. Again the accused might wish to adduce evidence of his good character in support of his defence (e.g. where the accused's alibi is that he was committing a less serious offence than the offence with which he is charged at the time when the offence with which he is charged was committed).

Gateway "c"

Evidence of the accused's bad character may be admissible as important explanatory evidence.

Section 102 provides that important explanatory evidence (which is admissible as prosecution or defence evidence under s.101(1)(c)) is evidence without which the court or the jury would find it impossible or difficult properly to understand other evidence in the case and which has substantial value for understanding the case as a whole. For example, in *R. v Chohan* (2005), where an identification witness knew the accused because the accused had been supplying the witness with drugs for a considerable time, the Court of Appeal held that evidence of the accused's drugs dealing had properly been admitted as important explanatory evidence in order to explain how the witness had been able to identify the accused. Similarly, evidence of the accused's bad character might be admissible as important explanatory evidence where the evidence relates to the background history of the offence with which the accused is charged. For example, in *R. v Haigh* (2010) , the evidence of members of the accused's family was admitted to prove that the accused, who was charged with murdering her son, had not been a good mother.

There appears to appear to be a degree of overlap between the section 101(1)(c) gateway and s.98(a), which was considered above. The important point, however, is that whether evidence of misconduct on the part of the accused is admissible as important explanatory evidence under s.101(1)(c) or is admissible at common law because (having to do with the alleged facts of the offence with which the accused is charged) it does not amount to evidence of bad character due to the operation of s.98(a), in either event the evidence of the accused's misconduct will be revealed to the jury ((*R. v Tirnaveanu*).

It appears to be undesirable to admit evidence of the accused's bad character under s.101(1)(c) for the prosecution in circumstances in which the prosecution's real purpose is to rely on the evidence as evidence of the accused's propensity. Rather, in such circumstances it seems that the admissibility of the bad character evidence should be subject to s.101(1)(d) and s.101(3), which are considered immediately below (*R. v Davis* (2008)).

Where the prosecution wish to rely upon evidence of the accused's bad character as important explanatory evidence under gateway (c), whilst the s.101(3) unfairness test, which is considered below in relation to gateways (d) and (g), does not apply, it seems that the court possesses discretion to exclude such evidence, in the exercise of its exclusionary discretion, under s.78 of **PACE** (which was considered in Chapter 11, above) (*R. v Tirnaveanu*).

Gateway "d"

Evidence of the accused's bad character may be admissible where it is relevant to an important matter in issue between the accused and the prosecution.

Only the prosecution may adduce evidence of the accused's bad character under s.101(1)(d).

Evidence of the accused's bad character is potentially admissible under gateway (d) if it is relevant to an important matter in issue between them and the accused but, as is seen below, admissibility under gateway (d) is subject to the s.101(3) fairness test.

What is an "important matter in issue"?

Section 112 provides that an "important matter" is one which has substantial importance in the context of the case as a whole. Section 103(1) provides that the matters in issue between the accused and the prosecution may include both whether the accused has a propensity to commit offences of the kind with which the accused is charged (unless the possession of such a propensity by the accused would not make the accused's guilt more likely) and whether the accused has a propensity to be untruthful (unless the prosecution do not suggest that the accused's case is untruthful). It seems, however, that (other than where the telling of lies forms an element of the offence with which the accused is charged) it will be unusual for propensity to be untruthful to be an "important" matter in issue (*R. v Campbell* (2007)).

How may propensity be established?

Section 103(2) provides that the accused's propensity to commit offences of the kind with which the accused is charged may (without prejudice to other methods of establishing such propensity) be established by evidence that the accused has been convicted of an offence of the same description or of the same category as the one with which the accused is charged. Basically, an offence is of the same description as another offence if it is a conviction for the same offence as that with which the accused is charged. For example, a previous conviction for assault is a conviction for an offence of the same description where the accused is charged with assault. An offence will be of the same category as another offence if they both fall within a category drawn up by the Secretary of State in secondary legislation. Currently, only two categories of offences exist, namely, the theft category (which contains offences such as theft, burglary, robbery, etc.) and the sexual offences (persons under the age of 16) category.

Section 103(2) does not restrict the means via which the propensity of the accused to commit offences of the kind with which the accused is charged may be established to evidence of convictions for offences of the same description or the same category. The Court of Appeal in *R. v Hanson* (2005) recognised that the s.103(2) methods for establishing such propensity to which s.103(2) relates are not exhaustive of the methods via which such propensity may be established. Thus, in *R. v Weir* (2005), the Court of Appeal held that the fact that the offence of taking an indecent photograph of a child is not an offence of the same category (see below) as sexual assault, did not prevent the judge from admitting a conviction for the former offence under gateway (d) in a trial concerning the latter offence. Equally, in *R. v Brima* (2006), the Court of Appeal held that evidence of convictions for assault occasioning actual bodily harm and for robbery had properly been admitted at a murder trial as evidence of the accused's propensity to commit offences using knives (it should be noted that neither conviction was for an offence of the same description as murder and that there is no category of offences covering murder or offences of violence). Indeed, evidence may be admissible under gateway (d) to establish the accused's propensity to commit offences of the kind with which the accused is charged even though the evidence does not even take the form of previous convictions (*R. v Somanthan* (2005)). It should be noted, however, that where evidence of bad character in a form other than that of a previous conviction is admitted, this may require the jury to get involved in "satellite issues" (i.e. they will have to determine whether the bad character evidence is true). Thus, it seems that a degree of caution will be required before the court admits such evidence (*R. v McKenzie* (2008)).

Section 103(3) provides that s.103(2) does not apply where the court is satisfied that (due to the length of time since the previous conviction, or for any other reason) it would be unjust for s.103(2) to apply. Moreover, the Court of Appeal in *R. v Hanson* indicated that the fact that a conviction is for an offence of the same description or the same category as the offence with which the accused is charged will not necessarily be sufficient to establish a propensity on the part of the accused to commit offences of the kind with which the accused is charged.

In *R. v Hanson*, the Court of Appeal recognised that even a single conviction may potentially establish a propensity to commit offences of the type with which the accused is charged (e.g. if it shows that the accused tends to behave in an unusual way). The Court of Appeal indicated, however, that a single conviction will often not establish such a propensity and that the fewer the number of convictions the accused has, the weaker the evidence of the accused's propensity is likely to be. Thus, in *R. v Long* (2006), the Court of Appeal held that evidence of a single conviction for robbery should not have been admitted under gateway (d) at a robbery trial where the facts of the earlier and later robberies did not display any similarities.

The Court of Appeal in *R. v Hanson* also indicated that propensity to be untruthful is not the same as propensity to be dishonest. Thus, the Court of Appeal indicated that convictions are only likely to be relevant to establish such propensity either if the accused pleaded not guilty to the offence of which the accused was convicted and had given an account to the police or in court which the jury must not have believed or if the way in which the accused committed the offence of which the accused was convicted shows a propensity to be untruthful.

Multi-count indictments

Where the accused is charged with several counts (i.e. with several offences) in the same proceedings, whether or not evidence relating to one count will be admissible to prove that the accused committed another count may depend upon the operation of gateway (d). In such circumstances it seems that evidence relating to one count may be admissible to prove that the accused committed the other either because the similarities between the alleged facts of the two counts tend to prove that they were committed by the same person or because the fact that several complainants have made similar allegations against the same person tends to prove that the allegations are true (*R. v Freeman* (2009)). Thus, in *R. v Chopra* (see above), in which the accused was charged with indecently touching three different complainants on three different occasions, the Court of Appeal held that the evidence of the three complainants was cross-admissible under gateway (d). Their Lordships recognised that it was more likely that similar allegations brought by three complainants were true than would have been the case if they had been brought by a single complainant.

Exclusionary duty

LEGISLATION HIGHLIGHTER

Section 101(3) **Criminal Justice Act 2003**

The court must not admit evidence under subsection (1)(d) or (g) if, on an application by the defendant to exclude it, it appears to the court that the admission of the evidence would have such an adverse effect on the fairness of the proceedings that the court ought not to admit it.

Where evidence of the accused's bad character is admissible under gateway (d), the accused can apply to the court to have the evidence excluded under s.101(3). Upon such a defence application, the judge must exclude the evidence if its admission would have such an adverse effect on the fairness of the proceedings that it ought not to be admitted. In determining whether to exclude evidence of the accused's bad character under this provision, s.101(4) directs the court to have particular regard to the amount of time that has elapsed between the matters to which the evidence of bad character relates and the matters to which the charge against the accused relates.

The Court of Appeal (in *R. v Hanson*) has indicated that s.101(3) and s.103(3) (see above) are closely related. In *Hanson*, the Court of Appeal indicated that factors which are of relevance when the court is considering the issue of fairness under s.101(3) and the issue of what is just under s.103(3) (see above) in relation to the admissibility of previous convictions include:

- the degree of similarity between the previous offence and the offence with which the accused is charged;
- the relative seriousness of the previous offence and the offence with which the accused is charged;
- the strength of the case against the accused (as it is unlikely to be just to admit evidence of previous convictions where there is little or no other evidence against the accused); and
- the existence of a substantial time gap between the commission of the previous offence and the offence with which the accused is charged (as old convictions are likely to have a serious effect on the fairness of the proceedings unless they either share significant special features with the offence charged or they demonstrate a continuing propensity on the part of the accused).

Gateway "e"

Evidence of the accused's bad character may be admissible where it has substantial probative value in relation to an important matter in issue between the accused and a co-accused.

Section 104(2) provides that only a co-accused may adduce evidence of the accused's bad character under s.101(1)(e). Evidence of bad character is admissible for a co-accused under gateway (e) if it has substantial probative value in relation to an important matter in issue between the accused and the co-accused. Thus, evidence of bad character that has only marginal or trivial probative value will not be admissible under gateway (e). Once the requirements of gateway (e) are satisfied, however, the court does not possess discretion to exclude the evidence of the accused's bad character (*R. v Lawson* (2007)).

Section 78 of **PACE** does not apply where evidence of the accused's bad character is admissible under gateway (e) because evidence of bad character adduced under gateway (e) is defence evidence (the gateway not being available to the prosecution) and s.78 only applies to prosecution evidence. Thus, where evidence of bad character is admissible under gateway (e) the court does not possess power to exclude it on the basis of unfairness (*R. v Musone* (2007)).

Where a co-accused wishes to adduce evidence of the accused's bad character under gateway (e) to establish the accused's propensity to be untruthful, s.104(1) provides that evidence of the accused's bad character will only be admissible for this purpose if the nature or conduct of the accused's defence is such as to undermine the co-accused's defence. Alternatively, a co-accused may wish to adduce evidence of the accused's propensity to commit offences of the type with which they are jointly charged under gateway (e) if the co-accused's defence is, for example, that it was the accused, rather than the co-accused, who was responsible for the offence. Thus, in *R. v McLean* (2005), where accused and co-accused were jointly charged with wounding the victim with intent to cause grievous bodily harm and the co-accused asserted that it was the accused who had committed the offence, the Court of Appeal held that the trial judge had properly admitted evidence of the accused's previous convictions for offences of violence under gateway (e).

Where a co-accused does wish to establish the accused's propensity to be untruthful under gateway (e), it seems that the court is not required to exercise the same degree of caution before admitting previous convictions as evidence going to the accused's credibility under gateway (e) as would be the case in the context of a prosecution application under gateway (d) (*R. v Lawson*). Thus, the point made by the made by the Court of Appeal in *R. v Hanson* (see above) that untruthfulness and dishonesty are not the same thing appears to be less significant in the context of a defence application under gateway (e) than would be the case in the context of a prosecution application under gateway (d).

Gateway "f"

Evidence of the accused's bad character may be admissible to correct a false impression given by the accused.

Section 105(7) provides that only the prosecution may adduce evidence of the accused's bad character under s.101(1)(f). Gateway (f) applies where the accused is responsible for the making of an express or implied assertion which is apt to give a false or misleading impression about the accused, evidence of the accused's bad character which has probative value in correcting the false impression being admissible under gateway (f) (s.105(1)). The accused may be responsible for the making of such an assertion if the assertion was made by the accused during the trial, if the accused made the assertion when questioned under caution or when charged, if the assertion was made by a witness called by the accused, if the assertion was made by a witness during cross-examination by the accused in response to a question which was intended or likely to elicit the assertion or if the assertion adduces evidence of an assertion which was made by a person out of court (s.105(2)). Thus, an accused who is of bad character may, for example, give a false impression by giving evidence of his own good character when testifying in court, by asserting his good character when questioned under caution about the offence with which he is charged, by calling a character witness to give evidence of his good character, by having his counsel cross-examine witnesses called by another party concerning his good character or by adducing evidence of a statement made by another person out of court concerning his good character. Indeed, where it is just to do so, the court may treat the accused as giving a false impression via his conduct in court, (including his appearance or dress) (s.105(4) and (5)). The accused may, however, withdraw or disassociate himself from an assertion, in which case the accused will not be treated as responsible for making it (s.105(3)).

Where the accused does give a false impression, evidence of the accused's bad character will only be admissible under gateway (f) if the evidence goes no further than is necessary to correct the false impression that the accused has given. Moreover, gateway (f) does not apply where the false impression that the accused gives is not about himself (e.g. it did not apply where the accused, charged with a sexual offence, gave a false impression about the complainant) (*R. v Pickstone* (2005)).

Where the prosecution wish to rely upon evidence of the accused's bad character under gateway (f) in order to rebut a false impression given by the accused, whilst the s.101(3) unfairness test, which was considered above in relation to gateway (d) and is considered below in relation to gateway (g), does not apply, it seems that the court possesses discretion to exclude such evidence, in the exercise of its exclusionary discretion, under s.78 of **PACE** (which was considered in Chapter 11, above) (*R. v Tirnaveanu*).

Gateway "g"
Evidence of the accused's bad character may be admissible where the accused has attacked another person's character.

Section 106(3) provides that only the prosecution may adduce evidence of the accused's bad character under s.101(1)(g). Evidence of the accused's bad character may be admissible under gateway (g) where the accused or a witness called by the accused give evidence attacking the other person's character, where the accused adduces such evidence via cross-examination of a witness called by another party or where evidence is given of an imputation about the other person which the accused made when questioned under caution about (or charged with) the offence with which he is charged (s.106(1)). Section 106(2) provides that evidence of the accused's bad character is evidence that the person has either committed an offence or has behaved (or is disposed to behave) in a reprehensible way.

In *R. v Williams* (2007), the Court of Appeal held that the judge had properly admitted evidence of the accused's convictions for offences of dishonesty under gateway (g) where the accused (who was charged with doing an act prohibited by a sexual offences prevention order) had asserted that he had been "stitched up" by police witnesses. The judge had admitted evidence of the convictions as evidence of the accused's propensity to untruthfulness but had not admitted evidence of the accused's convictions for offences against children upon the basis that these would not be of assistance in relation to the issue of propensity to untruthfulness. The Court of Appeal recognised that the Court of Appeal in *R. v Hanson* (see above) had indicated that propensity to be untruthful is not the same as propensity to be dishonest, but distinguished *Hanson* upon the basis that *Hanson* was a gateway (d) case and that since the accused had attacked the character of the prosecution witnesses the jury were entitled to be aware of the accused's character in order to decide whether to believe the prosecution witnesses or the accused.

Exclusionary duty

Where evidence of the accused's bad character is admissible under gateway (g), the accused can apply to the court to have the evidence excluded under s.101(3). Upon such a defence application, the judge must exclude the evidence if its admission would have such an adverse effect on the fairness of the proceedings that it ought not to be admitted. In determining whether to exclude evidence of the accused's bad character under this provision, s.101(4) directs the court to have particular regard to the amount of time that has elapsed between the matters to which the evidence of bad character relates and the matters to which the charge against the accused relates.

It seems that it may be unfair for the prosecution to adduce evidence of an exculpatory statement made by the accused when questioned under caution by the police solely for the purpose of activating gateway (g) (*R. v Ball* (2006)). Moreover, the Court of Appeal has indicated that it will not usually be fair for evidence of the accused's bad character to be admitted under gateway (g) where the person whose character the accused attacked was neither the victim of the offence with which the accused is charged nor a witness (*R. v Nelson* (2006)). Presumably for this purpose, a witness includes a person who is not called to give oral evidence at the trial but whose hearsay evidence is adduced in evidence. Moreover, it may presumably be fair to permit the prosecution to adduce evidence of the accused's good character under gateway (f) where the person whose character the accused attacked is not a witness if the accused suggested that it was this person, rather than the accused, who committed the offence with which the accused is charged.

As was seen above, the s.101(3) fairness test is also applicable where the prosecution wish to adduce evidence of the accused's bad character under gateway (d). It seems that the fact that it is unfair to admit evidence of bad character under gateway (d) does not necessarily mean that it will be unfair to admit the same evidence under gateway (g) if the accused attacks a person's character. Thus, in *R. v Edwards* (2005)), the Court of Appeal held that the trial judge, having excluded evidence of the accused's elderly convictions when the prosecution applied to have them admitted under gateway (d), in consequence of their adverse effect on the fairness of the proceedings, had, in the context of a defence application under s.101(3), been entitled to admit the convictions under gateway (g).

Assessment of relevance or probative value

When the court is required to assess the relevance or probative value of evidence for the purposes of the bad character provisions of the **CJA 2003**, it does so on the assumption that the evidence is true unless, on the material before it, no court or jury could reasonably find it to be true (s.109). Thus, for example, in *R. v Chopra* (see above), the Court of Appeal indicated that unless no jury could reasonably believe their evidence, the question whether the evidence of the three sexual offence complainants was true was a question for the jury, and was not a question that the judge was concerned with when determining whether their evidence was cross-admissible under gateway (d).

It seems that where evidence relating to several counts is cross-admissible under gateway (d) and the accused asserts that the complainants have either colluded or have unconsciously influenced each other, the judge should direct the jury that they may only rely on the cross-admissible evidence for a purpose adverse to the accused if they are satisfied that it is true (*R. v Lamb* (2007)).

Stopping the case where the evidence is contaminated

Where evidence of the accused's bad character is admitted under any of gateways (c) to (g) above, the court must either direct an acquittal or discharge the jury and order a retrial if, at any time following the close of the prosecution case, it is satisfied both that the evidence is contaminated and that the contamination is such that, in view of the importance of the evidence to the case against the accused, the conviction would be unsafe (s.107).

Section 107(5) provides that a person's evidence is contaminated if it is false or misleading or is different from what it would otherwise have been in consequence either of an agreement or understanding between that person and one or more others or of the person being aware of something alleged by another person or persons whose evidence has, or may be, given in the proceedings. Thus, s.107 may apply not only where there has been deliberate collusion between witnesses/complainants but also in circumstances in which contamination may have occurred innocently/accidentally (*R. v Card* (2006)). In *R. v Card*, the Court of Appeal held that the judge should have stopped the trial where the evidence of two sexual offence complainants differed from what it would otherwise have been in consequence of a conversation between one of the complainants and her mother during which the other complainant was also present.

It seems that where s.107 applies, the section gives rise to a duty to stop the trial, not to a discretion, but that, as a general rule, the judge should not normally stop the trial under s.107 until after the evidence has been given at the trial (*R. v Card*).

The relevance of evidence of the accused's bad character and judicial directions to the jury

Where evidence of the accused's bad character is admitted under a s.101 gateway, the judge should give the jury a simple, common sense, direction concerning the relevance of the evidence (its relevance not being limited by the gateway under which it was admitted) and should warn the jury not to assume that the accused is guilty merely because he has bad character and not to attribute too much weight to the bad character evidence (*R. v Campbell* (2007)). Moreover, where evidence of the accused's bad character takes a form other than previous convictions, the jury must be directed that before considering the significance of the evidence they must first be sure that it is true (*R. v Lowe* (2007)).

Where evidence relating to different counts with which the accused is charged in the same indictment is cross-admissible under gateway (d), the judge should direct the jury to the effect that the greater the similarities between the evidence of each complainant the more likely it is that the evidence of the complainants is true because it is unlikely that they could all have coincidentally made up the same detailed lies (or made the same mistakes concerning detailed facts) against the same accused (*R. v Lamb* (2007)). The judge must also make clear to the jury, however, both that they are only entitled to regard the evidence of one complainant as evidence supporting the evidence of another if they are sure that the complainants have not colluded to fabricate evidence against the accused and that if they regard it as possible that the evidence of a complainant may have been influenced by hearing about a complaint made by another complainant, they must take this into account when considering the weight of the complainant's evidence (*R. v Lamb*).

Offences committed by children

Section 108 provides that where the accused is charged with an offence that he allegedly committed when aged 21 or over, evidence that the accused was convicted of an offence when under the age of 14 will only be admissible if both offences are triable on indictment only and the court is satisfied that the admission of the conviction is in the interests of justice and the evidence is admissible under a s.101 gateway.

Evidence of the bad character of persons other than the accused

Section 100 sets out the circumstances in which evidence of the bad character of persons other than the accused is admissible in criminal proceedings. The effect of s.100 is that such evidence is only admissible if one of the three s.100 gateways applies. The three s.100 gateways will each be considered in turn.

Evidence of the bad character of a person other than the accused may be admissible as important explanatory evidence

Evidence of the bad character of a person other than the accused may be admissible under s.100(1)(a) as important explanatory evidence, though s.100(4) provides that such evidence is only admissible with the leave of the court. Section 100(2) provides that important explanatory evidence is evidence without which the court or the jury would find it impossible or difficult properly to understand other evidence in the case and which has substantial value for understanding the case as a whole. For example, where the accused relies on the defence of self-defence, it seems that evidence of the victim's propensity for violence might be admissible under s.100(1)(a) or under s.100(1)(b) (see *R. v Carp* (2005)).

Evidence of the bad character of a person other than the accused may be admissible as evidence which has substantial probative value in relation to a matter in issue which is of substantial importance in the context of the case as a whole

Evidence of the bad character of a person other than the accused may be admissible under s.100(1)(b) if it has substantial probative value in relation to a matter in issue which is of substantial importance in the context of the case as a whole though s.100(4) provides that such evidence is only admissible with the leave of the court. Evidence of the bad character of a person other than the accused may be capable of satisfying the s.100(1)(b) test where, for example, the person has given evidence against the accused and the evidence makes it more likely that the witness is untruthful, where the accused suggests that the person, and not the accused, committed the offence with which the accused is charged or where (as in *R. v Carp*, which was considered immediately above), the evidence otherwise makes the accused's defence more likely to be true.

In assessing the probative value of evidence of bad character for the purposes of s.100(1)(b), s.100(3) directs the court to take into account any relevant factors and, specifically, to have regard to the following three factors:

(1) The court should have regard to the nature and number of the events or

things to which the evidence of bad character relates and when those events allegedly happened or existed.

(2) If it is suggested that evidence of the person's misconduct has probative value in consequence of the similarity between it and other alleged conduct, the court should have regard to the nature and extent of the similarities and dissimilarities between the alleged instances of misconduct.

(3) Where it is suggested that the person is responsible for the misconduct with which the accused is charged and the identity of the offender is disputed, the court is required to consider the extent to which the evidence tends to show that the same person was responsible both for the misconduct with which the accused is charged and for the misconduct to which the evidence of the person's bad character relates.

Where the accused wishes to attack the credibility of a prosecution witness under s.100(1)(b), it seems that the court is not required to exercise the same degree of caution before admitting previous convictions as evidence going to a person's credibility under s.100(1)(b) as would be the case in the context of a prosecution application under gateway (d) (*R. v Stevenson* (2006)). Thus, the point made by the Court of Appeal in *R. v Hanson* (see above) that untruthfulness and dishonesty are not the same thing appears to be less significant in the context of a defence application under s.100(1)(b) than would be the case in the context of a prosecution application under s.101(1)(d). Consequently, in *R. v Stevenson*, the Court of Appeal suggested that had the trial judge not misdirected himself, he might have concluded that evidence of the complainant's bad character for shoplifting and receiving stolen goods was capable of having substantial probative value in relation to an important matter in issue, namely, in relation to the complainant's truthfulness.

Evidence of the bad character of a person other than the accused may be admissible if the parties agree that the evidence should be admitted

Evidence of the bad character of a person other than the accused may be admitted by agreement between the parties, the leave of the court not being required.

The court's duty to give reasons for its rulings

Where the court makes a ruling concerning whether evidence amounts to evidence of bad character, whether evidence of bad character is admissible under s.101 or s.100 or whether the trial should be stopped under s.107 the Crown Court must state its reasons in open court (in the absence of the jury) and a magistrates' court must enter the ruling and the reasons for it in the register of proceedings (s.110).

Rules of court

Part 35 of the **Criminal Procedure Rules 2003 (CrimPR)** requires a party to criminal proceedings who wishes to adduce evidence of the accused's bad character to serve notice on the court and the other parties in accordance with time limits laid down by the rules. If a party who receives such a notice objects to the evidence being introduced, the party must apply to the court to have the objection determined, again, in accordance with time limits laid down by the rules..

CrimPR Pt 35 requires a party who wishes to adduce evidence of the bad character of a person other than the accused to apply to the court, serving the application on the court and on the other parties in accordance with time limits laid down by the rules. If a party upon whom such an application is served objects to the evidence being introduced, the party must serve notice on the court and the other parties, again, in accordance with time limits laid down by the rules.

CrimPR Pt 35 empowers the court to vary the time limits and to dispense with the notice requirements. The court does possess the power to refuse to admit evidence of bad character where there has been a breach of the requirements of **CrimPR** Pt 35, however, and whilst the court should be reluctant to exclude evidence of substantial probative value on this basis there may be circumstances in which the court will find it necessary to do so in order to ensure the fairness of the trial (*R. v Musone*).

EVIDENCE OF CHARACTER IN CIVIL PROCEEDINGS (SIMILAR FACT EVIDENCE)

Essentially, evidence of bad character is admissible as "similar fact evidence" in civil proceedings if it is relevant to an issue in the proceedings (i.e. if it has probative value in relation to an issue in the proceedings) (*O'Brien v Chief Constable of the South Wales Police* (2005)). Thus, for example, where the claimant asserts that the defendant has infringed his copyright in a musical work, evidence of other such infringements on the defendant's behalf may be admissible because it is relevant in determining whether the similarities between the claimant's musical work and the defendant's musical work were a coincidence (*Mood Music v De Wolfe* (1976)). Where such evidence is relevant to an issue in the proceedings, however, the court still possesses discretion to exclude it (under **CPR** 32.1, which was considered in Chapter 10, above), for example if the evidence is of limited probative value and its admission would add to the complexity or expense of the proceedings, would be unfair or would give rise to side issues that would unbalance the trial (*O'Brien v Chief Constable of the South Wales Police*).

KEY CASE

O'BRIEN V CHIEF CONSTABLE OF SOUTH WALES (2005)

After serving 11 years of a life sentence the claimant's conviction for murder was quashed and he brought proceedings against the chief constable for misfeasance in public office and malicious prosecution. He alleged that police officers investigating his case had used "specific operational methods which were oppressive, dishonest and unprofessional". He sought to adduce evidence that the same police officers had used similar methods in earlier cases that they had investigated.

Dismissing an appeal by the Chief Constable against a decision of the Court of Appeal that the evidence was admissible the House of Lords held that the test for admitting similar fact evidence in civil proceedings was a test of relevance only. Relevance is decided by looking at whether the evidence is "potentially probative of an issue in the proceedings". Their Lordships also recognised, however, that the civil court's possess discretion to exclude relevant evidence under CPR 32.1.

It should be noted that as was seen in Chapter 8 above, evidence of previous convictions may be admissible in civil proceedings under s.11 or s.13 of the **CEA 1968**.

Revision checklist

You should now know and understand:

- **what evidence of good character the accused is entitled to adduce in criminal proceedings and what form that evidence can take;**
- **what directions the jury should be given in relation to the significance of the accused's good character in criminal proceedings;**
- **what constitutes evidence of bad character in criminal proceedings;**
- **when evidence of the accused's bad character will be admissible in criminal proceedings through the operation of the s.101 gateways;**
- **when evidence of the bad character of a person other than the accused will be admissible in criminal proceedings;**

- how the jury should be directed in relation to the significance of bad character in criminal proceedings;

- the test for admitting evidence of bad character as "similar fact evidence" in civil proceedings.

QUESTION AND ANSWER

The Question

Frank and Michael are jointly charged with arson and both intend to plead not guilty. The prosecution allege that the two co-accused set fire to a barn. Frank claims that whilst he and Michael were both present in the barn when the fire started, it was Michael alone who started the fire and that he (Frank) had tried to stop Michael from doing so. Michael claims that whilst he and Frank were in the barn when the fire started it was Frank alone who started the fire and that he (Michael) had not been involved and had attempted to stop Frank from starting the fire. Michael intends to call Reverend Adams who will testify that Michael is a lay preacher at his church who is well respected in the community and who regularly takes part in sponsored activities to raise funds for the new church roof. Frank has two recent previous convictions for arson and two elderly convictions for offences of dishonesty. Michael has no previous convictions.

(a) Consider the admissibility and relevance of the evidence of Michael's good character.
(b) Consider the admissibility and relevance of evidence of Frank's bad character.

Advice and the Answer

(a) In relation to the issue of Michael's good character, the extent to which the accused may adduce evidence of his own good character is governed by the common law authority of *R. v Rowton*. In this case the court held that only evidence of the accused's general reputation in the community would be permitted; evidence of specific examples of good deeds or the witness's opinion of the accused would not. Applying the rule in *Rowton*, the Reverend Adams would be allowed to state that Michael is a lay preacher as this would be generally known.

Strictly, applying *Rowton*, the Reverend Adams should not be permitted to state that Michael regularly raises funds for the new church roof as this is a specific example of Michael's good character. Since *Rowton* was decided, however, a slightly more flexible approach has been adopted by the courts, as illustrated in *R. v Redgrave*, so it is possible that the trial judge might permit Reverend Adams to comment upon Michael's fund-raising activities, but this is uncertain.

If the Reverend Adams gives evidence of Michael's good character, such evidence will be relevant both to Michael's guilt (i.e. to show that, as a person of good character, he is less likely to have committed the offence with which he is charged) and to his credit (i.e. to show that he is more likely to tell the truth under oath) (*R. v Vye*). Michael will be entitled to a direction from the judge to the jury to this effect even though he is jointly charged with Frank who is of bad character (*R. v Vye*).

(b) The admissibility of evidence of bad character in criminal proceedings is governed by provisions of the **CJA 2003**. Essentially, for the purposes of these provisions, "evidence of bad character" is evidence of, or of a disposition towards, misconduct (s.98) and "misconduct" means the commission of an offence or other reprehensible behaviour (s.112). Evidence of bad character does not include evidence which has to do with the alleged facts of the offence with which the accused is charged or evidence of misconduct in connection with the investigation or prosecution of that offence (s.98). Thus, the previous convictions of Frank amount to evidence of bad character for the purposes of the 2003 Act's character provisions but the alleged facts of the offence with which Frank and Michael are charged do not amount to evidence of bad character for this purpose.

Frank's convictions will only be admissible if one or more of paragraphs (a) to (g) of s.101(1) of the 2003 Act are applicable (i.e. under one of more of the s.101(1) "gateways").

[*Note*: if the prosecution wish to adduce evidence of Frank's convictions under a s.101 gateway, they should comply with the notice requirements imposed by **CrimPR** Pt 35 and the defence, if they object to the admissibility of such evidence, should also comply with the **CrimPR** Pt 35 procedure.]

It is unlikely that gateway (a) or (b) will apply as, respectively, there seems to be no reason why Frank would agree to the admission of evidence of his convictions or would want to adduce such evidence himself.

If it becomes clear to the defence that the prosecution will be entitled to adduce evidence of Frank's convictions under one or more of the s.101(1) gateways but they have not already been adduced in evidence by the time when Frank testifies, Frank may decide that it would be beneficial for his counsel to adduce evidence of his convictions more sympathetically from him under gateway (b).

Gateway (c) does not appear to be relevant as his convictions do not appear to be relevant (as important explanatory evidence) for the purpose of enabling the jury to understand other facts in the case.

Under gateway (d), the question for the judge will be whether the convictions are relevant to an important matter in issue between Frank and the prosecution. The important matter may include evidence of the accused's propensity to commit offences of the type with which he is charged (unless the evidence makes his guilt no more likely) and may include evidence of his propensity to be untruthful (unless it is not suggested that his case is untruthful (s.103)). Whilst the accused's propensity to commit offences may be established in a variety of ways, two ways of proving it are either by proving that he has been convicted of an offence of the same description as that with which he is charged (e.g. an arson conviction in the context of an arson trial) or by proving that he has been convicted of an offence of the same category as that with which he is charged (s.103(2)).

Currently, only two categories have been prescribed by the Secretary of State, namely, the theft category and the sexual offences (persons under the age of 16) category.

Whilst Frank's arson convictions are for an offence of the same description, this does not automatically mean that they will be admissible to establish his propensity to commit arson (*R. v Hanson*). The court will need to determine whether Frank's propensity to commit arson is an important matter in issue in the proceedings, whether the arson convictions are evidence of such propensity, whether (due to the length of time since the previous convictions, or for any other reason), it would be unjust for s.103(2) to apply and (upon the assumption that the defence make an application under s.101(3)), whether (paying particular regard to the time elapsed between the matters to which Frank's arson convictions relate and the matters to which the current charge of arson relates) admitting Frank's arson convictions would have such an adverse effect on the fairness of the proceedings that they ought not to be admitted. Upon the assumption that the judge admits evidence of Frank's arson convictions as evidence of his propensity to commit arson (which appears to be likely as there are two convictions and they are recent) the judge will be required to direct the jury as to the relevance of the convictions and make clear to them that they should not convict solely or mainly because the accused has previous convictions (*R. v Hanson*; *R. v Campbell*). It is submitted that the two elderly dishonesty convictions have no relevance to Frank's propensity to commit arson and are unlikely to be admissible as evidence of his propensity to be untruthful (as they are elderly and, as the Court of Appeal recognised in *Hanson*, dishonesty and untruthfulness are not the same thing).

Frank claims that he was not at the scene of the crime; Michael claims that he and Frank were both present but asserts that whilst Frank was involved in its commission, he (Michael) was not and, indeed, had attempted to prevent Frank from committing it. Gateway (e) may thus be applicable to Frank's arson convictions upon the basis that Frank's arson convictions have substantial probative value in relation to an important matter in issue between Frank and Michael, namely, which of them started the fire (the convictions being relevant both to establish Frank's propensity to commit arson and in relation to Frank's credibility). It should be noted that the s.101(3) unfairness test does not apply to gateway (e) and that the court's discretion to exclude evidence on the basis of unfairness under PACE s.78 only applies to prosecution evidence (and evidence of Frank's bad character adduced under gateway (c) would be defence evidence) so the court has no discretion to exclude evidence of bad character which is admissible under gateway (e) (*R. v Lawson*). Thus, even if the judge rules that the arson convictions are not admissible under gateway (d), it seems that they may well be admissible under gateway (e). Moreover, if the judge does not admit the dishonesty convictions for the prosecution under gateway (d), he may well admit them for Michael under gateway (e) as s.104 provides that where one co-accused's defence undermines another's defence, evidence of the former co-accused's bad character may be admissible as evidence of his propensity to be untruthful, and the Court of Appeal in *R. v Lawson* indicated that the courts would not be so cautious in admitting evidence of dishonesty convictions as evidence of credibility under gateway (e) as would be the case under gateway (d).

So far as we are aware, Frank has not given a false impression about himself and therefore gateway (f) does not appear to be relevant.

Finally, even if the judge was not prepared to admit evidence of Frank's arson convictions for the prosecution under gateway (d), he might be prepared to do so under gateway (g) upon the basis that Frank had attacked the character of another person (i.e. that of Michael). Admissibility under gateway (g) would, like admissibility under gateway (d), be subject to the s.101(3) unfairness test (see above). In particular, if the judge was not prepared to admit evidence of Frank's dishonesty convictions for the prosecution under gateway (d) he might still be prepared to do so under gateway (g) as it seems that the courts may be more willing to admit dishonesty convictions as evidence of credibility under gateway (g) than is the case under gateway (d) (*R. v Williams*).

If the convictions were admitted for the prosecution under gateway (g), the nature of the gateway they were admitted under would not determine their relevance (*R. v Highton*), it being for the court, applying common sense, to direct the jury concerning the relevance of the accused's convictions (*R. v Campbell*).

Handy Hints and Useful Websites

14

HANDY HINTS

Once you have studied the preceding chapters, you might like to test your knowledge and understanding by pitting your wits against the examination checklist of questions given below. If your knowledge is hazy and you need to jog your memory, refer back to the appropriate point in the relevant chapter. Use this method as part of your revision.

It should also be helpful, when revising, to review once more the sample questions and answers given at the end of each chapter. You will have seen that, in addition to either a model answer or an answer plan, there is general guidance on examination questions on the particular topic and how to approach them.

In addition to committing the law to memory, thinking about how you will answer questions on a particular topic is an important part of your preparation for the examination. Obviously, in an unseen examination you will not know the particular questions and topics that will come up in the examination. But by carefully reviewing questions that your tutors have set you in seminars and former or mock exam papers, where available, you should learn something about the *type* of questions that are likely to face you in the examination. Even on professional courses such as the BPTC, where evidence is assessed by multiple choice questions, a topic-by-topic structure to your revision is essential for your understanding of the subject.

EXAMINATION REVISION CHECKLIST

CHAPTER 1

(1) Who bears the legal burden of proof and what is the required standard of proof in criminal proceedings?

(2) Where the accused bears the legal burden of proving a defence will this result in a violation of art.6 of the **European Convention on Human Rights**?

(3) Who bears the legal burden of proof and what is the required standard of proof in civil proceedings?

CHAPTER 2

(4) What is the test for competence in criminal proceedings and when can a witness give sworn evidence?

(5) Give two examples of a witness who is not compellable in criminal proceedings.

(6) What is the test for competence in civil proceedings?

(7) Can an adult witness give unsworn testimony in both criminal and civil proceedings?

CHAPTER 3

(8) What type of direction may be given where there is an evidential basis for believing a witness to be unreliable?

(9) In what circumstances should a *Turnbull* direction be given and what are the elements of the direction?

(10) In what situation should the judge give the jury a *Lucas* direction and what are the elements of the direction ?

CHAPTER 4

(11) Explain what must be established before an inference can be drawn from the silence of the accused under s.34 of the **Criminal Justice and Public Order Act 1994**

(12) What must the accused fail to account for before an inference can be drawn under s.36 of the **Criminal Justice and Public Order Act 1994**?

(13) What must the accused fail to account for before an inference can be drawn under s.37 of the **Criminal Justice and Public Order Act 1994**?

(14) What would constitute "good cause" to prevent the drawing of an inference under s.35 of the **Criminal Justice and Public Order Act 1994**?

(15) Can a conviction be based solely on the silence of the accused?

(16) Can an inference from silence be drawn at common law?

CHAPTER 5

(17) Define a leading question.

(18) What is a previous consistent statement?

(19) Under s.120 of the **Criminal Justice Act 2003** what must be established before a victim's complaint about an offence may be admissible in evidence?

(20) When may a witness refresh their memory from a document in criminal and civil proceedings?

(21) What is the difference between an unfavourable witness and a hostile witness?

(22) What is a collateral matter?

(23) What is a previous inconsistent statement?

(24) On what basis may a witness be eligible for a special measures direction?

(25) Can the accused personally cross examine a sexual offence complainant?

(26) Can a sexual offence complainant be cross-examined about his/her sexual behaviour?

CHAPTER 6

(27) In civil proceedings when will a non-expert witness be permitted to give evidence of opinion?

(28) When is expert opinion evidence admissible in civil proceedings?

(29) When is expert evidence admissible in criminal proceedings?

(30) In criminal proceedings can an expert rely upon the findings of another expert who will not give evidence in the proceedings?

(31) In civil proceedings will an expert witness give oral evidence in court?

(32) What are the duties of an expert witness?

CHAPTER 7

(33) Explain the operation of the without prejudice privilege.

(34) On what basis is a person entitled to claim the privilege against self incrimination?

(35) What are the two types of legal professional privilege?

(36) What must the dominant purpose of a communication be in order for litigation privilege to attach to it?

(37) Can public interest immunity be waived?

CHAPTER 8

(38) When may a party plead a cause of action estoppel?

(39) What is the effect of the decision in the case of *Henderson v Henderson* (1843)?

(40) What is the effect of admitting a criminal conviction into civil proceedings under s.11 of the **Civil Evidence Act 1968**?

(41) What is the effect of admitting a criminal conviction into civil proceedings under s.13 of the **Civil Evidence Act 1968**?

(42) Explain the terms "autrefois acquit" and "autrefois convict".

CHAPTER 9

(43) Under s.114(1) of the **Criminal Justice Act 2003** what are the only four situations in which hearsay evidence is admissible?

(44) In criminal proceedings when is a statement used as evidence of the matter stated?

(45) Explain the common law exception to the hearsay rule preserved by s.118(1)(4)(a).

CHAPTER 10

(46) What is the effect of s.1 of the **Civil Evidence Act 1995**?

(47) What is the effect of failing to give notice of an intention to rely upon hearsay evidence under s.2 of the **Civil Evidence Act 1995**?

(48) How might a party seek to controvert a hearsay statement adduced in evidence by the opposing party?

CHAPTER 11

(49) Define the term "confession".

(50) When is a confession admissible in criminal proceedings and who is it admissible against?

(51) On what basis should a confession be excluded in criminal proceedings?

(52) What is the effect of s.78 of the **Police and Criminal Evidence Act 1984**?

(53) Where evidence is discovered in consequence of an inadmissible confession will the evidence be admissible?

(54) What is a voir dire?

CHAPTER 12

(55) Explain the operation of s.116 of the **Criminal Justice Act 2003**

(56) Under what section of the **Criminal Justice Act 2003** may a hearsay statement contained in a document be admitted into criminal proceedings and what are the additional requirements attached to documents created for the purposes of criminal proceedings or for a criminal investigation?

(57) What are the additional requirements for the admission of "multiple hearsay" under s.121 of the **Criminal Justice Act 2003**?

(58) What is the effect of s.114(1)(d)of the **Criminal Justice Act 2003**?

(59) Will the admission of hearsay evidence for the prosecution result in a violation of art.6 of the **European Convention on Human Rights**?

CHAPTER 13

(60) To what two matters is evidence of the good character of the accused relevant in criminal proceedings?

(61) Define "bad character".

(62) Which of the "gateways" contained in s.101(1) of the **Criminal Justice Act 2003** can only by used by the defence?

(63) What will always constitute an important matter in issue between the defence and the prosecution?

(64) Explain the test contained in s.101(3) of the **Criminal Justice Act 2003**, to which two "gateways" does it apply?

(65) How do the bad character provisions of the **Criminal Justice Act 2003** operate in the context of a multi-count indictment?

USEFUL WEBSITES

http://www.bailii.org—The British and Irish Legal Information Institute website contains British and Irish case law and legislation, European case law, Law Commission reports and other law related British and Irish material.

http://www.judiciary.gov.uk—This site contains information relevant to the judiciary of England and Wales including publications by the Judicial Studies Board (JSB) such a specimen directions to the jury.

http://www.justice.gov.uk—The website of the Ministry of Justice containing, amongst other things the Civil Procedure Rules and the Criminal Procedure Rules.

http://www.lawcom.gov.uk—The site contains reports of the Law Commission on proposals to reform the law, including the 2009 consultation *The Admissibility of Expert Evidence in Criminal Proceedings*.

http://www.legislation.gov.uk—A site delivered by the National Archives and provides primary and delegated legislation on evidence and other legal subjects, including the Youth Justice and Criminal Evidence Act 1999 and the Criminal Justice Act 2003.

http://www.privy-council.org.uk—The site contains law reports of the decisions of the Judicial Committee of the Privy Council.

http://www.supremecourt.gov.uk—the site contains reports of recent judgements of the Supreme Court.

Index

This index has been prepared using Sweet and Maxwell's Legal Taxonomy. Main index entries conform to keywords provided by the Legal Taxonomy except where references to specific documents or non-standard terms (denoted by quotation marks) have been included. These keywords provide a means of identifying similar concepts in other Sweet and Maxwell publications and on-line services to which keywords from the Legal Taxonomy have been applied. Readers may find some differences between terms used in the text and those which appear in the index.